Stride Out

Chico State, long known as a party school—*Playboy* magazine ranked it number one in the nation from 1987 through 2002—offered students an inviting environment in which to enjoy social life on and off campus while pursuing their studies. The non-athletic scholarship school drew runners to Chico like San Juan Capistrano beckons swallows homeward. One reason was Bidwell Park, which stretches miles and miles from downtown to the upper reaches of Chico Creek Canyon. In recognition of its beauty, a Warner Brothers Studio crew ventured 500 miles north from Hollywood in 1938 to film "The Adventures of Robin Hood" (a motion picture starring Errol Flynn) in Chico's "Sherwood Forest." An attraction for some was the surname of the men's cross country and track coach. He was a college All-American in football, who had played for the Green Bay Packers professional football team for a short time under Vince Lombardi, whose well-known mantra was, "Winning isn't everything, it's the only thing." The coach's brother was a world-class miler and two-time Olympian. The women runners came under the tutelage of three successive women coaches. A solid Chico State PE teacher preceded two remarkable women athletes—both former hurdlers. The second coach was an international-level competitor, and decades later a head Olympic coach. Her successor was an even better athlete, having competed in the 1964 Olympics Games. This is the story of Wildcat and Lady 'Cat runners who came under very different coaching philosophies in the 1969-1979 era. One hundred eleven photographs; appendices; and an index to full names add value to this work.

To Chico State middle-distance and distance runners, past and present.

Stride Out

David D. Bruhn

HERITAGE BOOKS
2023

HERITAGE BOOKS
AN IMPRINT OF HERITAGE BOOKS, INC.

Books, CDs, and more—Worldwide

For our listing of thousands of titles see our website at
www.HeritageBooks.com

Published 2023 by
HERITAGE BOOKS, INC.
Publishing Division
5810 Ruatan Street
Berwyn Heights, Md. 20740

Copyright © 2023 Cdr. David D. Bruhn, USN (Retired)

All rights reserved. No part of this book may be reproduced or transmitted in any form or by any means, electronic or mechanical, including photocopying, recording or by any information storage and retrieval system without written permission from the author, except for the inclusion of brief quotations in a review.

International Standard Book Number
Paperbound: 978-0-7884-3011-4

Heritage Books by Cdr. David D. Bruhn, USN (Retired)

Battle Stars for the "Cactus Navy":
America's Fishing Vessels and Yachts in World War II

Enemy Waters:
Royal Navy, Royal Canadian Navy, Royal Norwegian Navy,
U.S. Navy, and Other Allied Mine Forces Battling the
Germans and Italians in World War II
Cdr. David D. Bruhn, USN (Retired)
and Lt. Cdr. Rob Hoole, RN (Retired)

Eyes of the Fleet:
The U.S. Navy's Seaplane Tenders and
Patrol Aircraft in World War II

Gators Offshore and Upriver:
The U.S. Navy's Amphibious Ships and Underwater Demolition Teams,
and Royal Australian Navy Clearance Divers in Vietnam

Guns Up, Depth Charges Readied:
U.S. Navy, Commonwealth, and Other Allied Escort Ships
Shepherding Convoys, and Battling German and Italian Air
and Naval Forces in the Mediterranean in World War II

Guns Up:
Naval Action in the Yellow Sea off Korea, 1950–1953

Home Waters:
Royal Navy, Royal Canadian Navy, and U.S. Navy
Mine Forces Battling U-Boats in World War I
Cdr. David D. Bruhn, USN (Retired)
and Lt. Cdr. Rob Hoole, RN (Retired)

Ingram's Fourth Fleet:
U.S. and Royal Navy Operations Against German Runners, Raiders,
and Submarines in the South Atlantic in World War II

Intercept:
The U.S. Navy's Intelligence-Gathering Ships
("Cold War Spy Fleet") 1961–1969, 1985–1989

Kissing Cousins:
U.S. Navy Wooden Minesweepers and Variants (YMS, PCS, AGS)
and USN and Royal Australian Navy Bomb and Mine Disposal
Personnel in the Pacific in World War II, 1944–1945

MacArthur and Halsey's "Pacific Island Hoppers":
The Forgotten Fleet of World War II

Nightraiders:
U.S. Navy, Royal Navy, Royal Australian Navy, and
Royal Netherlands Navy Mine Forces Battling
the Japanese in the Pacific in World War II
Cdr. David D. Bruhn, USN (Retired)
and Lt. Cdr. Rob Hoole, RN (Retired)

On the Gunline:
U.S. Navy and Royal Australian Navy Warships off Vietnam, 1965–1973
Cdr. David D. Bruhn, USN (Retired)
and STGCS Richard S. Mathews, USN (Retired)

Queenstown Bound:
U.S. Navy Destroyers Combating German U-boats
in European Waters in World War I

Ready to Haul, Ready to Fight:
U.S. Navy, Royal Australian Navy, and British Merchant
Navy Cargo Ships in the Pacific in World War II

Salvation from the Sky:
U.S. Navy, Royal Australian Air Force, and Royal New Zealand Air
Force Heroic Air-Sea Rescue in the Pacific in World War II
Cdr. David D. Bruhn, USN (Retired)
and Stephen Ekholm

Send Some King's Ships:
U.S. Navy, Royal Naval Patrol Service, and Royal Canadian Navy Ships
Combating German U-boats off North America's Eastern Seaboard,
and RNPS and South African Naval Forces Vessels in
African Waters as well, 1942–1945
Cdr. David D. Bruhn, USN (Retired)
and Lt. Cdr. Rob Hoole, RN (Retired)

Support for the Fleet:
U.S. Navy and Royal Australian Navy Service
Force Ships That Served in Vietnam, 1965–1973

We Are Sinking, Send Help!:
The U.S. Navy's Tugs and Salvage Ships in the African,
European, and Mediterranean Theaters in World War II

Toe the Mark

Turn into the Wind:
Volume I: US Navy and Royal Navy Light Fleet Aircraft Carriers
in World War II, and Contributions of the British Pacific Fleet

Turn into the Wind:
Volume II: US Navy, Royal Navy, Royal Australian Navy, and
Royal Canadian Navy Light Fleet Aircraft Carriers in the
Korean War and through End of Service, 1950–1982

Stride Out

Wooden Ships and Iron Men:
The U.S. Navy's Ocean Minesweepers, 1953–1994

Wooden Ships and Iron Men:
The U.S. Navy's Coastal and Motor Minesweepers, 1941–1953

Wooden Ships and Iron Men:
The U.S. Navy's Coastal and Inshore Minesweepers, and
the Minecraft that Served in Vietnam, 1953–1976

Contents

Foreword by Jack Leydig	xiii
Foreword by Kim Ellison	xv
Foreword by Laura de Ghetaldi	xvii
Acknowledgements	xxi
Preface	xxvii
1. 1969 "Track Cats" - Great Milers Abound	1
2. Wildcats Third in the Nation	11
3. Dawning of the 1970s	19
4. 1970 Wildcat Cross Country	29
5. Kim Ellison Arrives on Campus	37
6. 1971 Harriers	47
7. Ellison Attempts Sub-4-Minute Mile	51
8. Bob Darling's Participation in the Olympic Trials	61
9. 1972 Cross Country Season	65
10. 1973 "Track Cats" Win FWC Championship	73
11. Harriers Sixth at Nationals – Shuman an All-American	83
12. 1974 Track Season	91
13. 1974 Cross Country Season	99
14. 1975 "Track Cats"	103
15. No Wildcat Cross Country in 1975	111
16. 1976 Track Season	113
17. 1976 Men's and Women's Cross Country	121
18. 1977 Men and Women "Track Cats"	127
19. 1977 Men and Women Harriers	135
20. 1978 Track and Field Season – Toni Ruggle's Finale	145
21. Jill Symons Arrives on Campus	151
22. Final '70s Track Season	157
23. End of a Decade – the 1979 Cross Country Season	165
Postscript: Wildcat All-Americans, 1969-1979	175
Appendices	
A. Wildcat Athletes' Track Times, 1969-1979	185
B. Lady 'Cat Athletes' Track Times, 1969-1979	189
Notes	191
Index	203
About the Author	211

x Contents

Photographs

Foreword-1: *Nor-Cal Running Review* magazine cover	xiii
Foreword-2: Laurie de Ghetaldi	xvii
Foreword-3: 1972 Chico State Women's Track Team	xviii
Acknowledgements-1: West Valley Track Club members	xxi
Acknowledgements-2: Jack Leydig	xxii
Acknowledgements-3: Plato Yanicks	xxiv
Acknowledgements-4: Hank Lawson	xxiv
Acknowledgements-5: Rick Reaser	xxv
Acknowledgements-6: Joe Mangan	xxv
Preface-1: Bill Gregg	xxix
Preface-2: Gary Towne	xxix
Preface-3: Chico State Track Team members	xxxiv
1-1: Gene Meyers in the 1968 NCAA Regional Championships	2
1-2: Athlete of the Week Gene Meyers	3
1-3: Duwayne Ray running a 4:02.9 mile in the West Coast Relays	6
1-4: Duwayne Ray, Rob Laxson, Gene Meyers, and Flynn Johnson	8
2-1: Chico State Cross Country team members, and Bob Darling	11
2-2: Wildcats Gene Gilligan, Dan Mulloy, and Duwayne Ray	12
2-3: Coach Larry Burleson and Nationals-bound team members	15
2-4: Top fifteen finishers in the 1969 National Championships	16
2-5: Meet program and Mike Dailey's All-American certificate	17
2-6: Individual and team awards from the National Championships	17
3-1: Baton exchange between Flip Rowland and Mike Porter	21
3-2: Rob Laxson, Jim Estes, and Ralph Patten in 880-yard race	22
3-3: Mike Porter after being passed baton by Gene Meyers	23
3-4: Mike Dailey competing in the steeplechase	24
3-5: Charles Banks out sprinting Dick Brignolo to win relay race	25
3-6: Chico State Men's Track Team together in bleachers	26
3-7: Deanne Carlsen practicing hurdling on a grass surface	28
3-8: Coach Deanne Carlsen at 1974 National T&F Championships	28
4-1: Howard Miller at the Long Beach Invitational	29
4-2: Chico State 1970 Cross Country Team	30
4-3: Tom O'Connor leading Chico Invitational cross country race	32
4-4: Wildcats Bob Darling and Mike Dailey	34
5-1: Wildcats Juan Dura, Jim Estes, Mike Dailey, and Ralph Patten	39
5-2: Ralph Patten kneeling exhausted following a 3-mile race	39
5-3: Gene Meyers, Mike Dailey, and Kim Ellison breaking the tape	41
5-4: John Staple winning an 880-yard race	46
5-5: Head U.S. Olympic team women's coach Deanne Vochatzer	46
7-1: Wildcat Kim Ellison winning mile race with time of 4:01.4	55

7-2: Pat Stordahl in Placerville, California — 57
7-3: T-shirt from 1972 NCAIC Track and Field Championships — 59
8-1: Bob Darling wearing 1972 Olympic Trials Marathon t-shirt — 61
8-2: Bob Darling and Bill Scobey in a race in Golden Gate Park — 62
8-3: Bill Scobey leading Mark Covert in PA-AAU one-hour run — 64
9-1: Athlete of the Week Pat Stordahl — 65
9-2: Mike Leonard, Mike Fornaciari, Pat Finn, and Scott McVey — 66
9-3: Pat Stordahl in a meet against San Francisco State — 66
9-4: Eddie Silva competing in the PA-AAU 20k Championships — 66
9-5: The Doobie Brothers in concert at Chico State — 69
10-1: Jack West winning a race on the track — 74
10-2: Chico State graduate Kim Ellison — 74
10-3: Eddie Silva competing in the District 20k Championships — 76
10-4: Chico State women coaches and runners at the track — 80
10-5: T-shirt from the 1973 AIAW National Championships — 81
10-6: Chico State Lady 'Cats 440-relay team — 82
11-1: Oroville High's Calvin Lantrip winning a 2-mile race — 84
11-2: Jim Nuccio battling Dwayne "Peanut" Harms in a race — 86
11-3: Greg Griffin leading Tom Brown and Jim Price in a race — 86
11-4: Chico State 1973 FWC champion team members — 88
11-5: Wildcat Mark Shuman on eve of making All-American — 89
12-1: Jim Price, Jack West, and Toni Ruggle racing on the track — 92
12-2: All-American Tom Brown clearing a steeplechase barrier — 94
12-3: T-shirt from the 1974 AIAW National Championships — 97
12-4: Sandy Wiseman's adidas spikes — 97
12-5: Merill Cray and Sandy Wiseman at the Samoa Cookhouse — 98
13-1: Coach Larry Burleson — 99
14-1: Laurie de Ghetaldi leading her race — 107
14-2: Laura de Ghetaldi's track spikes — 108
14-3: T-shirt from the 1975 AIAW National Championships — 108
14-4: Athletes waiting in the shade to race at the Nationals — 108
16-1: Walt Schafer running the Trail's End Marathon — 115
16-2: Coach Cherrie Sherrard with Trainer Tara Lepp — 118
16-3: Olympic Gold Medalist Jack Yerman — 118
16-4: Lisa Foy winning an 880-yard race — 119
16-5: Kathy Sullivan in a cross country race — 119
17-1: Toni Ruggle working to regain top form — 121
17-2: Kent Pease winning a mile race — 122
17-3: Doug Avrit leading Kent Pease during a cross country race — 123
17-4: Angelo Martinez leading Bill Britten and Jim Birnbaum — 124
18-1: Charlie Griffin relaxing on the infield at the track — 127
18-2: Mark Hulbert, Tony Mezzapelle, and Tony Webb in race — 128

18-3: Gordon Innes winner of steeplechase and the 5,000 meters   130
18-4: Leaders in a 10,000-meter race won by Bill Britten   130
18-5: Kathy Sullivan on her way to a win in the 5,000 meters   134
19-1: Start of the Chico Invitational men's race   135
19-2: Wildcat Tom Olson running a cross country race   135
19-3: Chico High's 1977 Girls' Cross Country Team   140
19-4: Coach Chuck Sheley observing a track meet   141
20-1: Toni Ruggle competing as a Wildcat on the track   145
20-2: Toni Ruggle leading the "Devil Mile" at the Cow Palace   147
21-1: Kent Mulkey crossing the finish line in a race   152
21-2: Suzanne Richter finishing a race on the track   154
22-1: Jill Symons on her way to record for the 5,000-meter run   161
22-2: Alice Trumbly, Suzanne Richter, Jan Oehm, Sally Metteer   162
23-1: Mike Wright competing in the steeplechase race   165
23-2: Marcos Silva, Kurt Vineyard, and Eddie Teague   166
23-3: Lady Wildcats competing in a cross country race   167
23-4: Julia Orri during a race in Bidwell Park   169
23-5: Jill Symons, a 1979 Cross Country All-American   173
23-6: Jack Leydig's 1968 VW Van   174
Postscript-1: Duwayne Ray and Rob Laxson   175
Postscript-2: Gene Meyers   176
Postscript-3: Mike Dailey   177
Postscript-4: Bob Darling   178
Postscript-5: Jim Estes   179
Postscript-6: Kim Ellison   180
Postscript-7: Mark Shuman   181
Postscript-8: Tom Brown   182
Postscript-9: Karl Schaechterle   183
Postscript-10: Jill Symons   184

Map

Preface-1: Northern California   xxxi

Foreword
The Running Boom!

Photo Foreword-1

Nor-Cal Running Review magazine cover.
Courtesy of Jack Leydig

This era (at least in US distance running) has usually been credited as the result of mass participation in "jogging" by the general populace after Frank Shorter won the 1972 Olympic Marathon in Munich, West Germany. While the 1970's certainly marked the start of high numbers of road races and participation by the general public, this trend started in certain areas around the country well before that time. I didn't start running (cross country and track) until the fall of 1960 at Hillsdale High in San Mateo. At that time there were just a handful of road races in northern California, including the Bay to Breakers, Dipsea, and Statuto, and they had very small numbers of entrants. What used to be hundreds of runners in the Bay to Breakers grew to 50,000+ in the following decades. Most of the participants in these events were "fun runners." In the earlier years the runners were highly competitive, even if their times were not stellar.

In the 1960's there were very few running clubs (AAU sanctioned) where athletes could continue their sport once they graduated from college. And the vast majority of those running were high caliber. The Bay Area had clubs such as Marin AC, West Valley TC, NorCal Seniors TC, Athens AC, Golden Gate TC, and the Dolphin South End RC. These clubs provided base where runners could continue training and competing after graduation. In the 60's and into the early 70's women were not even (officially) allowed to compete in distance events. The first Olympic women's marathon did not occur until 1984 in Los Angeles, despite the fact that the world record was in the low 2:20s. Local running clubs in the Bay Area and in other "hot spots" around the country (New York, southern California, Boston, Minnesota, Washington, etc.) provided opportunities for top runners, but also families who wanted exposure to the sport. The first Boston Marathon that allowed women to run was not until 1972!

As I am now approaching my 80th birthday, I have over 60 years of exposure to the distance running scene in Northern California and around the country. Races used to be timed with handheld sweep-hand stopwatches, but now runners simply wear numbers with chips that record their times. Entries used to be done through the mail, but now they are mostly done online and there are often limits to the number of entries allowed. The USATF Club scene has expanded greatly all over the country, with many clubs providing coaches and training groups for those that are serious competitors. If you were a part of the distance running scene in the 60s and 70s, then YOU were part of the running boom, although you did not know it at the time! The preceding photo is from May 1977 with over 10,000 participants in the *Examiner* Bay to Breakers race. Thank you for being a part of the movement!

Jack Leydig

Foreword

It's Not About Times or Records; It's About Relationships

The older we get, the better we were.

—Old Guys Rule tee shirt and hat slogan. Also, the motto of "The Worn Out (Nike) Waffles," a group of old, mostly Chico State distance runners who still often gather at Chico home and away meets and tell sometimes somewhat true (?) tales of the past.

The author, David Bruhn, found it curious that several runners mentioned in this book all came to Chico State from Southern California. In fact, Karl Springer, Jim Estes, Bob King and myself all attended high schools in the San Fernando Valley that were only a mile or two apart. All four of us knew "of" each other, but none of us ever dreamed we would all end up together as "Wildcat" teammates. At the time, Chico State was totally off my friends' radar and when it finally became known to them, they found out that Chico didn't even offer athletic scholarships. So, what was the "draw" to this small college and small town in the northern end of the Sacramento Valley? I can't speak for the others, but here is my story.

I first set foot on the Chico State campus in the Spring of 1964. My English teacher and cross country coach the previous Fall, Jim Roulsten, brought three teammates and myself from the San Fernando Valley north to Chico. As the former Student Body President at Chico State and one of its most vocal off-campus cheerleaders, Coach Roulsten wanted to show us his old alma mater. We met the then track coach (and legendary coach of everything) Willie Simmons. We strolled down 1st Street that had great old Victorian homes (mostly fraternity and sorority houses) staring right across the street at what is now the Administrative building. We were continually *STUNNED* by countless people passing by on campus and in town who often waved to us and said, "Hello," or "Good morning." I remember asking Coach Roulsten, "Do you know these people?" His response was, "No. We're in Chico." Add to those friendly folk the beauty of Bidwell Park, the almond trees in blossom, Chico Creek meandering through a storybook college campus.

I knew I'd be back.

Fast forward a few years through the rest of high school, an unpleasant experience at a "scholarship" institution, and an all-expenses-paid two year tour to such exotic destinations as Fort Bliss, Texas; Fort Huachuca, Arizona; and Da Nang, South Viet Nam…and then, with those fond memories in the Spring of 1964, I was "drawn back" to Chico to finish my formal education and maybe get back in shape and run again.

Over the next few years in Chico, I would complete a BA in English and get a teaching credential. I would also meet and marry my wife, Nancy; that has been by far the best move I have made in my life, much better than any move I ever made on the track. During this time as well, I competed for Chico State in track and cross country, and, while doing so, I had too much fun competing and made many life-long running friends. While my running exploits are well in the past, my relationships with many of my old teammates still remain.

More than fifty years have gone by since most of us competed, but Bob King, Eddie Silva, Jim Estes, Bob Darling, Dave Wood, Jim Price, Toni Ruggle, Jack West and I can still be found from time to time at Chico State track and cross country meets. Sometimes we talk about times and records; this is when George Wright and Tom Cushman correct us. Mostly, we are laughing; telling tales of the past that are sometimes somewhat true; or (in good Chico form) greeting people with a "Hello," even if we don't know them. I remember with fondness training and competing "back in the day" with all my teammates. That remembrance and those old relationships make these "from time to time" gatherings with my old friends treasures as coveted as any track gold medal.

Kim Ellison

Foreword

For a long time, I did not know if I was born too late, too early, or just at the right time for involvement in women's athletics. Let me explain. I grew up when there were no real compatible sports for girls. I studied Ballet. I learned to cheer on my brothers at their sports. In high school, I became a Pom-Pom Girl. We had GAA (Girls Athletic Association) "in school" opportunities to "play," but it was not the same as training and competing. In high school, I trained with the boys' track team and was celebrated by the coach. He requested of the league coaches that I be allowed to compete with and against the boys! He/I was voted down. This was 1970.

Photo Foreword-2

Laurie de Ghetaldi (center) and other Pom-Pom girls of Serramonte High School, Daly City, CA, Spring of 1971. Courtesy of Laura de Ghetaldi

I knew what I wanted to study long before High School and that was Physical Education with a California K-12 credential. I knew of only one college I would want to attend. That college was Chico State. In 1971, I started my first year there.

I walked onto the track as a freshman and was greeted by Coach Larry Burleson. He put me through assessment in a variety of track events and finally determined I was meant for middle and long distance.

I remember track season, Spring semester of 1972. I volunteered as the team manager and I also trained and competed. I noticed the uniforms were very old, stiff, and scratchy material. The budget and travel expenses fell far short of what we needed, especially for National Championships.

Miracles do happen, though! With the passage of Title IX, the rights for young girls and women athletes began to change. Budgets improved and travel increased (even for those qualifying for Nationals.) Print articles began to increasingly cover our meets. The Men's Track Team welcomed us, and we became family.

Photo Foreword-3

1972 Chico State Women's Track Team sitting together in bleachers; Deanne Carlsen's first year as head coach, 1972-73. I am in the front row second in from the right. Assistant Coach Betty Best (head Tennis Coach) is at the upper right on the top level; Deanne Carlsen is third from the left, on the upper level.
Courtesy of Laura de Ghetaldi

With Title IX, the Athletic Department had money for travel and essentials like modern uniforms. A brand-new world opened for me to train and compete. Girls and women across America soon began to experience growing opportunities and new realities I never imagined as a young girl growing up in the 50s and 60s.

Years later, in 1999, I watched Brandi Chastain successfully score the final shoot-out at the World Cup. The USA Women's Soccer Team had won the World Cup! It was a triumphant moment. And then it hit me; as she dropped to the ground and threw her arms up in celebration, I cried. The cameras filming her, then zoomed in to pan the little girls in the stands. They were cheering in joyful celebration of their heroines. Yes, it hit me—I wept tears of happiness.

In my opening to this Foreword, I stated that I was not sure if I was born too soon, too late, or just at the right time. I answer that now: I was born just at the perfect time! I was able to experience this change. I was able to experience the transition of increasing support for girls and women in sports.

I am eternally grateful to the support we women "Tracksters" received from the Chico Track/Athletics programs and Chico State. Thank you to our coaches, the men's teams, and to the passage of Title IX.

Dr. Laura de Ghetaldi
(EdD Education, Physical Education, Adapted PE)
Chico Track member 1972-1975

Acknowledgements

Before acknowledging the many individuals, who contributed to or influenced this book, I would first like to thank Debbie Riley, Heritage Book's editor and book designer for her sensational cover art. Pictured on the front cover are Duwayne Ray and Jill Symons and, on the back, Kathy Sullivan and Mike Dailey. (Readers will learn much more about these individuals in the book.)

I am deeply appreciative of Jack Leydig, Kim Ellison, and Laura de Ghetaldi's generosity in reviewing the text, as well as penning forewords for the book offering their very unique and valuable perspectives. Jack also generously allowed use of photographs and materials from the *Nor-Cal (Northern California) Running Review*, which he started and edited during its existence from November 1969 through Spring 1981.

Photo Acknowledgements-1

L-R: Marcel Hetu, Sean O'Riordan, Jack Leydig, Ken Napier, and Mike Duncan. *West Valley Newsletter*, November 1969

The "bible" of running sports in northern California, the *Review* began as the *West Valley Newsletter*. A photograph from the first issue depicts The West Valley Track Club's top five runners responsible for taking the team title in a race described thus: "In what must have been the wettest and muddiest race in the history of the PA-AAU, West Valley Track Club displayed good team depth in putting all of its finishers in the top 16. The course wound through the hills around Searsville Lake in Woodside [San Mateo County, California] and traversed a rain-swollen creek three times, much to the disliking of the runners."

While working at the Hunters Point Naval Shipyard in San Francisco, mostly as a computer programmer, and training and competing as a top-flight runner, Jack found time to put out the *Review* for over a decade.

Photo Acknowledgements-2

Jack Leydig, circa 1998. (signed photograph)

Milestones

1969: New President of the West Valley Track Club
1969: WVTC club newsletter launched
1970s: Started Northern California points-based running race circuit
1971: Newsletter renamed the *Nor-Cal Running Review*; a decade later, merged with one known today as *California Track & Running News*
1977: Jack's Athletic Supply established, following years of selling running equipment out of a vintage '60s VW van

Much information and photographs used in the book came from the Chico State student newspaper *Wildcat* (later renamed *Orion*) and Chico State *The Record* student yearbooks. I am grateful to the California State University, Chico Meriam Library Special Collections and University Archives for allowing their use, and to Ryan Browar, who assisted me in making this possible.

I am also indebted to Kim Ellison, who served as content editor for *Stride Out*, and also penned a foreword sharing the insights of an All-American 4:01 miler, who ran for the Chico State Wildcats in the early 1970s, and then went on to a lengthy teaching and coaching career. Readers will learn about Ellison's athletic background in Chapters 5-7.

Dr. Laura de Ghetaldi, a "Lady 'Cat" cross country and track athlete at Chico State in the early 1970s, describes in her foreword the dramatic effect that Title IX had on women's sports all across America and, directly benefited her and teammates, at Chico State. An excerpt from Title IX of the Education Amendments of 1972 declared:

> No person in the United States shall, on the basis of sex, be excluded from participation in, be denied the benefits of, or be subjected to discrimination under any education program or activity receiving Federal financial assistance.

Laura continued to train and took up road racing following her competitive years in college, noting the accrued benefits of her "running the oval" while a Lady Wildcat:

> I'm so thankful that I had the opportunity to run for Chico State. It was an important part of my education. It provided structure, discipline, physical and mental challenges, built confidence, independence, and lifelong friendships. I continued to run on and off after college, mostly 5 and 10K road races but just before turning 50, I started training to run marathons and trail runs. In the fall of 2006, I ran my first 32K trail run, two weeks later ran the Hood to Coast Relay and then ran the Portland Marathon.

Hank Lawson, Rick Reaser, and Joe Mangan served as "gap fillers," providing me information from their archives, or ones they have access to, that helped "flesh out" *Stride Out* accounts.

Hank Lawson (CIF Central Coast Statistician) is the Curator for the Plato Yanicks Archives. Primarily San Francisco Bay Area focused, the Archives are scrapbooks of not just High School track and field (T&F)/cross country (XC) results, articles, meet programs and annuals. They also cover Jr. College, College and Open/Club/Pro competitions dating back to 1897. The Archives cover National and World results as well and, in addition to T&F/XC, the Archives also have scrapbooks on Football, Basketball, Baseball, Swimming, Wrestling, Gymnastics and other sports.

Photo Acknowledgements-3

Photo Acknowledgements-4

Left: Plato Yanicks, and at right, Hank Lawson running the Dipsea road race in 1993. Courtesy of Hank Lawson

Rick Reaser is an NCAA Division I and USATF Track and Field/Cross Country Meet Director and USATF Long Distance Running Race Director. He is also an active Track and Field/Cross Country historian and statistician for San Diego State University, Women's Athletics and California High Schools. He has compiled the complete history of San Diego State's Track and Field/ Cross Country programs going back to 1921. He researched and compiled the first complete history of the AIAW Cross Country Championships that were held from 1975 to 1981. He led a small team that researched and documented the most complete and up-to-date history of the California State High School Meet going back to 1915.

Reaser is a 1978 graduate of the US Air Force Academy and retired as a Colonel in 2006. In addition to his passion for all things Track and Field/Cross Country, he likes to swim, bike and run.

Celebrated former College of San Mateo head coach Joe Mangan was particularly adroit in sleuthing out hard to find results from track and cross country meets five decades ago. Part of this ability is born of his being a member of the Track Attic staff, which offers at its website https://trackattic.xyz/ a lot of historical results.

Photo Acknowledgements-5

Photo Acknowledgements-6

Rick Reaser at left and, at right, Coach Joe Mangan, College of San Mateo. Courtesy of Rick Reaser and Joe Mangan

Much of Mangan's expertise results from his lengthy involvement with student athletes. While serving as head coach at College of San Mateo from 1996 to 2016, he guided 96 conference champions, 24 regional champions and 12 state champions in track & field along with nineteen top-10 regional finishes and five top-10 state finishes as a team. In cross country, he coached three regional individual champions and five top-10 individual finishers at the junior college state championships.

I am particularly appreciative of all the assistance All-American Bob Darling lent this project, a man who readers will also be introduced to in the book. In addition to providing much information gleaned from research, he also allowed use of a compelling account of competing in the 1972 U.S. Olympic Trials Marathon. Athletes then experienced very austere conditions and meager support. Darling's account comprises Chapter 8 of *Stride Out*.

Many others—all runners, mostly ex-Wildcats—also assisted with this book. They include current Chico State head Track and Cross Country coaches Oliver Hanf and Garry Towne; ex-UC Berkeley Golden Bear Suzanne Richter; ex-Oregon State Beaver Tom Cushman; and ex-Wildcats Mike Buzbee, Pat Buzbee, Merill Cray, Mike Dailey, Jim Estes, Pat Finn, Charlie Griffin, Greg Griffin, Rob Laxson, Calvin Lantrip, Kent Pease, Toni Ruggle, Pat Stordahl, Jill Symons, Nick Vogt, and Jack West.

Finally, a tip of the hat to Lynn Marie Tosello, my stalwart and long serving editor, who has now run (vicariously) in the footsteps of those mentioned within the book, and others from the 1970s.

Preface

Vintage Chico State Wildcat Logo.[1]

Stride Out is meant to honor Wildcat distance runners of the 1970s. I authored a previous book, titled *Toe the Mark*, about the distance running dynasty developed at Chico High School in northern California in the 1970s. Coach Chuck Sheley's efforts resulted in his fielding the strongest groups of boy and girl distance runners of any high school to date in the Northern Section. His 1977 girls Cross Country Team was ranked second in the nation by *Harrier* magazine.

L-R: Doug Avrit, Pat Buzbee, Kim Ellison, and Jill Symons.

I wrote *Toe the Mark* in the first person because I was part of the leading edge of that dynasty and, by doing so, I could add some context and perspective to the book. I attended Chico State following an enlistment in the Navy but was not a Wildcat runner, so the only place first person voice will be found is in this preface. The observations about coaching and running expressed in the next few paragraphs are mine alone, and do not necessarily reflect those of any Wildcat runner.

In 1973, 74, and 75, Chico High teammate Mark Burch and I occasionally trained with the Wildcats, mostly in our off-seasons between Cross Country and Track, and Track and Cross Country. Meet ups were easy because Chico State University (then college) is located across Warner Street from Chico High School. Larry Burleson, the head coach, was always cordial and friendly to Mark and me, although I don't recall many conversations with him. When we, of our own initiative, showed up for workouts, he would allow us to join his runners. When doing long Sunday runs to Paradise or Cohasset with the Wildcats, he would load us, along with them, in the back of his red pickup truck at the run's completion, and return us to Chico.

Following graduation from high school, I attended nearby Butte College for a year and ran for Coach Gene Meyers. Geno was a former Wildcat miler/half-miler who readers will be introduced to in the first chapter. After the 1975-76 school year, I transferred to American River College (ARC) in Sacramento to run for legendary Coach Al Baeta. I was immensely impressed with him then and remain so to this day.

I did not know back then, while being coached by Meyers, that he had set school records in the mile, half-mile, and three-mile while at Chico State and was an All-American, nor that Baeta had been a great runner at UC Berkeley (Cal) in the 1950s. Regarding Coach Baeta, we knew that he had run for Cal while in college, but not that he had run a leg on the two-mile relay team at the LA Coliseum Relays in 1954 that broke the world record with a 7:28.5, only to lose the competition to Fordham's new mark of 7:27.3. Knowing this now provides an answer to how, in 1976, he could hang with us for a good portion of our distance workouts. We would cruise along on a six-mile run at about 5:30 mile pace, look back, and see our coach, who would remain there for three miles or so.

Many, perhaps most, running coaches draft workout plans, put their athletes through their paces and, if they have a sufficient number of well-trained, uninjured athletes at season's end, achieve success. Great coaches don't believe that "one size fits all" and are able to identify exactly what each athlete needs to reach his/her potential, and tailor workouts to each of them. In his book *Bowerman and the Men of*

Oregon, former Oregon Duck and Olympian Kenny Moore describes how University of Oregon coach Bill Bowerman would occasionally wrap a large hand around a runner's throat at the end of a workout to take their pulse. He used this, admittedly, rudimentary means to determine their level of effort that particular day and whether more rest was needed the following day(s).

The ability of a coach to optimize the abilities of their individual athletes, while avoiding injury and "peaking them" at the same time to achieve great success at season's end in championship races, is rare. If this was not exceedingly difficult, anyone could do it. At ARC, we had a sub-4:10 miler who could only run at most 50 miles a week or he would be injured. Another teammate (a sub-9:10 2-miler) declared that he could run 130 miles a week on asphalt roads and not get injured. Baeta was able to determine what each of us required and provide it. His prowess was recognized by his selection as an assistant coach to the U.S. National Track and Field Team in 1973, which led to him landing a spot as an assistant coach on the 1992 U.S. Olympic Track and Field Team.[2]

Two current area coaches—Bill Gregg and Gary Towne—also have the "Midas touch." Bill modestly attributes his great success to the influence of his former coaches. These were legendary Chico State swim coach Ernie Maglischo, Chico High's Chuck Sheley, and Butte College's Gene Meyers and successor Kim Ellison.

Photo Preface-1

Photo Preface-2

Left: Davis High School Head Cross Country and Track & Field Coach Bill Gregg, and at right: Chico State University Head Cross Country and Assistant Track & Field Coach Gary Towne.
Courtesy of Bill Gregg and Gary Towne

Acknowledging the important impact of these individuals, I believe that Bill (a former teammate), who was a competitive swimmer and runner, understands fully the importance of physiology, work and rest, and motivation of athletes. His Davis High School "Blue Devils" have garnered twenty-two Sac-Joaquin Section Cross Country Championship Team titles, and finished in the top ten at the California State Championships fifteen times. Bill's girls' Cross Country teams were runners up at the Nike National Cross Country Championships in 2015 and 2016. Four former Blue Devils, his children Brendan and Kaitlin, Chelsea Reilly Sodaro, and Fiona O'Keeffe, competed in the U.S. Olympic Track & Field Trials. Last October (2022), Sodaro won the World Ironman Championship in Kona, Hawaii; and O'Keeffe the USATF 10-mile National Road Championships.

Following a career in the Navy, I returned with family to Chico and was gratified to learn that Chico State's Cross Country and Track teams greatly aided by superlative distance runners, had gained and sustained national prominence under the guidance of Gary Towne.

As of this writing, Coach Towne is in his 27th year as Chico State men's and women's Cross Country head coach, as well as serving as the distance coach for the Wildcats' Track & Field teams. Towne's great success spans parts of four decades, in which 42 of his Cross Country teams have finished in the top 10 nationally (18 of his women's teams and 24 men's teams) and boast 35 CCAA conference titles. From these teams have come 295 All-California Collegiate Athletic Association (CCAA) runners, 208 All-Region runners and 72 All-Americans.[3]

Towne has also been instrumental in the great success enjoyed by the Chico State Men's and Women's Track teams, coaching 102 All-American distance runners over the past 25 years. These include National Champions Scott Bauhs (10k in 2007, 5k in 2008), Charlie Serrano (5k, 2007) and Sarah Montez (3k, 2008). Towne's middle distance and distance runners have helped the Wildcats win 25 CCAA team track & field championships and rack up eight national top 10 finishes.[4]

NORTHERN / CENTRAL CALIFORNIA COMPETITORS

The following map and table below it, offer a quick reference to the colleges and universities against which Chico State regularly competed. Not all were in the same conference, and all the colleges identified were eventually upgraded to universities.

Map Preface-1

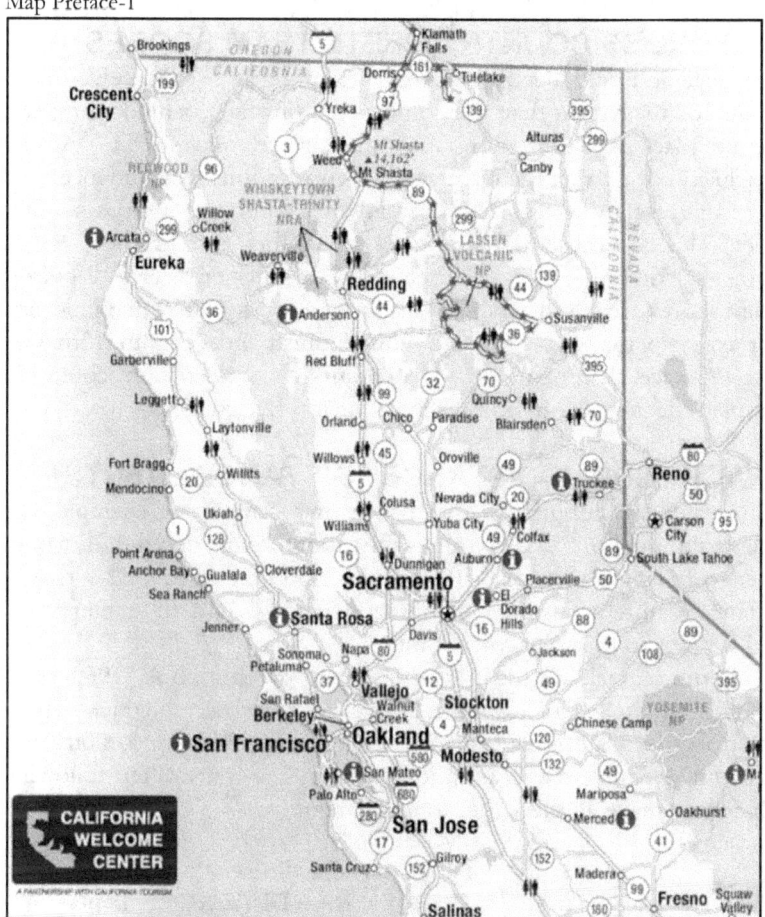

College/University	City/Town	Team Name/Mascot
Chico State	Chico	Wildcats ('Cats)
Fresno State	Fresno	Bulldogs
Hayward State	Hayward (near Oakland)	Pioneers
Humboldt State	Arcata	Lumberjacks ('Jacks)
San Francisco State	San Francisco	Golden Gators (Gators)
San Jose State	San Jose	Spartans
Sonoma State	Rohnert Park (N. of SF)	Cossacks
Stanislaus State	Turlock (near Stockton)	Warriors
UC Berkeley	Berkeley	Golden Bears (Bears)
UC Davis	Davis	Aggies
Uni. of Nevada, Reno	Reno	Wolf Pack

DIFFERENCES BETWEEN TRACK & FIELD MEETS, AND CROSS COUNTRY MEETS TEAM SCORES

At a track and field meet, an individual winning an event receives more points for their team than the competitors finishing behind them; and second place is worth more than third place, and so on. At the conclusion of a meet, the team with the most points wins the meet.

Conversely, the team with the lowest score wins a cross country meet. This is because runners' scores reflect their race finishes. A race winner's score is 1 point. The second-place finisher receives 2 points. Team scores are based on the collective scores of its first five finishers. For example, if a team's top five runners finish 2nd, 7th, 8th, 13th, and 20th in a race, their team score is 50 points. A perfect team score is 15 points, reflecting 1-2-3-4-5 finishes of its top five runners.

TRACK MIDDLE-DISTANCE / DISTANCE EVENTS

Runners, like other athletes, have their own slang. For example, if a miler told a cohort, "I ran a three-fifty 1,500," this declaration would refer to having a time of 3:50.0 for the 1,500-meter run. This race, a distance of three-and-three-quarter laps of a standard 400-meter track, is also referred to as the "metric mile."

During much of the period covered by this book, 1969-1979, runners ran the 880, mile, 2-mile, 3-mile, and 6-mile on the track. These distances were later changed to 800m, 1,500m, 3,200m, 5,000m, and 10,000m, concurrent with adoption of the metric system. The following tables may make all this easier to understand:

440-yard Track

Race Distance	Lap(s)	Race Distance	Lap(s)
880-yard run	2 laps	2-mile run	8 laps
mile run	4 laps	3-mile run	12 laps
3,000-yard steeplechase	7½ laps	6-mile run	24 laps

400-meter Track

Race Distance	Lap(s)	Race Distance	Lap(s)
800-meter run	2 laps	3,200-meter run	8 laps
1,500-meter run	3½ laps	5,000-meter run	12½ laps
3,000-meter steeplechase	7½ laps	10,000-meter run	25 laps

LIMITATIONS OF THE BOOK

A former Chico State Wildcat or Lady 'Cat reading this book may find that they are not included in the summary of cross country team members, or track team middle-distance and distance runners found at the head of their respective chapters. This is because these lists were compiled from race results available to the author, and additional information provided by contributors to the book. As might be expected, unless someone preserved to this day, all results from five decades ago, gaps exist in the tapestry of amassed information.

Similarly, former runners consulting Appendices A and B, might know that, for example, they ran a faster time for the mile than the one listed. In recognition of this shortfall, the titles of Appendices A and B contain the words "Track Times," not "Best Times," because they (like the lists of cross country team members and those of track team middle-distance and distance runners at the heads of each of their respective chapters) were compiled from available meet results.

TG-4 "Marathon" racing flat

Olympiade XIX spikes

TG-22 "Road Runner" racing/training shoe

With this overview behind us, it's time to proceed into the heart of the book, and run in the footsteps of Chico State's best from 1969-1979. Deanne (Carlsen) Vochatzer recently recalled this vibrant period while a college student and her ensuing stint as coach of the Lady 'Cats:

> I was a college freshman in 1967—born and raised in Chico. I originally enrolled at University of Hawaii because they actually began a women's track team, then realized how far it was from the mainland for track meets so I headed back home. Chico State had such a wonderful 'family' campus and a phenomenal Physical Education faculty (my major) it was a relief to come back home. The campus seemed to be a regular stop for great musicians and I cherished every performance in the North Gym (now Acker) from artists like Ike & Tina Turner, the Doobie Brothers, Janis Joplin, and others. So much of Chico, and other on-campus activities such as Pioneer Week, made the college experience exciting and fun.

Photo Preface-3

Members of the 1974 Chico State Men's and Women's Track teams, posing for a group photo prior to a popular outing on a hot day, going "tubing" on the Sacramento River. Courtesy of Laura de Ghetaldi

1

1969 "Track Cats" – Great Milers Abound

"Class" is a word used in the sporting world to describe an athlete of exceptional ability—approaching the world's best. The 1969 Wildcat track team had one, with at least two on the way. At the head of the class was miler Duwayne Ray who ran a 4:02.9 mile at the Modesto Relays and was expected to break the four-minute barrier in the summer. Ray picked Chico State over a host of "big time" track schools because, well, it's a groovy place. And the track coach, Larry Burleson is the brother of a former Olympic miler besides being a nice guy. Two on the way to "class" are local products, Gene Meyers and Rob Laxson. Meyers, from nearby Oroville, is FWC [Far West Conference] half-mile champion and had a season's best of 1:50.1 in that race. Laxson, of Chico, ran the half in 1:51.9 and the mile in 4:08.7 And all three come back next year!

—Praise for Chico State's three best distance runners during the 1969 Track and Field Season found in The Record 1969, published by the Associated Students of Chico State College.[1]

**Chico State College
1969 Men's Track Team
Distance / Middle-Distance Runners**

Gene Gilligan	Jim Moyle
Rob Laxson	Tom O'Connor
Joe McNally	Duwayne Ray
Gene Meyers	Karl Springer

Wildcat Track & Field

The Chico State Track Team opened its 1969 season at Stockton, California, in a dual meet against University of the Pacific. Among the distance runners expected to figure prominently in the forthcoming season was miler Gene Meyers, a sophomore who had recorded a 4:14.9 as a freshman. The best of the newcomers was ace Duwayne Ray, the 1968 California State Junior College mile champion—having garnered the title while at Modesto with a 4:05. Rob Laxson and Karl Springer came to Chico with 1:53 half miles to their credit.[2]

In addition to local kids and high school athletes from other nearby northern California towns, runners came from all over the state to attend Chico State. As described by a former Wildcat from that era, Chico State didn't offer athletic scholarships, so that wasn't the draw. Instead, athletes learned by word of mouth that Chico offered a close-knit college environment and friendly townspeople. Wanting to escape the "concrete jungle" of large cities, or desolate central California, or take a break from the laid-back lifestyle of Southern California, or the staid existence of the San Francisco Bay Area, runners came to Chico to pursue their studies and compete in their sport(s). There was no need to do a lot of recruiting to ensure a constant stream of eager athletes.

Eugene "Gene or Geno" Meyers was born and raised in Oroville, twenty-five miles from Chico. Duwayne Ray was from Modesto in the central valley, Karl Springer was from Los Angeles, and Rob Laxson was from Chico. In 1970, the population of the city proper was 19,580. Over that decade, the number of people living within Chico's city limits grew to 26,716 by 1980.

Photo 1-1

Frosh miler Gene Meyers 4:14.9 highlighted Chico's showing in the 1968 NCAA Regional Championships.[3]

A week after its season opener against University of the Pacific (UOP), Chico State lost a dual track meet to the talented Humboldt State Lumberjacks, 83½-69½, but head coach Larry Burleson was pleased with his team's overall performance. Most of the athletes improved on their marks from the UOP contest, and two school records were broken—a very credible accomplishment that early in the season. Gene Meyers with a 4:12.5 mile erased the record of Bill Schipper set in 1964, and both Duwayne Ray and Rob Laxson eclipsed the previous mark of 1:55.4 in the 880, also set by Schipper. Ray's new record was 1:54.1 and Laxson's time 1:55.3.[4]

Photo 1-2

Gene Meyers was selected as the Athlete of the Week by the Chico State College (CSC) coaching staff for his outstanding performance in the mile.[5]
Wildcat, March 13, 1969

The next contest slated for Chico State was with UC Davis and Sonoma State in a three-way track meet at the Wildcat track. In this meet, Ray would have his "first go" at his specialty, the mile. Meyers would switch to the 880, and Burleson looked for both runners to eliminate each other's records. These expectations would prove too optimistic for the forthcoming competition.[6]

Demonstrating their depth, the Aggies outscored the Wildcats 86-65, while Sonoma managed only nine points. Duwayne Ray and Gene Meyers won their races as expected, but did not produce their best performances this early in the season.[7]

CHICO STATE DISTANCE RECORDS FALL IN MEET WITH HUMBOLDT STATE 'JACKS AND THE UNIVERSITY OF NEVADA WOLF PACK

In a three-way meet with the University of Nevada, Reno, and Humboldt State, Wildcats Joe McNally and Duwayne Ray broke school records. In the 7 ½-lap steeplechase over wooden barriers and a water jump, McNally followed a Lumberjack setting the pace for nearly the entire race, before surging ahead with about 600 yards to go. After that he never looked back and finished with a record setting time of 9:36, breaking the old record of 9:47.2 set the previous year.[8]

The steeplechase is a very hard race, run over obstacles which for the men are 36 inches high, and for women 30 inches. These barriers are heavy and don't move. If an athlete hit one, he would go down, not the massive hurdle. (There was then no women's track team at Chico State, nor at other colleges and universities.)

Competing against the best runners in the conference, Duwayne Ray ran away from his competitors as he clipped eight-tenths off the mile record held by teammate Gene Meyers, winning in 4:11.7. Ray also teamed up with Mike Hulsey, Flip Rowland, and Gene Meyers to lower Chico State's mile relay mark one full second to 3:18.2.[9]

Ray and Meyers both had blazing speed. Coming around the last curve in the half-mile race contested earlier, Meyers had unleashed a tremendous kick, quickly separating from a pack of four of which he had been a part, and winning by as much as five yards.[10]

HORNETS TOPPLE 'CATS IN TRACK

> *For the most part, it was 14 first places for the Hornets compared to three for the Wildcats that was the deciding factor in a meet marred by a hot asphalt track.*
>
> —Except from an article in the *Wildcat*, titled "Hornets topple 'Cats in track."[11]

In Chico's next track meet, in Sacramento, against Sacramento State and San Francisco State, the mile and half-mile runs were the only events in which the Wildcats showed any strength, taking first, second, and third in both. Duwayne Ray cruised to a win in the mile with a 4:25.6, well off his school record in the previous week's meet. Joe McNally and Karl Springer finished in the next two spots with times of 4:26.2 and 4:27.4, respectively. Ray also won the half-mile in 1:55.0, followed by Rob Laxson's 1:55.3 and Gene Meyers's 1:55.5.[12]

In other races, Wildcats Karl Springer (15:34.1) and Jim Moyle (15:56.8) finished second and fourth in the three-mile, and Gene Gilligan (10:21.3) and Tom O'Connor (10:37.7) third and fourth in the steeplechase.[13]

WILDCATS BEST AGGIES

Nearing the end of their track season, Chico State prevailed in a rematch at Davis against UC Davis and Sonoma State, in which the 'Cats took 12 first places compared to the Aggies' five. One of the big surprises was the emergence of Kirk Freitas (future Chico State head track coach) in the 100-yard dash. Although he finished third, he had shown improvement and was expected to be ready for the conference meet.[14]

FINAL CONFERENCE MEET

Despite heavy winds and intermittent rain, the Chico State Wildcats tied Cal State Hayward 77-77 Saturday at College Field.

Duwayne Ray, Gene Meyers and Kirk Freitas highlighted an outstanding performance by the entire team as all three trackmen took first in their events with Ray and Meyers establishing school records.

—From an article in the *Wildcat* titled "Cats, Pioneers deadlock; Freitas, Ray outstanding."[15]

In the final conference meet of the season, Chico State battled Hayward State to a 77-77 draw on its home track. Under challenging conditions, Duwayne Ray and Rob Laxson coasted around the track in the mile run, finishing together with a 4:30.7 clocking. In the 3-mile, Ray followed a runner from Hayward who kept up a torrid pace the entire race. But it was Ray's great kick over the last 110 yards that made the difference. His time of 14:26.2 smashed the existing school record of 14:46 set the previous year by Tom Castro.[16]

Gene Meyers also set a new school record in the 880, lowering Ray's mark of 1:54.1 to 1:53.5. Paced by Karl Springer, Meyers was followed closely by Hayward's Larry Woods. Woods made his move on the final curve but Meyers, not to be denied a win, unleashed a tremendous kick and hit the tape two seconds ahead of Woods.[17]

Kirk Freitas scored 13 points in the 100-yard dash, 220, and 440 relay for his most outstanding performance of the year. Taking the baton from Flip Rowland on the anchor leg of the relay, he never gave an inch to the strong Hayward runner and broke the tape with a 42.4 clocking. In the 100, teammate Dan Stevens edged Freitas at the tape for first place, but both ran times of 9.9. In his final event of the day, Freitas edged Rowland for the win in the 220 with both clocking 22.6. Chico State also set a school record in the mile relay. Hulsey, Laxson, Rowland and Meyers teamed to lower the mile relay record from 3:18.2 to 3:17.8, in a losing effort to Hayward's time of 3:16.[18]

WEST COAST RELAYS

The week following the track meet with Hayward, Coach Larry Burleson took twelve of his top athletes to the West Coast Relays. This annual meet, which featured many outstanding athletes from all over the country, was intended to be a tune-up for the Wildcats, who needed to be at their best in the Far Western Conference Championships the following weekend. Composition of the relay teams was as follows:

Mile Relay:
Mike Hulsey, Dan Stevens, Flip Rowland, Rob Laxson
2-Mile Relay:
Duwayne Ray, Gene Meyers, Karl Springer, Rob Laxson
Distance Medley:
Mike Hulsey, Rob Laxson, Gene Meyers, Duwayne Ray[19]

Five Wildcats were competitors in individual track and field events. These men were Rich Carter (shot put), Don McAlister (pole vault), Tom Wilson (high jump), Silas Sanchez (javelin), and Flynn Johnson (440 intermediate-hurdles).[20]

Chico State performances were highlighted by Duwayne Ray's 4:02.9-mile anchor leg on the distance medley. Had this exceptional time been achieved in an open event, it would have smashed his existing school record of 4:11.7, set earlier in the season in a meet against Humboldt State and the University of Nevada. (Relay splits don't count for record purposes.)[21]

Photo 1-3

Photo in *The Record 1969*, with associated caption quoted at chapter's head highlighting that Duwayne Ray ran a 4:02.9 mile in the West Coast Relays.[22]

Chico's distance medley team had surprised the nearly 45,000 fans at the meet. Running against top teams from around the country, the unheralded Wildcat team finished only a few strides behind the winner, University of New Mexico. Brigham Young University, San Jose State, and UC Berkeley were among those finishing behind the 'Cats.[23]

The West Coast Relays, which are no longer held, were a "big deal." An athlete who ran for Chico State in the late 1970s recounted that his father had, decades earlier, been awarded engraved West Coast Relay belt buckles for his victories in the sprints.

FAR WESTERN CONFERENCE CHAMPIONSHIPS

> *Ray, Johnson, Meyers take firsts in conference.*
>
> —Headline of an article in the *Wildcat*, declaring that three members of the track team were conference champions. Two of them, Ray and Meyers, set school records in earning these laurels.

Winning the mile, 880, and 440 intermediate-hurdles events, Chico State placed third in the Far Western Conference in Track and Field. Duwayne Ray let highly regarded Bill Scobey of Humboldt State set the pace for the first three laps in the mile, until Scobey fell back. With 110 yards to go, he and teammate Rob Laxson sprinted the remaining distance, like 440-yard relay anchor men, to finish one, two, in the event. Ray won in a time of 4:05.5 (a new school record) with Laxson at 4:06.7, the best performance for the "blond bomber."[24]

With Sonoma State's Bill Gillingham having set a new conference record of 1:52.1 on Friday in the meet trials, the second greatest event of the meet promised to be close. The first lap of the two-lap race was completed in 56 seconds. There was elbowing as the runners jockeyed for position, and no one in the first group gave any ground to the others. On the second lap, with the final curve in sight, spectators waited to see who would be the strongest in the final 110 yards. Gene Meyers, Chico's only competitor in the event, turned on a kick—similar to those of his teammates in the mile—and powered his way to a first-place finish in 1:52.2.[25]

Flynn Johnson, the conference's number one intermediate-hurdler, was the other winner for Chico. In an equally exciting and satisfying race, Johnson held off a last-minute challenge from a Sacramento State competitor to win the race in a time of 54.1.[26]

Photo 1-4

At left: Chico State's Duwayne Ray and Rob Laxson finishing first and second in the mile race at the 1969 Far Western Championship Meet. Gene Meyers (top right) and Flynn Johnson (bottom right) were victorious in the 880 and 440 intermediate-hurdles events, respectively.
Wildcat, May 19, 1969

1969 NCAA COLLEGE DIVISION CHAMPIONSHIPS
At the NCAA College Division Track and Field Championships, held June 10, 1969 in Ashland, Ohio, Duwayne Ray won the mile race, becoming an All-American and National Champion. Teammate Gene Meyers finished third in the 880, and also earned All-American honors.[27]

**Chico State College
1969 Women's Track Team**

Distance / Middle-Distance Runners
Nancy Hartwig and Nancy Wedel

National Championships: May 8-9, San Marcos, Texas

VICTORIOUS IN EARLY SEASON TRI-MEET

Launching its season, Coach Mary Ruby's Chico State College Women's Track Team easily ran, threw, and jumped to victory in an early season meet against UC Davis and Lassen Junior College. The "Wildkittens" scored 87 points, while Davis had 24 and Lassen 20. In the only distance run contested, Chico's Nancy Wedel and Nancy Hartwig finished first and second in the 880 with times of 2:41.2 and 2:49.6.[28]

CHICO STATE INVITATIONAL TRACK & FIELD MEET

On April 26th, the Wildkittens played host for the annual Chico State College Track and Field Meet, and emerged victorious. Chico captured first place with 129 points, trailed closely by San Jose State College (122) and Humboldt State College (116), and further back, University of Nevada (47), UC Davis (27), Sonoma State College (15), and Hayward State College with four points.[29]

The women's team next travelled to San Jose State College for a meet on the Spartans' oval, in which over nineteen teams were expected to participate. The Wildkitten squad was the defending champion for this meet, having won the previous year from a field that included San Jose State College, Stanford University, and the University of California, Los Angeles.[30]

SAN JOSE COLLEGE INVITATIONAL MEET

This time around, the Chico State "cindergals" tied with Cal-Poly Pomona for fourth. Los Angeles Harbor College took top honors, San Jose State finished second, and Humboldt State, third.[31]

HUMBOLDT STATE TRACK AND FIELD MEET

Everyone is pleased with the growth of women's track and field in Northern California. There were more schools in competition this year than ever before.

This has been a profitable year for us. Each of the girls has improved tremendously in her individual event. Our growth as a team has been remarkable.

—Coach Mary Ruby quoted in *Wildcat*, May 19, 1969.

Closing out their season in a meet at Arcata, Chico State finished third behind Humboldt State, the winning team and meet host, and San Jose State which took second. Chico's Nancy Wedel took third place in the mile with a time of 6:18.9. Demonstrating her versatility, she also placed third in the 200-meter hurdles and ran the first leg of the fourth-place 880-yard medley relay.[32]

NATIONAL WOMEN'S TRACK CHAMPIONSHIPS

The 1st Annual National Intercollegiate Women's Track and Field Championships was held May 8-9, 1969, in San Marcos, Texas, under the auspices of the the Division for Girls' and Women's Sports (DGWS). The meet was a great innovation—fifteen universities and colleges took part—but was marred by a lack of communication to interested institutions. For example, no California schools sent competitors.[33]

To bring in more coordination, the AIWA (Association for Intercollegiate Athletics for Women) was founded in 1971 to govern collegiate women's athletics and to administer national championships. In 1982, two championships were held, as the competing AIAW and NCAA both staged meets. That was the last of the AIAW; in 1983, for the first time, men and women competed together in just one national championship.[34]

```
Sites, dates of championship meets

1969  DGWS  May 8-9         San Marcos, Texas   SW Texas St. College
1970  DGWS  May 29-30       Urbana, Illinois    Univ. of Illinois
1971  DGWS  May 14-15       Cheney, Wash.       Eastern Wash. Univ.
1972  DGWS  May 12-13       Knoxville, Tenn.    Univ. of Tennessee
1973  AIAW  May 11-12       Hayward, Calif.     Cal. St.-Hayward
1974  AIAW  May 17-18       Denton, Texas       Texas Women's Univ.
1975  AIAW  May 16-17       Corvallis, Ore.     Oregon State Univ.
1976  AIAW  May 13-15       Manhattan, Kans.    Kansas State Univ.
1977  AIAW  May 19-21       Los Angeles, Cal.   UCLA
1978  AIAW  May 25-27       Knoxville, Tenn.    Univ. of Tennessee
1979  AIAW  May 24-26       E. Lansing, Mich.   Michigan St. Univ.
1980  AIAW  May 21-24       Eugene, Oregon      Univ. of Oregon
1981  AIAW  May 28-30       Austin, Texas       Univ. of Texas
1982  AIAW  May 27-29       College Station,Tx  Texas A&M
1982  NCAA  May 31-June 5   Provo, Utah         Brigham Young U.
1983  NCAA  May 30-June 4   Houston, Tex.       Univ. of Houston
```

2

Wildcats Third in the Nation

Photo 2-1

Left: Group of Chico State Men's Cross Country Team members training and, at right, Wildcat Bob Darling in 1969.
The Record 1970, CSU Chico Digital Collections

Chico State College 1969 Men's Cross Country Team		
Steve Adams	Rob Laxson	Tom O'Connor
Mike Dailey	Gene Meyers	Duwayne Ray*
Bob Darling	Howard Miller	Ralph Patten
Jim Estes	Jim Moyle	Bob Wear
Gene Gilligan*	Dan Mulloy*	

* Returning members of Chico State team that won the 1968 Far Western Conference Cross Country Championship, and were kicked off the 1969 team in early season.

The Chico State Men's Cross Country Team began its 1969 season as the defending Far Western Conference champions. But, scarcely had the season begun when three returning members—Duwayne Ray, Gene Gilligan, and Dan Mulloy—were kicked off the team by head coach Larry Burleson. An article by Mike Borkowski in the *Wildcat* (school newspaper), titled "Three track men dropped," noted that "Three lettermen, all of whom were injured last year [previous track season], returned to run for Chico State, but now find themselves without a team and little chance of finding one."[1]

On October 25th, the day before a meet with Humboldt State, the team had discussed the length and appearance of a teammate's hair, and decided that it was respectable. Five members of the team, including Ray and Mulloy, went to Burleson's home that evening to talk things over. However, before any dialogue could begin, the coach kicked Mulloy off the cross country and track teams, and dropped Ray from the cross country team, and gave him one month to decide if he wanted to run track in the spring.[2]

Coach Burleson later issued a statement for print, "Both individuals were considered to be detrimental to the growth and development of the CSC [Chico State College] Cross Country and Track teams." Burleson had earlier dropped Gilligan from the team because the runner was unwilling to participate in Sunday afternoon workouts in the mountains. Married, father of a baby girl, and working as well as attending classes, Gilligan wanted to run on his own Sunday mornings and spend afternoons with his family.[3]

Ray had hurt his Achilles tendon the previous track season, rested during the summer, and showed up out of shape. Two weeks after being given 4-5 weeks to run on his own while his injury continued to heal, Burleson wanted him to run regular workouts, including speedwork—which Ray believed would hinder rather than help his condition.[4]

Photo 2-2

L-R: Gene Gilligan (singlet #73), Dan Mulloy (#74), Duwayne Ray (#71), and Coach Larry Burleson.
Wildcat, November 6, 1969

The Chico State Cross Country Team had launched its '69 season earlier that month when the Wildcats hosted the Chico State Cross Country Invitational at the Bidwell Park Golf Course. The invitational layout provided an excellent opportunity for spectators to view the race. From an area just below the Easter Cross in upper Bidwell Park, approximately seventy-five percent of the course was visible.[5]

Twelve colleges and six junior colleges made up the field, which Burleson observed, "is the strongest group of competitors ever assembled for the invitational." Competing for the 'Cats were Junior lettermen Rob Laxson and Gene Meyers along with junior college transfers Steve Adams, Jim Estes, Mike Dailey, Bob Darling, Ralph Patten, and Bob Wear. Duwayne Ray was injured, as was Howard Miller (another promising JC transfer), and they did not compete.[6]

Running in their own invitational, the 'Cats placed a strong second to the University of California at Berkeley (Cal Berkeley). Moreover, Chico defeated every other team from the Far Western Conference, including UC Davis, fourth place finisher in the Small College Nationals in 1968. Berkeley's Bob Waldon won the 5-mile race in an outstanding time of 24:24.6. Leading the 'Cats, Bob Darling was fourth in 25:28; Rob Laxson, 10th; Jim Estes, 14th; Ralph Patten, 17th; and Gene Meyers, 27th.[7]

On October 26th, Chico's harriers beat the Humboldt State College team with a 26-30 score. For readers not familiar with the sport of cross country, the finishing places of a team's first five runners across the finish line are added together to arrive at an overall team score. If a team's sixth runner beats the fifth runner of another team, one point is added to the other runner's place. If both the sixth and seventh runners beat the fifth runner, it results in two additional points. A perfect team score of 15 points signifies that the first five runners on one team crossed the finish line in the 1st through 5th places.[8]

Mike Dailey finished nine seconds behind the race winner, Bill Scobey of the Lumberjacks. Bob Darling had been giving Scobey a good race when he tripped and fell with one-half mile left in the 5-mile race. As Jim Estes stopped to help Darling, Dailey raced by the two. Darling, returning to his feet, finished sixth. Trailing them, Ralph Patten was seventh, team captain Rob Laxson, ninth, and the tenth place finisher was veteran Jim Moyle.[9]

Next on the schedule for the undefeated 'Cats was a meet at Sacramento against Sacramento State and San Francisco State, then, a week later, one against tough UC Davis.[10]

Chico State remained undefeated in Far Western Conference by easily beating Sacramento and San Francisco in the three-way meet.

Chico had the low score of 22, while Sacramento finished second with 33, and San Francisco far back. Wildcats Mike Dailey and Bob Darling tied for first place; with Jim Estes, third; Rob Laxson, sixth; and Howard Miller, tenth in the race. Miller, who had been sidelined with injuries the first part of the season, showed with this finish, he was returning to form.[11]

WILDCATS CONTINUE DOMINANT SEASON

> *Burleson couldn't say enough about the tremendous team effort and especially the job done by first place finisher Jim Estes who broke the course record by 51 seconds.... "It was the fastest and most interesting course to run in the Far Western Conference. Davis' fine coach Bill Adams did an excellent job setting it up and our team really enjoyed it. I was pleased with the entire team."*

—Excert from a *Wildcat* article titled "CSC Hosts Cal St."[12]

In the ensuing meet at Davis against UC Davis and Sonoma State, Chico prevailed against the Davis Aggies which had finished fifth in the NCAA Small College Nationals the previous year. Close on the heels of winner Jim Estes, came Bob Darling and Mike Dailey in third and fourth, with Ralph Patten only three seconds behind Dailey in fifth, and Rob Laxson in eighth place. Significantly, Wildcat results over the past few weeks evidenced both depth and versatility with different individuals leading the team.[13]

Following a very impressive 21-36 triumph over top contender UC Davis, Chico's next contest would be at home, hosting Cal State Hayward on the Bidwell Park Course. This meet was to be the Wildcats' final preparation for the NCAA Nationals in Wheaton, Illinois, on November 15, 1969.[14]

Using only two of its top seven runners, Chico State easily defeated Cal State Hayward on the Bidwell Park Course. (The Wildcats' top five men were rested for their trip back to Wheaton, Illinois.) Hayward's Dick Hunter took top honors with Chico sweeping the next five places: Howard Miller (2nd), Jim Moyle (3rd), Tom O'Connor (4th), Gene Meyers (5th), and Bob Wear (6th). Wildcat runners also finished ninth, eleventh, and fifteenth in the race.[15]

NATIONAL SMALL COLLEGE CHAMPIONSHIPS

The three big guns for Chico this year have been Dailey, Darling and Estes, but it will take a team effort to win at the national competition. The other four runners going to the nationals will decide the fate of Chico at the nationals as they must run well to give Chico a low enough score to cop the title.

—*Wildcat* article titled, "Thin-clads on way to nationals."[16]

Photo 2-3

Five of the seven Wildcats who competed in the 1969 NCAA College Cross Country Championships at Wheaton, Illinois, on the eve of the race. From L-R: Coach Larry Burleson, Jim Estes, Jim Moyle, Howard Miller, Ralph Patten, and Mike Dailey. Rob Laxson and Bob Darling were not present.[17]
Wildcat, November 14, 1969

Coming off an undefeated dual-meet season, the Chico State harriers were considered contenders for the National title, but competitors from the eastern United States were an unknown factor. The official Far Western Conference crown was to be decided at UC Davis one week after the Nationals, when all the member teams would race in one big meet. Cross country seasons ended earlier back east and in the midwest, due to cold weather beginning there, before the west.[18]

Running in 27-degree chill with swirling snow and wind, the Chico State Cross Country Team placed third in the Small College Nationals behind winner Eastern Illinois and second place Eastern Michigan. The Wildcats effort marked the best finish in cross country history at Chico State. Individual places for the top five Wildcats were:
- 10th Mike Dailey
- 14th Bob Darling
- 21st Jim Estes
- 47th Ralph Patten
- 99th Rob Laxson[19]

Photo 2-4

Top fifteen finishers in the 1969 NCAA College Division Cross Country Championship Meet at Wheaton, Illinois. The runners competed in the snow on one of the coldest days of the year but managed to put on a top-notch performance for everyone attending. Mike Dailey is the second person from the left in the top row, and Bob Darling (four places to his left) the sixth person from the left in that row. Missing was Bill Scobey. Courtesy of Bob Darling

Top 15 Finishers, and Chico State College 3rd, 4th, and 5th Runners

Place	Name	School	Time
1	Ron Stonitsch	C. W. Post	24:53
2	John Cragg	St. Johns University	25:06
3	Arjan Gelling	North Dakota University	25:14
4	Martin McIntire	Eastern Illinois	25:17
5	Jerome Dirkes	St. Cloud	25:25
6	Phil Stirrett	Eastern Illinois	25:32
7	Alan Taylor	Illinois State University	25:36
8	Bill Scobey	Humboldt State	25:38
9	Don Yehle	Alma College	25:42
10	Michael Dailey	Chico State College	25:45
11	Larry Mayse	Eastern Illinois	25:46
12	Wayne Seiler	Eastern Michigan	25:47

13	James Skinner	Eastern Illinois	25:49
14	Bob Darling	Chico State College	25:50
15	David Calloway	Eastern Michigan	25:51
21	James Estes	Chico State College	26:02
47	Ralph Patten	Chico State College	26:28
99	Rob Laxson	Chico State College	27:58

Photo 2-5

Left: Original program from the National Championships. Right, Mike Dailey's All-American certificate. Dailey was Chico State's first All-American cross country runner in the history of the school and Bob Darling was the second.
Courtesy of Mike Dailey

Photo 2-6

At left, Bob Darling's individual award for finishing 14th at the National Championships and, at right, Chico State College's team award. The inscriptions on these awards, intended for display on a tabletop, read "1969 NCAA COLLEGE DIVISION CROSS COUNTRY CHAMPIONSHIPS FOURTEENTH," and "1969 NCAA COLLEGE DIVISION CROSS COUNTRY CHAMPIONSHIPS THIRD PLACE TEAM."
Courtesy of Bob Darling

Other Far Western Conference teams garnered high finishes with Humboldt State fifth, and UC Davis seventh. Cal-Poly San Luis Obispo was the other West Coast team with a top finish, placing tenth in the Nationals.[20]

FAR WESTERN CONFERENCE CHAMPIONSHIP

Chico State easily defended its 1968 title at the Far Western Conference Championships following the Nationals. Running over the picturesque arboretum course at Davis, the Chico runners started out somewhat slowly, but in the third and fourth miles of the race, moved up considerably, to coast in to the finish and the championship. Chico's first five runners were all in the top ten.[21]

Ralph Patten finished second overall in the race, with a fine time of 24:57; breaking the top time by a Chico runner of 25:01 set by Jim Estes earlier in the year. Bob Darling was third in 24:58, Gene Meyers sixth in 25:17, Mike Dailey eighth in 25:21, and Jim Estes tenth in a time of 25:25. Meyers, hampered all season by injury, filled in for the injured Laxson, cutting more than a minute off his season's best for a 5-mile race, and finishing strongly.[22]

When the meet officials called up the top ten finishers to be presented their medals for making the All-Conference Team, five of the receipients were wearing sweats with CHICO STATE on the back.[23]

3

Dawning of the 1970s

Wildcat Track & Field

**Chico State College
1970 Men's Track Team
Distance / Middle-Distance Runners**

Mike Dailey	Howard Miller
Bob Darling	Tim O'Connor
Jim Estes	Flip Rowland
Rob Laxson	Ralph Patten
Gene Meyers	Mike Porter
Jim Moyle	Karl Springer

We finally have depth.

—Observation by head track coach Larry Burleson on the eve of the 1970 track season, which was to open in a home meet against the University of the Pacific Tigers.[1]

As Chico State opened its 1970 track season, head coach Larry Burleson had some help—coach Don Batie (Burleson's chief assistant), and new assistant coach Dan Hagenbuch—with great expectations. A *Wildcat* article previewing the 'Cats opening meet with University of the Pacific at Chico's home stadium (termed College Field), advised:

> Under sunny skies (hopefully!), you not only will get a chance to get a pre-spring burn, but you will be able to watch one of the best meets of the year. UOP has a very strong team with a class sprinter and an outstanding freshman miler who ran a 4:14 in high school.[2]

Wildcats from Chico's nationally-ranked cross country team were entered in the three- and six-mile races. Rob Laxson, second in the mile at the Far Western Championships the previous year, and Gene Meyers, first in the 880, headed Chico's entries in the mile, in which Jim Estes and Ralph Patten were also to compete. Alas, the meet was cancelled owing to a rain-caused muddy dirt track.[3]

This disappointment behind them, Chico's 1970 track season was to open in Arcata, on the northern California coast. Rain or shine, the Humboldt Lumberjacks-hosted meet would take place on their all-weather track. The 'Jacks boasted one of the top three milers in the nation in "Mad Dog" Bill Scobey, and would field a team that had beaten conference contender Hayward State 94-60 the previous week. (It should be noted that "in the nation" referred to the NCAA small colleges category of which Chico and Humboldt were a part.)[4]

Since both teams had good distance squads, a new event was to be run in the meet. A 4-mile relay would take the place of the standard mile and, for this "16-lapper," the Wildcats would field Gene Meyers, Ralph Patten, Howard Miller, and Jim Estes. There was also to be a separate matchup in the 880 between Humboldt's Vince Engel and Gene Meyers, and other competitors.[5]

Running in the rain, with field events contested in a field house, Chico overcame Humboldt 85-68 in its opening meet of the young season. The big event of the day, the 4-mile relay, proved to be a big disappointment. With Howard Miller getting sick on the way to Arcata, the 'Cats could not keep up with Bill Scobey and his cohorts. However, Chico distance runners prevailed in other events. Mike Dailey's time of 9:26.8 in the steeplechase erased Joe McNally's old record of 9:36 by ten seconds; and Jim Estes easily won the 880, albeit with a slow time of 1:56 caused by a downpour.[6]

WOODY WILSON RELAYS AT DAVIS

The Wildcats next traveled to Davis, California, to take part in the Woodrow Wilson Relays traditionally held on UC Davis' Picnic Day. At this meet, Chico State finished second to Cal State Hayward in team competition. Highlights by the Wildcats included a new meet record in the two-mile relay. Premier quartermiler Mike Porter (who had already run a 47.9 440 in the first leg of the sprint medley) moved up in distance and ran a 1:55.7 leadoff leg. Ralph Patten (1:59.1), Gene Meyers (1:54), and Jim Estes (1:56.4) then took the baton in succession and easily broke the old record by six seconds with a time of 7:45.4.[7]

ENSUING MEETS

Chico's next meet was at Hayward in the San Francisco East Bay area. For this meet, Burleson doubled and tripled Wildcat athletes in many of the events and, by this means, bested Hayward and Sonoma State in team competition. Before the 3-mile run, the score was Chico 73

Hayward 67. Wildcats finished 1-2-3 in this race to secure the team win. Howard Miller (14:55.4) edged teammate Bob Darling (14:55.4) at the finish line, and Bob Ware (15:06.2) took third place.[8]

In a repeat meet with Humboldt State, at Chico, the Wildcats easily beat the Lumberjacks 93-61 in team scoring. All-American Bob Darling (1969 cross country) waved to the crowd with one lap to go in the six-mile run, and continued on to finish in a time of 30:50.0. This result broke the old school record held by Tom Castro and set a new stadium record also.[9]

In a much more hotly contested and anticipated matchup between Bill Scobey and Gene Meyers in the mile, Meyers clocked 4:08.9 coming away with a tremendous win.[10]

In the 880, Wildcat Karl Springer finished second to Lumberjack Vince Engel who won with a slow time of 1:57.1. Engel and Springer sat behind the lead pack of runners for the first lap, then Engel took the lead. Springer matched him stride for stride for the first 330, but could not maintain contact over the final 110 yards of the race.[11]

WILDCATS HOST AGGIES AT HOME

The attendance really helps the performance of the athletes. I only wish we could fill the stands for the home meets.

—Coach Larry Burleson remarking on the eve of a home meet against UC Davis, of the importance of fans in the stands.[12]

Photo 3-1

Baton exchange between Wildcats Flip Rowland and Mike Porter in the mile relay; part of a winning team effort against the Aggies. *Wildcat*, April 13, 1970

For an upcoming meet against UC Davis, Gene Meyers was scheduled to compete in the three-mile with Bob Darling; although Darling (who had broken the school record in the six-mile the previous week) might not be able to run because of blisters. Jim Estes, still recovering from tendonitis, was questionable, but proved ready to go. Karl Springer usually competed in the the 880, but for this meet was to move up to the mile, joining Howard Miller and Ralph Patten.[13]

Photo 3-2

A UC Davis runner entered the home stretch leading the 880-yard race. Rob Laxson overtook him, and Jim Estes came up on his outside to draw even and tie with Laxson in a first-place finish. Ralph Patten, barely visible, finished third for Chico.
Courtesy of Jim Estes

On a wind-swept Saturday, Chico State defeated the Aggies 114-39, improving its perfect dual-meet record. In the quartermile relay, Dan Stevens, Kirk Freitas, Rick Call, and Dick Brignolo set a new school record of 41.4, breaking their previous one of 41.6 set a week earlier. Brignolo, getting the handoff after two preceding flawless exchanges, exploded down the grandstand straightaway to finish twenty yards ahead of the Aggies and Tahoe Paradise Junior College.[14]

In the distance events, Aggie Ed Haver won the steeplechase with a time of 9:19.3. Wildcat Gene Meyers collected a first in the three-mile, and teammates Rob Laxson and Jim Estes tied for first in the 880.[15]

FINAL HOME MEET SLATED

> *"I will definitely beat Gene Meyers in the two mile,"* remarked a confident Patten.... To Patten's challenge, Meyers promptly retorted, *"I can beat Patten on my hands and knees."*
>
> —Playfull exchange between teammates Ralph Patten and Gene Meyers prior to a scheduled home meet with the San Francisco State Gators at Chico State's College Field stadium.[16]

Although San Francisco's distance running corp did not have a lot of depth, Gene Meyers was to battle the Gators' top miler who had a 4:14 to his credit in the mile race. As indicated in the preceeding quoted material, the 2-mile race conducted later in the meet was expected to feature one Wildcat against another.[17]

Wildcats Gene Meyers (4:18.3) and Bob Wear (4:18.4) beat San Francisco's Steve Noland (4:19.0) to the tape in the mile race. Meyers (9:24.5) also won the two-mile with teammates Ralph Patten (9:29.0) and Bob Darling (9:39.5) in second and third behind him. Mike Dailey set a new school record in the steeplechase, as Chico swept the first three places—Dailey (9:04.9), Tom O'Connor (9:53.3), and Jim Moyle (10:08.0). The 'Cats also took 1-2-3 in the 880-yard run with Mike Porter (1:55.0) leading Karl Springer (1:59.0) and Darryl Brock (1:59.4).[18]

FINAL COMPETITION OF DUAL-MEET SCHEDULE

Photo 3-3

Mike Porter beginning his anchor leg of a victorious 'Cat effort in the mile relay after being passed the baton by Gene Meyers. *Wildcat*, March 6, 1970

24   Chapter 3

On a day marked by 105 degree weather at the capital city, Chico State edged Sacramento State 81-73 in a meet hosted by the Hornets. The distance races were characterized by slow times, owing to hot temperatures on the track causing blisters on the feet of competitors circling the track many times. In the mile relay, the final and deciding event, Flip Rowland led off with a 48.5 leg to give the 'Cats a six-yard lead. Jim Estes, a middle-distance runner, then matched up against Sac's top sprinter, Charlie Young. Young overtook Estes, giving a lead to his teammate running the third leg, during which Gene Meyers kept pace with the Hornet. The anchor leg matched Mike Porter against Sac's Clay Wilson. Running a little behind for most of the lap, Porter took the lead coming off the final turn, and victory was assured. The winning relay time was 3:18.2, with the Wildcats—two of them middle-distance runners—averaging 49.55 per quarter mile.[19]

WEST COAST RELAYS

Photo 3-4

Mike Dailey competing in the steeplechase at the West Coast Relays.
Courtesy of Mike Dailey

The next challenge awaiting Chico State in the remainder of its quickly closing 1970 season was the annual West Coast Relays. It was the top attraction in the nation that weekend as far as track and field was concerned—attracting teams from schools such as New Mexico State, Villanova, and Kansas along with a host of others from all over the country. Sixteen Wildcats were to participate, including the sprinters, middle-distance, and distance runners identified below:

440-Yard Relay
Dick Brignolo, Kirk Freitas, Dan Stevens, Randy Washington

Two-Mile Relay
Mike Porter, Flip Rowland, Rob Laxson, Jim Estes

Distance Medley
Jim Estes, Mike Porter, Rob Laxson, Gene Meyers

Steeplechase	**Three-Mile**	**5,000-Meter Run**
Mike Dailey	Ralph Patten	Bob Darling[20]

In the open 100-yard dash, in which Dick Brignolo was to compete, were some of the best sprinters in the world—including John Carlos (co-holder of the world record of 9.1) who would be running unattached (individual competitor without a team).[21]

FAR WESTERN CONFERENCE CHAMPIONSHIPS

Photo 3-5

Sac State's top sprinter Charles Banks outlegged Chico's Dick Brignolo to win the 440-yard relay at the Far Western Conference Championships.
The Record 1970, CSU Chico Digital Collections

The final challenge for the Wildcats was the Far Western Conference Championships, contested at Sonoma State over a two-day period in mid-May. At this meet would be an abundance of talent in the middle-distance and distance races. Most imposing was Humboldt's Bill Scobey—the defending national champion in the three-mile run—who would highlight the distance events.[22]

In the steeplechase, Davis Aggie Ed Haver, ranked eighth in the country with a best of 9:01, was the favorite. Chico's Mike Dailey with a best of 9:04 was ranked second in the conference and ninth in the nation. Next came Haver's teammate, Bryon Spradlin, tenth ranked and third in the conference behind Dailey with a time of 9:06.[23]

Humboldt State was also expected to field tough contenders in the 880 with Vince Engel (1:52) and Bill Scobey (1:52). The event favorite was Hayward's Larry Woods who had a best time of 1:50.1.[24]

Coach Larry Burleson believed that any one of four conference teams could emerge from the championship meet victorious. In the end, Chico finished a disappointing third behind Sacramento State, which successfully defended its title, and also Hayward State. An article in the *Wildcat* offered a reason for the results:

> Chico's specialties, the sprints and the distance events, seemed to fall apart. Sprinter Dick Brignolo and distance ace Gene Meyers were upset in their specialties.[25]

Wildcats Flynn Johnson and Will Mathews garnered first place honors in the intermediate-hurdles and discus, respectively, and triple jumper Bruce McLain finished second.[26]

Photo 3-6

Photo accompanying an article titled "Track leads the season; takes third in FWC," in *The Record 1970*.

> ## Chico State College
> ## 1970 Women's Track Team
>
> Deanne Carlsen
>
> **National Championships: May 29-30, Urbana, Illinois**

CONFERENCE CHAMPIONSHIPS

In 1970, the Chico State Women's Track Team won its first NCIAC Championship crown. (This acronym stands for Northern California Intercollegiate Athletic Conference.). Beneath the title, "CSC Wins Gals Track and Field Meet at Davis," an article in the *Chico Enterprise-Record* reported that "Chico State College's women's track team won the first Invitational Women's Track and Field Meet at the University of Davis." (This likely referred to the NCIAC meet). The team scores were: Chico State (107 points), San Jose State (100), Humboldt State (77), Brigham Young (75), Hayward State (55), UC Davis (33), and University of Nevada, Reno with 23 points.[27]

NATIONAL CHAMPIONSHIPS

The 2nd Annual DGWS (Division for Girls' and Women's Sports) National Intercollegiate Track and Field Championships were held at Urbana, Illinois, on May 29th and 30th, 1970. At this meet, Lady 'Cat Deanne Carlsen finished third in the 100-meter hurdles with a wind-aided time 13.9, earning All-American honors. More about Deanne follows in the book. A soon-to-be international-caliber athlete, she later took up the reins as coach of the Chico State Women's Track Team.

Photo 3-7

Photo 3-8

Left: Deanne Carlsen practicing hurdling, running barefoot on the grass.
Right: Coach Deanne Carlsen with her Chico State Women's Track Team at the 1974 National AIAW Track & Field Championships hosted by Texas Women's University at Denton, Texas.
Courtesy of Deanne (Carlsen) Vochatzer and Laura de Ghetaldi

4

1970 Wildcat Cross Country

This will be the best cross-country team that I have ever coached.

—Assertion by Chico State's cross country coach Larry Burleson as he talked about his team's upcoming season.[1]

Photo 4-1

Chico State Wildcat SPORTS

1970 Cross Country Schedule

DATE	OPPONENT	TIME	SITE
Sept. 19	Long Beach Invitational	10:00	Long Beach
Sept. 24	Southern Oregon College	3:00	Ashland
Sept. 25	Oregon College of Education	3:00	Monmouth
Sept. 26	Oregon All Comers Meet	11:00	Newberg
Oct. 3	Chico Invitational	11:00	CHICO
Oct. 10	Sacramento Invitational	12:00	Sacramento
Oct. 17	U.C. Davis & Cal Hayward	11:00	Hayward
Oct. 24	Humboldt State College	11:00	CHICO
Oct. 31	Sacramento State College	11:00	Sacramento
Nov. 7	Far Western Conference	11:00	Sonoma
Nov. 14	NCAA College Division	11:00	Wheaton, Ill.

Howard Miller was Chico State's second runner to finish at the Long Beach Invitational on September 19, 1970, helping the 'Cats to fourth place in the meet.[1] *Wildcat*, September 21, 1970

Chico State College 1970 Men's Cross Country Team

Brett Barham	Bob King	Howard Miller
Mike Dailey	Manny Mahon	Bob Wear
Bob Darling	Gene Meyers	Mike Vanderford
Jim Estes	Tom O'Connor	Nick Vogt
	Ralph Patten	

Photo 4-2

Chico State 1970 Cross Country Team. L-R: Bob Darling, Bob King, Manny Mahon, Bob Wear, Ralph Patten, Howard Miller, Brett Barham, Mike Dailey, Gene Meyers. Courtesy of Bob Darling

The 1970 'Cats were to start their cross country season five hundred miles south of Chico at the Long Beach Invitational. Running in the university division, they would compete against the likes of USC, UCLA, San Diego State, Long Beach State, etc., all whose enrollments were well over twenty-three thousand students. Burleson believed that if his harriers ran as well as they had done in the past, the Wildcats would make a good showing. The 'Cats were expected to be stronger with the addition of three top JC runners. They were Bob King from L.A. Valley College, coming up from Los Angeles in Southern California, and Brett Barham (Diablo Valley College), and Manny Mahon (DeAnza College), journeying from the San Francisco Bay Area.[2]

Making up the remainder of the team were veterans from the last season, but Estes had to sit this one out due to injury.[3]

Chico State could have competed in the college division, but as explained in a *Wildcat* article, Burleson "chose to make a go of it in the higher division to give the boys a shot at the big ones, as well as to show his confidence in them." His optimism was rewarded by a fourth place team finish behind winner Long Beach State, Cal State Fullerton in second, and San Diego State in third. The Wildcats looked tough with

Gene Meyers finishing eighth and Howard Miller eleventh overall in the race. No other northern California institutions competed in the meet, at least as far as team standings were concerned.[4]

SERIES OF MEETS IN OREGON

> *It was more of a tour than a trip. We traveled all across the state of Oregon. We visited the state capital, and had a real good time. I wanted to give them an opportunity to race up there, and they really enjoyed it.*
>
> —Coach Larry Burleson explaining why he arranged for the 'Cats to compete in three sequential, day-apart meets in Oregon.[5]

Between September 24-26, the Wildcat Cross Country team "toed the line" three days in a row against Oregon opponents in their home state. Larry Burleson and his famous brother Dyrol—a world-class miler and two time Olympian—were raised in Cottage Grove, Oregon. Larry attended Linfield College, earned All-American honors in football, and was drafted by the Green Bay Packers professional football team. After playing for the Packers in 1960-61, he decided to pursue a career teaching (physical education) and coaching.[6]

The 'Cats were victorious in three out of three shots, beginning with a 16-57 rout on Thursday against Southern Oregon in the first meet at Ashland. Chico's first five runners finished 1-2-3-4-6. But for Southern Oregon's top athlete crossing the finish line in fifth place, the 'Cats would have achieved a perfect team score of 15 points. This occurred the next day, Friday, in a meet with Oregon College at Monmouth. All eight Wildcat runners crossed the finish line of the 4-mile race together in a time of 21:20.[7]

The real test came on Saturday at the first annual George Fox All-Comer Invitational Cross Country Meet at Newberg. Three Oregon State runners finished in the top ten, including individual winner Spencer Lyman, who blazed to a time of 18:36 over the four-mile course. However, Chico had five runners in the top ten whose places combined for an overall score of 21 points for the team win; Oregon State was second with 44 points. Mike Dailey led the 'Cats with a second place finish (18:41), followed by Ralph Patten (3rd, 18:49), Gene Meyers (4th, 18:50), Bob Wear (6th, 18:58), and Brett Barham bringing up the tenth spot with a time of 19:02. Wildcats Bob King and Manny Mahon finished eleventh and twenty-first, respectively.[8]

CHICO INVITATIONAL

Photo 4-3

People don't realize how hard it is for them to psych themselves up meet after meet.

We will go with the studs there, and you will really see some action!

—Coach Burleson explaining why he didn't field his top runners at the Wildcat-hosted Chico Invitational, and what to expect a week later at the Sacramento State Invitational.[9]

Chico State's Tom O'Connor leading early in the race at the Chico Invitational. *Wildcat*, October 5, 1970

At the Chico Invitational on October 3rd, the Wildcat "B Squad" finished sixth in the university division with 156 points; behind UC Davis (53), Humboldt State (61), Cal State Hayward (70), UC Berkeley (72), and Southern Oregon (105), and ahead of seventh place San Francisco State (165). Tom O'Connor was the top 'Cat harrier, finishing 24th, with teammates Mike Vanderford (27th) and Nick Vogt (28th) close behind. The individual winner was Bill Scobey of Humboldt State with a very fast time of 25:04 for the five-mile course. In the junior college division, future Wildcats Jim Price and Mike Leonard, both of Shasta College, finished first and second with times of 27:03 and 27:07, respectively.[10]

SACRAMENTO INVITATIONAL

We will be faced with our sternest test this Saturday at the Sacramento State Invitational.
—Coach Larry Burleson.[11]

Heat, wind, and a somewhat unconventional course made for real difficult going Saturday at the Sac. State Cross Country Invitational. Runners from all parts of California and some from Nevada were showing their discomforts as times were slow and facial expressions were unbecoming.

—*Wildcat*, October 12, 1970.[12]

Chico State's top eight Wildcat runners—Dailey, Darling, Patten, Meyers, Wear, Miller, King, and Barham—travelled to Sacramento to compete against Stanford, Nevada, San Jose, and possibly USC, in addition to Far Western Conference opponents. The competition was expected to be tough. Behind the efforts of the nation's top two small college steeplechasers, Byron Spradlin and Ed Haver, UC Davis had captured the Chico Invitational the past weekend. Bill Scobey, easily winning the race, had led Humboldt to a second-place team finish.[13]

At Sacramento, high heat and wind adversely affected most teams, except perhaps Stanford, whose top runners finished one, two, and the Cardinal easily won the competition. The victory was contentious, however, as the first seven runners including three from Stanford had inadvertently cut the course in an area poorly marked. A *Wildcat* article reporting meet results, asserted:

> If the results remain as they now stand, it will be Stanford winning, West Valley Track Club in second, Cal State Fullerton third, Humboldt State fourth, San Jose State fifth, Chico sixth, Fresno State seventh, Cal State Hayward eighth, and the University of Nevada ninth.[14]

The Wildcat contingent finished in close proximity to one another; Bob Darling was 20th, followed by Howard Miller, Bob King, Ralph Patten, and Brett Barham. The following week would bring the first conference meet for the Chico Staters, with the 'Cats taking on UC Davis and Cal State Hayward, at Hayward, on Saturday.[15]

CHICO RUNNERS ROMP AT CAL STATE HAYWARD

> *Davis has a very strong team.... They will give us a good race, so the team has got to do the job.*
>
> *It was a complete reversal of the way we ran last week.*
>
> —Comments by Coach Larry Burleson before and after a meet at Hayward against two conference rivals.[16]

At Hayward, the Wildcats came out on top in a three-way meet with Davis and Hayward. Three-way meets also constituted two dual meets. Chico claimed both of these also, beating Davis 26-33 and dumping Hayward 27-44. Aggie Byron Spradlin won the five-mile race with a time of 24:24, followed closely by Chico's Mike Dailey in second with a time of 24:29. Gene Meyers was fourth, followed by Bob Darling (5th), Howard Miller (8th), Ralph Patten (9th), Brett Barham (11th), and Bob King (12th).[17]

Coach Burleson had individual praise for Dailey, who he said ran well, and also for Manny Mahon who finished sixteenth with a time of 26:09, which was a tremendous improvement for him.[18]

In their next contest the Wildcats were to battle Scobey, who had been extremely possessive of first place honors in the meets he had run that season. Humboldt also boasted two surprising freshmen, Craig Streichman and Ron Elijah, with veterans Howard Labrie and Gary Miller rounding out a team that had run to an easy victory over Sacramento State the previous weekend.[19]

WILDCATS TOP LUMBERJACKS

> *I am very pleased with our showing. We were deeply concerned about Humboldt, as they had beaten us earlier in the year at the Sacramento Invitational.*
>
> —Coach Larry Burleson.[20]

In their home meet with the Lumberjacks, the Wildcats prevailed in the greatly anticipated competition on the Bidwell Park Course. Bill Scobey won the race, keeping his season's unbeaten streak intact. All five of Chico's scoring runners crossed the finish line in the top ten. Mike Dailey and Bob Darling sparked the 'Cats victory with a tie for second—sealed by, on their heels, Gene Meyers in fourth, Ralph Patten sixth, and Howard Miller seventh.[21]

Photo 4-4

L-R: Bob Darling and Mike Dailey. *Wildcat*, October 26, 1970

FINAL CONFERENCE DUAL MEET

> *Manny Mahon and Bob Wear both showed they are getting stronger and will be in top shape for this weekend's conference finals at Sonoma.*
>
> *Humboldt, Hayward, and UC Davis are capable of giving us a tough time.*
>
> —Coach Burleson praising the performance of two of his runners in a team victory over Sacramento State, and acknowledging the strengths of competitor teams on the eve of the Far Western Conference Championships.[22]

An article in the *Wildcat*, noted about Chico's final conference race hosted by Sacramento State that "the Wildcats apparently were not bothered by the hard asphalt track at Sacramento." Top runner Bob Darling was held out due to the flu, but Mike Dailey won the race in a time of 26:14. Sacramento's Noel Hitchcook and Kevin Furey picked up the second and third places. Then came 'Cats in quick succession. Howard Miller was fourth, trailed by Ralph Patten (5th), Gene Meyers (6th), Manny Mahon (7th), Bob King (9th), and Bob Wear in tenth place.[23]

DISAPPOINTING SEASON'S END

> *Davis was up for the race, and won handily. Humboldt's phenom Bill Scobey placed first. Chico was third overall.... What could be responsible for the recent letdown? The Cat harriers have umpteen workouts a week, which is fine for condition. They also run with pressure—from the coach, fans, and school—which is fine too, if they can take it. The job of the mentor is to see that too much doesn't hit at once, evenly spreading the efforts of the team as well as giving them the will to win.*
>
> —From an article in the November 13, 1970 issue of the *Wildcat*.[24]

An article penned by the sports editor of the *Wildcat*, criticizing the performance of both the 1970 Wildcat Track and Cross Country teams in championship meets at season's end, spurred a response from a former Wildcat distance runner. (The preceding quoted material represents gentler portions of the rebuke of the team's head coach and of Gene Meyers for retiring from the race with muscle cramps.)

Two paragraphs of a letter from an ex-Wildcat runner, defending his former coach and team, follow:

> First of all, I would like to say that Burleson and the Chico State Cross Country team are the best unit Chico State—or the Far Western Conference—has ever seen. They were undefeated in dual meets (like last year's track team), they were favored (like last year's track team)—but this year I know for a fact Ralph Patten, Meyers and most of the other runners had the flu—if not during the meet—the week before, which made them a little weaker physically and mentally.
>
> Gene Meyers is the hardest working distance runner I have ever known—last year I had the opportunity to train with him—if you think that the fact Gene was unable to finish was unimportant to the Chico team you should turn in your note pad. Meyers is the type of runner that makes Chico the great team it is. You can bet one thing—If Meyers had to quit he was hurting very, very bad. Had Meyers finished in the place he was in when he developed cramps Chico would have won—it would have been close—but they would have won.[25]
>
> Thank you for equal time,
Karl Springer
X-country runner
Butte College cross country coach

5

Kim Ellison Arrives on Campus

In addition to Meyers and King in the distance events, the 'Cat cindermen have Mike Dailey returning in the steeplechase, and have added Juan Dura from Spain in their 880 unit.

—*Wildcat* article, February 26, 1971.

Wildcat Track & Field

**Chico State College
1971 Men's Track Team
Distance / Middle-Distance Runners**

Mike Dailey	Manny Mahon
Bob Darling	Gene Meyers
Juan Dura	Howard Miller
Kim Ellison	Ralph Patten
Jim Estes	Nick Vogt
Bob King	

The Wildcats first meet of the 1971 track season was scheduled to be against University of the Pacific at Stockton. The 'Cats were again blessed with a strong core of able distance and middle-distance runners, which included Gene Meyers and Mike Dailey. Meyers was the school record holder in the 880 with a time of 1:50.5; Dailey had lowered the steeplechase record by nearly 20 seconds the preceding track season; and augmenting the middle-distance runners was Spaniard Juan Dura.[1]

Due to some major adjustments in the UOP track program, the Tigers were not able to compete on a team basis during the '71 season. On the bright side, the program had obtained well-known coach, Dick Purcell, who had led Cal-Poly San Luis Obispo to two NCAA College Division National Championships. Moreover, Purcell's move to Stockton had spurred some Cal-Poly "cindermen" as well as other four-year school trackmen to transfer to UOP—which was expected to result in a powerhouse team for years to come.[2]

Among the Cal-Poly athletes accompanying their coach to Stockton was two-time defending NCAA college division 880 champion Mathyas

Michael. On the eve of the meet, Burleson expected Gene Meyers and Bob King would be up against Michael in the mile, which could make it the feature event. Meyers had run two spots behind Michael in the 880 at the Nationals two years earlier when his third place earned him 1969 All-American laurels.[3]

Amid a strong wind and intemittent rain, Chico State opened its 1971 season on a victorious note, compiling 80 ½ points in besting the Stockton Track Club (58) and San Francisco State (35 ½). University of the Pacific also competed but did not count in team scoring.[4]

Wildcat distance runners produced good efforts for the first meet. Senior Gene Meyers won the mile in 4:12.0 to defeat the Stockton Track Club's Mathyas Michael (4:15.6). Michael, with a best of 1:47.0 in the half-mile last year, came back to win the 880 in 1:55.1. Kim Ellison, a transfer from Butte College, clocked 4:18.2 to finish third in the mile. Mike Dailey won the two-mile in 9:25.6; Ralph Patten in second place received the same time. Chico's half-milers were also strong; Jim Estes was second to Michael with a 1:55.9 and Juan Dura was fourth at 1:56.5.[5]

MEET AGAINST THE UNIVERSITY OF NEVADA AND FRESNO PACIFIC UNIVERSITY

In early season competition at Reno, the Chico State Track Team used its field-event strength to surprise the powerful U of N's Wolf Pack. Chico finished with 80 points to Nevada's 68 and Fresno Pacific's 44 points. Contested in good weather with the temperature in the low 70s, the meet produced five stadium records. Mike Dailey set one in winning the 3,000-meter steeplechase with a time of 9:37.4. Nevada's Peter Duffy, an Englishman, broke the mile record with a 4:11.6 win. Nevada's 4 x 440 relay team zipped around the oval in 41.4 to set a new stadium and school standard. A fourth stadium record came in the mile relay when Flip Rowland, Don Crawford, Jim Estes, and Mike Porter put together a 3:14.7. The fifth record was by a Wolf Pack pole vaulter.[6]

Leading other Wildcat top-five, middle-distance and distance finishes was Jim Estes with a time of 1:55.0 in winning the 880-yard race. He was followed by teammates Juan Dura (3rd, 1:56.0) and Manny Mahon (4th, 1:59.0). Finishing well behind Dailey was Bob Darling (All-American in cross country, but rookie-steeplechaser) with a 10:30.5 fourth-place effort. Chasing Duffy in the mile, Kim Ellison finished second (4:15.6) and Gene Meyers third (4:18.4) in the event.[7]

Photo 5-1

Wildcat Juan Dura winning a 880-yard race later in the season. Jim Estes, in lane two, finished second and teammate Mike Dailey, inside him, third place. Trailing behind on the curb, Ralph Patten finished fourth.
Courtesy of Jim Estes

'CATS WIN AT HOME AGAINST THE 'JACKS

Photo 5-2

Wildcat Ralph Patten kneeling exhausted in the long jump pit, following a third-place finish in the 3-mile race.
Wildcat, March 8, 1971

In early March before a large partisan crowd, the Chico State Track Team chalked up its first Far Western Conference dual-meet victory with a score of 97-57 over Humboldt State. Bob Darling and Howard Miller both broke the school record of 30:50 in the six-mile run while finishing one-two. Darling hit the tape with a 30:22.6, followed by Miller, 15 seconds later. Gene Meyers also prevailed in the mile race.[8]

Chico State's next scheduled meets were the UC Davis Track Relays, followed by a dual meet with Central Washington.

'CATS HOST CENTRAL WASHINGTON AT HOME

> *[Lloyd] Jhanson with a 4:15 clocking in the mile already this season will put the pressure on the locals Gene Meyers (4:12), Kim Ellison (4:14) and Bob King (4:18). Burleson has been extremely impressed with Ellison so far. Combined with Meyers and King, he gives the Wildcats the depth they need.... Manny Mahon is beginning to come around and should give excellent depth in the 880 as he will team with Juan Dura and Jim Estes.*
>
> —*Wildcat* article offering a prospectus of a forthcoming track meet between Chico State and Central Washington.[9]

On March 20th, Chico State bested Central Washington with a score of 91-67 in their meet at College Field. In the mile, Gene Meyers and Kim Ellison were deadlocked at the end with a time of 4:23.2; Bob King finished a close third to sweep the event. The Wildcats also swept the three-mile race. Bob Darling slowed to allow his teammates to finish with him, resulting in a four-way tie for 1st place, there being no chance of being caught by the opponents. Rounding out the winners list for Chico was Jim Estes, who raced to victory in the 880 with a time of 1:54.3.[10]

SACRAMENTO STATE RELAYS, AND DUAL MEET AT SONOMA STATE

In a non-scoring meet in Sacramento, Chico garnered a trio of relay victories in impressive times. The two-mile relay team of Juan Dura, Kim Ellison, Gene Meyers, and Jim Estes clocked a fast 7:44.1—an average of 1:56 per half-mile leg. Flip Rowland (440), Dura (880), Ellison (1,320), and Meyers (mile) won the distance medley in 10:17.9. In the sprint relay, Mike Porter (440), Kirk Freitas (220), Rick Call (220), and Jim Estes (880) clocked 3:27.9.[11]

In a third-place effort by the 'Cats four-mile relay team—Ralph Patten, Bob Darling, Manny Mahon, and Mike Dailey—Dailey ran his anchor leg in 4:14.7, a personal best for the mile.[12]

In an ensuing dual meet at Sonoma State, the Chico State "cindermen" easily outmatched their opponents in scoring 129 points with 14 firsts in the 19 events. San Francisco State gained 57 points, while Sonoma State managed only nine.[13]

HOME MEET UNDER THE LIGHTS

Photo 5-3

L-R: Wildcats Gene Meyers, Mike Dailey, and Kim Ellison breaking the tape together in the 3-mile race, in a dual meet against Hayward State. *Wildcat*, May 21, 1971 (photo published well after the associated meet)

On April 24th, a Wildcat-hosted home meet against Hayward State conducted under stadium lights began at 6:30 P.M. In this meet, Chico piled up points in nearly every event while capturing 13 of 19 first places. Among the numerous 'Cat winners were Mike Dailey in the steeplechase (9:13.0); Jim Estes in the 880 (1:58.1); and, finishing the 3-mile race together, Gene Meyers, Mike Dailey, and Kim Ellison.[14]

WILDCAT DISTANCE RUNNERS BREAK RECORDS IN MEET AGAINST UC DAVIS

> *Gene Meyers doubled up to produce a 4:12.3 (mile) and a 1:53.0 (880) for the second fastest mile-880 combo ever in the FWC. Willie Eashman from Hayward [doubled] to produce times of 4:08.6 and 1:53.0 last year. Meyers' mile effort combined with Kim Ellison (4:13.0) and Jim Estes (4:13.8) established the best mile run ever by a fine school.*
>
> —*Wildcat*, May 4, 1971 article.

In early May, the Chico State Track Team faced little difficulty in winning its 20th consecutive dual-meet victory, dating back over the past three years, as the Wildcats easily bested UC Davis 115-57. Mike

Dailey set a new school record in the 3-mile by trimming 2.5 seconds off Duwayne Ray's 1969 mark of 14:26.2, but finished second to Aggie Byron Spradlin's 14:10.5. Bob Darling lowered his own 6-mile record by a minute to 29:22.8, but also came in second behind a Davis runner.[15]

Chico's final two track meets of the season before the Far Western Conference Championships began on Thursday, May 20th, were the West Coast Relays in Fresno, followed by a dual meet with two-time defending FWC champion Sac State.[16]

WEST COAST RELAYS IN FRESNO

On May 8th, at the annual West Coast Relays, Friday's portion of the big meet was postponed by rain, and all competition had to be conducted on Saturday. It was sunny and cool that day with little rain, and a heavy track from the day before. Wildcat Mike Dailey led the distance-running contingent by clocking a 9:02.8 in the 3,000-meter steeplechase, breaking the school record of 9:04.6 he set a year earlier.[17]

Chico State also placed in the open-division distance medley and the college-division two-mile relay. Villanova won the distance medley in 9:38.1, with Olympian Marty Liquori running the anchor leg. University of Houston (9:41.9) finished second, University of Utah (9:52.5) was third, and unheralded Chico State (10:03.2) fourth place.[18]

Running for Chico were Jim Estes (880), Flip Rowland (440), Kim Ellison (1,320), and Gene Meyers (mile). Kim Ellison recalled about this race, "Flip ran a great leg; Jim, Geno and I had run the 2-mile relay about an hour before the distance medley and were still feeling the effects...but we had a lot of fun!" The two-mile relay of Kim Ellison, Jim Estes, Gene Meyers, and Juan Dura had earlier finished second to Occidental with a time of 7:43.3, which had an identical time.[19]

CHICO WINS MEET AGAINST SAC STATE, BUT...

Chico State prevailed over Sacramento State in its final dual meet of the season, but Cal State Hayward, Sacramento State, and Chico State were all considered strong contenders to win the team title at the Far Western Conference Finals to be hosted by Chico State. A prospectus article in the *Wildcat* titled, "FWC Track Finals," cautioned:

> In dual meet competition, Chico has defeated both Hayward and Sacramento, but could be in trouble in the league finals because of the strengths of "non-favorite schools."

Humboldt State and U.C. Davis with its excellent distance runners, could take valuable points away from the 'Cats and may be darkhorses for the title.[20]

FAR WESTERN CONFERENCE CHAMPIONSHIPS

Chico State finished third in the FWC Finals at College Field. Hayward State won the meet with 170-1/3 points. Sacramento State tallied 143-1/3 points, and Chico State, 141, to take second and third in the team competition.[21]

Wildcats Gene Meyers and Jim Estes combined for three wins in middle-distance and distance events, with two of their victories being upsets. Meyers won the mile with a time of 4:06.7, then upset UC Davis' Ed Haver in the three-mile with a time of 14:07.2. Estes was at his very best in nipping Willie Eashman of Hayward State in the 880 with a time of 1:51.8. Eashman finished a whisker behind in 1:51.9.[22]

MEYERS AND ELLISON GARNER ALL-AMERICAN HONORS AT NCAA COLLEGE DIVISION NATIONAL CHAMPIONSHIPS

The 1971 NCAA College Division Track and Field Championships were held in Sacramento, California. At this meet, Far Western Conference distance runners fared well as evidenced by the following summary and complete results. Wildcats Gene Meyers and Kim Ellison finished second and sixth in the mile, earning All-American honors. This made Meyers a two-time All-American, his having finished third in 1969 in the 880-yard race.

Far Western Conference All-American Middle-Distance/Distance Runners

Event	Runner	School	Place	Time
880	Willie Eashman	Hayward State	4th	1:51.1
Mile	Gene Meyers	Chico State	2nd	4:06.2
	Kim Ellison	Chico State	6th	4:09.0
Steeplechase	Ed Haver	UC Davis	1st	8:51.1
	Daniel Mullens	Humboldt State	3rd	9:06.2
	Byron Spradlin	UC Davis	4th	9:07.7
	Kevin Furey	Sacramento State	5th	9:12.4

1971 NCAA College Division Track and Field Championships
Middle-Distance and Distance Events Results

880—1. Jay Fabian (Ashland) 1:48.3 (New record, old 149.3 by Rick Herrmann, San Diego State, 1966), 2. Eugene Weiss (Montclair State) 1:49.5), 3. Curt Thompson (Fullerton State) 1:51.0, 4. Willie Eashman (Hayward State) 1:51.1, 5. Ken Jacobi (Eastern Illinois) 1:51.2, 6. Dennis Bohlayer (US Coast Guard Academy) 1:51.5.

Mile—1. Wayne Seller (Eastern Michigan) 4:06.2, 2. Gene Meyers (Chico State) 4:06.2, 3. Dave Kampa (North Dakota State) 4:67.7, 4. Arthur Botterill (Southwest Louisiana) 4:08.4, 5. Thomas Carr (Hamilton) 4:09.0, 6. Kim Ellison (Chico State) 4:09.0.

Three Mile— 1. Gordon Minty (Eastern Michigan) 13.36.4 (New record, old 13:-56.0 by Ron Stonitsch, CW Post, 1970), 2. Mike Slack (North Dakota State) 13:-37.2, 3. Mark Covert (Fullerton State) 13:46.8, 4. John Casso (Fullerton State) 13:49.5, 5. William Ryan (Cal Poly Pomona) 13:50.2, 6. Rick Twedt (Northern Iowa) 13:52.0.

Six Mile—1. Gordon Minty (Eastern Michigan) 28:45.7, 2. Richard Bowman (Wabash) 28:46.1, 3. Mark Covert (Fullerton State) 29:09.4, 4. William Ryan (Cal Poly Pomona) 29:13.3, 5. Jimmy Howell (North Carolina) 29:22.5, 6. James Alexander (Denison) 29:28.2.

3,000-Meter Steeplechase—1. Ed Haver (UC Davis) 8:51.1 (New record, old 8:54.9 by Gary Tuttle Humboldt State, 1969), 2. John Costello (Central Michigan) 8:58.0, 3. Daniel Mullens (Humboldt State) 9:06.2, 4. Byron Spradlin (UC Davis) 9:07.7, 5. Kevin Furey (Sacramento State) 9:12.4, 6. Jeff Renneberg (St. Cloud State) 9:14.3.

Chico State College
1971 Women's Track Team
Deanne Carlsen

National Championships: May 14-15, Cheney, Washington

Deanne has competed in indoor meets at Bakersfield, Los Angeles, San Diego and San Francisco. She tied the meet record in the 100-meter hurdles in the LA Times Meet.

The next two meets are quite a distance from Chico. She hopes to compete in the Pan-American Games Trials April 29-30 that will be held in Quantico, Virginia. A week later the women's national intercollegiate championships are scheduled in Chicago, Illinois.

Former Chico High School track coach Mel Jones still helps Mrs. Carlsen. She'll be trying to qualify in both the 440-yard dash and 100-meter hurdles in the Pan-Am events. If she qualifies in the top four in either she'll earn a trip to the Games in Columbia, South America.

—Chico Enterprise-Record article, April 24, 1971, soliciting donations by individuals or community businesses to assist Deanne Carlsen, one of the most prominent women's track athletes in the United States. At this time, expenses for Finals were paid by the AAU (Amateur Athletic Union), but individuals had to pay their own costs until that time.

Women's Sports
Injury to Deanne Carlsen Puts Spotlight on Other Performers

A subsequent article in the *Enterprise-Record* on September 11, 1971, informed the public that an injury during the Pan American Games trials in the early part of May sidelined Carlsen from competition until July, causing her to miss the intercollegiate championships. The article went on to highlight other women athletes at Chico State, noting as a prelude to discussion about them:

> Although it may be hard to believe, the entire women's athletic program at CSC didn't collapse as a result of the unfortunate hamstring pull suffered May 1 by Deanne Carlsen. Rather the limelight had an opportunity to scatter its beam over the sundry sections that compose women's athletics on the local campus.

Carlsen was leading her heat by four yards, while competing in the Pan American Games trials in Quantico, Virginia, when she suffered a severely torn hamstring muscle. The injury forced her out of further competition, and she was unable to participate in the intercollegiate championships.[23]

MEL JONES AND COACHING ASSISTANCE

The Chico High track coach assisting Deanne Carlsen in training was a legendary figure. Melvin Richard Jones had served as a Radarman aboard the amphibious attack transport USS *Mellette* (APA-156) in World War II, and earned the Purple Heart Medal for being wounded in combat. Following the war, Jones first attended Marin Junior College, then transferred to Chico State, where he participated in baseball, track, and boxing, becoming a Far Western Conference boxing champion in 1950. Mel was the founder of the Chico Invitational Track Meet in 1958 and in 1998 the Chico High Track was dedicated as the "Mel Jones Track and Field Complex." Mel passed away on September 3, 2019, at age 94, greatly beloved in the Chico community.

One day in the spring of 1967, Deanne, then a student-athlete at Chico State, visited Chico High during the instruction portion of the day, to seek Coach Jones' assistance. Part of his help that day took the form of a slip of paper from the front office delivered to sophomore John Staples in class. Originated by Jones, it instructed Staples to leave class immediately, to "suit up," and to meet the coach out at the track.[24]

It was an overcast and rainy day. Staples must have wondered what was up. To his amazement, there stood a slight, blonde runner on the track, in the fog, waiting to hurdle. John had been taken out of his class to serve as a "rabbit," sprinting alongside and slightly ahead of Deanne Carlsen, a local Chico sports figure and legendary athlete, as she worked on her speed and technique over the single lane of hurdles set up.[25]

She blew out of the starting blocks over and over again. At the completion of this training session, high school sophomore John Staples, who would later run middle-distance races for the Wildcat Track Team, returned to class. Following her competitive career, Carlsen embarked on a career of teaching and coaching, which culminated in her selection as head women's coach of the 1996 U.S. Olympic Track and Field Team. When asked about the incident described, she recalled that training session at Chico High's dirt track and, to this day, appreciates the efforts of her young rabbit on that occassion.[26]

Photo 5-4

Photo 5-5

Left: John Staples winning an 880-yard race in 1:55.9, his senior year at Chico High School. Right: Head women's coach of the 1996 Olympic Track & Field Team, Deanne (Carlsen) Vochatzer.
Chico Enterprise-Record, May 10, 1969, and courtesy of Deanne (Carlsen) Vochatzer

6

1971 Harriers

"We are young and inexperienced, but we have a lot of talent and will be tough in the future."

Coach Burleson believes that his runners will have a good season. The track mentor feels that as soon as Kim Ellison, Bob King and Jim Estes return to action his team will be tough to beat

—*Wildcat* article quoting Coach Larry Burleson, and providing his assessment of team prospects after his harriers kicked off the 1971 cross counry season the previous weekend.[1]

Chico State College 1971 Men's Cross Country Team

Brett Barham	Mike Fornaciari	Jim Price
Tom Brown	Bob King	Junior Torres
Kim Ellison	Mike Leonard	Nick Vogt
Jim Estes	Scott McVey	Dave Wood

In pre-conference action, the '71 Wildcat Cross Country Team travelled to Oregon and Idaho for a series of meets. They opened their season with an 18-42 victory over Southern Oregon at Ashland, Oregon, and, the following day, "carded" a 24-36 win over Ricks College (which is today Brigham Young University–Idaho). In their third meet in three days, the Chico harriers went up against Boise State on Saturday and were beaten 22-54.[2]

The Wildcats were next to host their own meet, the Chico Invitational. The UC Berkeley (Cal) team was expected to honor the small town of Chico (population then a little over 20,000) by showing up for the meet. Also on hand would be the six Far Western Conference schools, with Cal and Humboldt State as the favorites. Davis was thought to be a "darkhorse" competitor.[3]

The race in Bidwell Park proved that the Cal Cross Country Team could beat all the schools in the Far West Conference. The Bears easily won the meet with 44 points, with Chico State finishing a surprising second with 64 points, and UC Davis a close third with 67. Scott

McVey, a Junior College transfer, was the top placer for the 'Cats with a sixth-place finish. Coming in ninth, Tom Brown, from Oroville (as was Gene Meyers), was another talented and tough runner produced by that nearby town. Kim Ellison grabbed the tenth spot.[4]

Chico's next meet was the Sacramento Invitational. Burleson believed that the competition would be extremely difficult, but in a very strong and satisfying showing, the Wildcats finished fourth behind Cal State Fullerton, San Diego State, and defending champion Stanford University. Junior Torres and Kim Ellison were the "top 'Cats," finishing in 16th and 19th places.[5]

Following this invitational, the Wildcat harriers travelled to Sonoma State in the third week of October, for a three-way meet with San Francisco State and Sonoma. Chico swept the first five places in the 5-mile race with Wildcat leaders Dave Wood, Nick Vogt, and Jim Price tying for first while setting a course record of 27:22.2. Chico also finished second through fifth with Nick Vogt, Mike Fornaciari, Brett Barham, and Mike Leonard, the fourth through seventh Wildcats across the line. Team scores were Chico State 15, San Franciseo 48, and Sonoma 85.[6]

PLEASANT HILL INVITATIONAL

We had a rough week and we were tired.

—Observation by Coach Burleson after the Wildcats finished fourth at the Pleasant Hill Invitational in Hayward.[7]

Near the end of October, Chico travelled to the Pleasant Hill Invitational, in the East Bay of the San Francisco Bay Area. Cal State Hayward was among the nine teams competing and dual meet scoring between Chico and Hayward would count as a meet. Among the other teams entered were Fresno State, Westmont College, Eastern Washington, and U.S. International.[8]

Chico State bested Hayward State, which was the prime objective of the weekend, led by Kim Ellison, who finished eighth. In the team competition, Chico finished fourth behind winner Westmont College, Fresno State in second, and Whitworth in third (a participating school from eastern Washington), only one point ahead of the Wildcats.[9]

The following weekend, the 'Cats were to travel to Davis for a meet with the Aggies and Sacramento State. At that point in the season, Davis was number one in the conference.[10]

UC DAVIS HARRIERS DOMINANT

In the dual meet between Chico and the Aggies on the Davis course, the host defeated the 'Cats by a 20-35 score. John Sheehan won the race in a time of 24:35, followed by a teammate in second. Kim Ellison finished fourth in 24:51, but Chico was disadvantaged owing to two of the Wildcat runners being out with injuries.[11]

The next contest, the Conference Championships in Arcata, was to be hosted by the Humboldt Lumberjacks. The meet would also determine who would qualify for the NCAA College Division Championships in Wheaton, Illinois, the following weekend.[12]

FAR WESTERN CONFERENCE CHAMPIONSHIPS

In the FWC Championship race at Arcata, Davis star John Sheehan won the race in a time of 24:58, leading the Aggies to a team victory. Humboldt State took second place, followed by Chico State, Hayward State, Sacramento State, San Francisco State, and Sonoma State.[13]

Running one of his best races, Kim Ellison grabbed second place with a fine time of 25:08. The next Chico finisher was Dave Wood in the fourteenth position. Leaving Arcata, Ellison might have another week of practice, depending on whether the Chico State Finance Board decided, in the forthcoming week, to pay the costs for him to travel to and compete in the College Division Finals at Wheaton.[14]

7

Ellison Attempts Sub-4 Minute Mile

Wildcat Track & Field

**Chico State University
1972 Men's Track Team
Distance / Middle-Distance Runners**

Tom Brown	Scott McVey
Dan Chapman	Pat Stordahl
Juan Dura	Junior Torres
Kim Ellison	Nick Vogt
Gil Escoto	Dave Wood
Bob King	

The Chico State Track Team opened its 1972 season on an impressive note by taking 13 out of 19 events, scoring an easy victory over San Francisco State and University of the Pacific. In distance events, Kim Ellison won the mile with an exciting early season time of 4:09.3, and teammates Tom Brown and Pat Stordahl raced to wins in the 3,000-meter steeplechase and 3-mile run, respectively.[1]

Kim Ellison kept rolling in an ensuing meet at home in which the Wildcats piled up 126 points while easily beating two FWC rivals: San Francisco State with 70 ½ points and Sonoma State's 12 ½. Streaking to a win in the two-mile, Ellison set a new school record of 8:59.8—one of the fastest times by a college division runner all year. The 'Cats also won eleven other events, including victories by Dave Wood in the mile, and Juan Dura in the 880-yard race.[2]

Following this impressive showing, Chico next traveled to Arcata, to take on arch-rival Humboldt State.

At the Arcata competition the Wildcats buried the Lumberjacks 113-59. Doing their part, Chico's middle-distance/distance runners won five events and scored additional points with other finishes.[3]

Ellison posted another personal best of 4:08.8 in the mile, finishing ahead of Humboldt's Dan Mullens (4:13.0) and teammate Scott McVey in third with a fast 4:15.1. Dave Wood nosed out Humboldt's Hersh Jenkins in a quick 880, clocking a 1:55.5 to his 1:55.6. Freshman Tom Brown ran away from the field in the 3,000-meter steeplechase while lowering his best to a time of 9:18.8.[4]

The 'Cats were also victorious in two other distance races. Junior Torres and Dan Chapman both clocked a 31:08.5 in tying for first in the six-mile. Pat Stordahl ran 14:17.3 to win the three-mile, in which Ellison finished in second place.[5]

Following this series of meets, the Wildcats were idle until April 1st when they hosted Boise State College at home. Gaining some measure of revenge for Chico's previous Camellia Bowl football loss to Boise State, the 'Cats achieved an easy 96-55 victory over the Broncos. As in previous meets, stalwarts Tom Brown won the steeplechase, Kim Ellison, the mile, and Pat Stordahl captured first in the three-mile. Next on the 'Cats' schedule were the Sacramento and Davis Relays on sequential weekends.[6]

SACRAMENTO AND DAVIS RELAYS

At the Sacramento State Relays, Chico's four-mile relay quartet—Tom Brown, Dave Wood, Pat Stordahl, and Kim Ellison—clocked a 17:11 (averaging 4:17.75 per mile); brought home to victory by Ellison's 4:06.5 anchor leg. Ellison also anchored the distance medley team of Don Crawford (440), Scott McVey (880), Brown (1,320) and Ellison (mile) to a second-place finish. Placing fourth in the two-mile relay were Wood, McVey, Gil Escoto, and Juan Dura.[7]

The following week at the Davis Picnic Day Relays, Pat Stordahl set a new meet record while racing to a 9:09.2 in the two-mile—edging UOP's John Caldwell and Sacramento State's Noel Hitchcock at the tape in a brilliant race. Caldwell and Hitchcock finished in the same time for second and third. In relay competition, Chico's distance medley team of McVey (880), Dura (440), Brown (1,320), and Ellison (mile) clocked a 9:58.8 for second place behind University of the Pacific.[8]

After these two relay meets, the Wildcats were slated to return to FWC dual-meet action at Cal State Hayward the following Saturday.

STREAK OF DUAL-MEET WINS BROKEN

Chico State's record of 28 straight dual-meet wins came to an end in Hayward, when the Pioneers edged the 'Cats 85-78 in team competition. Leading Hayward State (the defending FWC team champion), were miler Willie Eashman and field events-standout Art McCollum. In the feature race of the meet, Eashman nipped Ellison at the tape, finishing with a 4:05.0 clocking to Ellison's 4:05.1 in the mile. Ellison doubled back in the three-mile, finishing second with a time of 14:46.0 behind teammate Pat Stordahl who won the race in 14:26.8. In other distance action, Tom Brown and Scott McVey finished one-two in the steeplechase with times of 9:32.1 and 9:46.8, respectively; and Dave Wood broke the tape in 1:55.9 to win the 880-yard run. Bypassing the 880, in which he would normally doubleback, Eashman ran a leg on the victorious mile relay, which decided the meet as Hayward crossed the finish line in 3:18.5 to Chico's best of the season 3:18.8.[9]

MEET AGAINST UC DAVIS AT HOME

> *"Go for Four!" will be the slogan for this Saturday night's Chico State track meet with U.C. Davis.*
>
> *The meaning has nothing to do with Chico's recently ended 28-consecutive dual meet victories nor with the majority of the evening's activitites, which will begin at 6:30 P.M.*
>
> *It will, in fact, deal with only one race of the evening, The Mile Run.*
>
> *Kim Ellison, Chico's crack miler, who recorded a 4:05.1 clocking last week against Hayward, will be going out for the North Valley's first ever sub-four-minute mile.*
>
> —*Wildcat*, April 28, 1972 article previewing the expected feature event, a mile race focused on Wildcat Kim Ellison, in a home meet against UC Davis at Chico's College Field.[10]

In the same article quoted above, Coach Larry Burleson explained:

> We had been planning for Kim to go for the four-minute mark in the Fresno West Coast Relays, but since this is an Olympic year, only the 1,500 meters will be run at the West Coast. Therefore, we decided to move up our schedule and make a run at the mark this Saturday night at College.[11]

The following account from the author's book *Toe the Mark* (a companion to *Stride Out*) provides amplifying information about Kim Ellison, frequent nighttime conditions at College Field, and results of the race the night of April 29, 1972.

Ellison had a storied past as an elite runner, interrupted by military service in Vietnam. After graduating high school in 1965, as the three-time L.A. City Section Cross Country champion and the Los Angeles City Section 2-mile champion with a time of 9:20.0 and a second-place finish at the State Meet, he attended California State University, Northridge, for a time on a track scholarship, before leaving school to take a position with Adidas, then a fledgling shoe company.

One day his laidback lifestyle came to an end while hanging out on a beach with some friends, when his brother, Kerry, came running up, waving an envelope, and yelling, "You got drafted." Kim's Army duty in Vietnam, at the Marble Mountain Army Airfield, south of Da Nang city, was, at first, as a clerk typist and later as a beach lifeguard. At the completion of his two-year obligation, Ellison was discharged from the Army and returned home.

Following the advice of Jim Roulsten, a former teacher and good friend, he headed to Chico, a small college town and agricultural community ninety miles north of Sacramento and enrolled at Butte College. Despite, understandably not training in Vietnam, he retained his immense talent and competitive nature, and a return to fitness quickly followed. Within a year, he was on the Chico State Track Team and racing for a national championship in the mile, while pursuing a degree in English. In his final year at Chico State, Ellison wanted to break 4 minutes on his home track in front of hometown fans.

One disadvantage of the open stadium at Chico State was that it was subject to mountain breezes (wind). To the east, lay the foothills of the Sierra Nevada mountains. In the evening when the sun had set and it was cooler at higher elevations than in the valley, cold dense air would flow downslope to fill the void left by rising warm air. This is the definition of wind—the movement of air masses from areas of higher density to areas of lower density—and the winds often picked up in the evenings in Chico. Moreover, unlike today, with the athletic fields at Chico State reduced to provide space for new buildings constructed since 1972, there were then practically no impediments to buffeting winds. As a result of this geography, it was generally more-windy during evening track meets than daytime ones. Despite this, it was exciting for the athletes to compete under stadium lights with more fans in attendance coming out for an evening after work.

On Saturday night, April 29th, hundreds of spectators were present in the stands at the track stadium at Chico State University to witness Ellison's attempt to break the 4-minute mile. This feat had first been accomplished by Englishman Roger Banister at Oxford on May 6, 1954. Many others had subsequently also broken this barrier, but no Wildcat (Chico State track athlete) to date. At that time, Jim Ryun held the World and American Records of 3:51.1, set on June 23, 1967.

THE MILE RACE

Wildcats Bury Aggies 120-51
Ellison Runs 4:01.4 Despite Cold Wind

—*Chico Enterprise-Record* headline in Monday's newspaper.

Photo 7-1

Wildcat Kim Ellison winning the mile race during a home meet on April 29, 1972.
Chico Enterprise-Record photograph

The following description of the exciting race is from the *Enterprise-Record*, found below a short, informative headline:

> Chico State College's premier miler Kim Ellison didn't get his sub-four-minute mile clocking at College Field Saturday evening but it was not because he failed to run a brilliant race.
>
> Despite a bitterly cold wind which swept the local track Ellison streaked to a 4:01.4 clocking and gave promise he'll crack the barrier in the near future.

Paced by teammate Bob King, Ellison was under 60 seconds after the first 440 and at two minutes for the 880. Midway the third lap Ellison was forced to take the lead. He finished the 1,320 at three minutes then sprinted hard the last quarter. He tightened some coming down the stretch but his 4:01.4 was a great race. He broke the CSC mark of 4:02.9 set in 1969 by Duwayne Ray.

Ellison's clocking also broke the stadium record of 4:06.7, set the preceding year by Wildcat Gene Meyers. Finishing behind Ellison, UC Davis' Dwayne "Peanut" Harms broke his school's record with a time of 4:07.1.

Two other Wildcat distance runners also garnered wins in the meet with UC Davis. Dave Wood won the 880 with a time of 1:55.1; and Pat Stordahl raced to victory with a 14:21.5 in the 3-mile.

Ellison's time of 4:01.4 on the dirt track would be the fastest mile of his life. Unfortunately, going sub-four wasn't in the cards for him. One week later, he tore ligaments in his foot from landing in pea gravel (in a French drain on the inside of the curb) during a race on Sacramento State's new all-weather track. The injury took about a year to heal, and Kim could not compete again at a high level.

A year later, while serving as a "rabbit" (pacesetter) for the open indoor mile at the Cow Palace (located in Daly City near San Francisco), and at the Bakersfield Invitational, Ellison found that he no longer had his "top-end gears." His ability to "kick" at the end of races was gone. Despite great disappointment that his competitive running was over, Kim finished school, earned his degree, and readily embarked on a teaching and coaching career.

Kim Ellison's school mile record of 4:01.4 stood for thirty-seven years until April 12, 2008, when Scotty Bauhs broke it with a time of 3:59.81. In doing so, he became the 308th American to break the magical 4-minute mile barrier.

FINAL DUAL MEET AT SACRAMENTO

Sacramento State prevailed over Chico 98-73 in the final meet of the season prior to the conference championships, but Chico dominated the distance events with four wins. Tom Brown won the steeplechase in 9:14.6; Kim Ellison, the mile (4:12.6); Dave Wood, the 880 (1:55.3); and Pat Stordahl, the three-mile. Stordahl's time of 14:26.6 was a minute faster than the second-place finisher.[12]

Following the meet with Sac State, Chico planned to send some competitors to the West Coast Relays at Fresno, but would not compete again as a team until the FWC Championships in Davis, May 18th-20th.

WILDCATS A DISAPPOINTING FOURTH

At the Far Western Conference Championships, Chico State finished fourth in the team competition with 107 points. Sacramento State took top honors with 150 points, followed by Hayward, a close second with 145. Humboldt was third with 115 points. During the rain-dampened meet, the only distance-event winner for the 'Cats was Pat Stordahl who set a school record in the three-mile by clocking a fast 14:06.4. Kim Ellison, who had hurt ligaments in his foot in an earlier meet against Sac State, had to settle for second in the mile at 4:14.9, which Willie Eashman of Hayward won in 4:07. Scott McVey of Chico State was fourth in 4:18.9. Freshman Tom Brown finished fifth in the steeplechase race with a time of 9:43.2, and Nick Vogt was sixth in the twenty-four-lap, 6-mile race (30:52.5).[13]

Photo 7-2

Pat Stordahl in Placerville, California, in summer 1972, at which he won the hilly 5¼-mile Hangtown road race hosted there. Courtesy of Calvin Lantrip

---

Chico State University
1972 Women's Track Team

Distance / Middle-Distance Runners
Shirley Miller, Regina Robinson, and Darlene Wallach

National Championships: May 12-13, Knoxville, Tennessee

THREE WAY TRACK MEET

Minutes before the running of the last event of a three-way meet with Hayward State and Cal-Poly San Luis Obispo, the Chico Ladies' Track Team learned that they were behind Hayward by 4 ½ points. (Sometime after 1969, the use of the moniker "Wildkittens" to describe Wildcat women's sport teams had fallen out of favor, and had been replaced with "Lady 'Cats.") If Chico could win the 880-yard relay, and Hayward place last, the Chico tracksters would win the meet. Leadoff runner Carol Stanley was ahead when she passed the baton to Sandy Cola, who stretched the lead. From there it was easy, Chico third and fourth runners—Karen Bulbeck and Nancy Wedel—were never challenged and Chico won the relay easily. Team excitement about this victory faded, however, when Hayward's anchor leg runner crossed the finish line in second.[14]

The final team scores were Hayward State 94 ½, Chico State 93, Cal-Poly San Luis Obispo 37 ½.[15]

Earlier that day, excitement was produced by three nationally-ranked exhibition runners, representing the Sacramento Road Runners Club, who weren't scored in the events in which they participated. Chico State student and Olympic hopeful, Deanne Carlsen, ran the 100-meter hurdles in 13.8. Finishing first for purposes of scoring, Hayward's Linda Vagmonde trailed well behind with a time of 15.3. United States-Soviet Union dual-meet winner, Kathy Hammond, raced to a time of 55.3 in the 440-yard dash. Kathy Medlin of Chico State ran a 64.9 for first place. In the 880, Nancy Mullen crossed the finish line in 2:23.2 with Chico's Regina Robinson first in the event with a time of 2:40.9.[16]

In the longest race of the meet (and run at that time for Ladies track), the mile run, Chico's Darlene Wallach and Shirley Miller finished first and second with times of 6:21.9 and 6:45.9.[17]

NCIAC AND NATIONAL CHAMPIONSHIPS

The 1972 Northern California Intercollegiate Athletic Conference (NCIAC) Championships at Davis offered one final opportunity for athletes to qualify for the National Championships. A photograph of a t-shirt from this meet follows:

Photo 7-3

T-shirt from the National Championships.
Courtesy of Laura de Ghetaldi

At the Fourth Annual DGWS National Championships, held May 12th-13th, 1972 at Knoxville, Tennessee, Chico State's Lynn Cannon threw the javelin 156 feet, 10 inches—good for second in the event and All-American honors for the Lady 'Cats.

8

Bob Darling's Participation in the Olympic Trials

Photo 8-1

Bob Darling qualified for the 1972 Olympic Trials Marathon with a time of 2:28:53 at the West Valley marathon in San Mateo, California, and competed in the Trials. Eight years later, he ran 2:25.54 at West Valley trying to qualify for the 1980 Trials, but by that time the standard for competing had dropped from 2:30 (1972) to 2:21:53 (1980). At the right is his later-framed race number from the 1972 trials. Courtesy of Bob Darling

Bob Darling (an All-American at the 1969 NCAA College Division Cross Country Championships) like many college athletes, continued to train and race after graduation—some for decades. This chapter is devoted to Darling's compelling account (contained within the brackets) of qualifying for, and taking part in, the 1972 Olympic Trials Marathon.

I qualified for the 1972 Olympic Marathon Trials on a whim. It was the first time there was a marathon trials qualifying standard for the 26-mile, 385-yard race at two hours and thirty minutes. Only 12 runners had run under 2:30 in 1971 (a time requiring a 5:43 average mile pace). I had decided to run the West Valley marathon in San Mateo in February 1972. My prior personal best (PB) was 2:43 in 1969.

I knew that I could run way faster than that. I was fit but did not do a special marathon training block. So, I surprised myself by running a PB 2:28:53. The last 10k was a super slow 40 minutes. Nevertheless, I was shocked and proud to qualify for the Olympic marathon trials. That race had 11 other qualifiers.

So, I joined another 99 fellow qualifiers from all across the United States in heading to Eugene, Oregon ("Track Town, USA"). The downside was that you had to pay for all your expenses. Some competitors had their club, school or military do so, but they were a minority. It was still the amateur days of the AAU (Amateur Athletic Union). Years later, the AAU did pay for all qualifiers.

Photo 8-2

Bob Darling, in center of photo wearing an RCS (Redwood City Striders) jersey, and to his left (right of photo), "Mad Dog" Bill Scobey competing in a race in 1972 at San Francisco's Golden Gate Park.
Courtesy of Bob Darling

In June, I got a ride up to Eugene (10 hours) in an old VW van driven by our crazy coach, Mike Ipsen. Qualifiers from the Redwood City Striders team were Mitch Kingery, age 16, Jose Cortez, age 19 and me age 22. We all had limited funds and decided to camp out at a local campsite. As were the circumstances, we could not afford the $10 daily fee for room and board in the University of Oregon dormitories. It rained the first two nights and our tent leaked. Here was the biggest race of my life and I'm sleeping on the ground!

The next day I ran into a former running friend Dan Best and found out his parents lived in Eugene. I got upgraded to their spare bedroom floor that night. I also found out too late that day that Nike was giving out a pair of prototype-running shoes to all the marathon qualifiers

(100). It was the first Nike shoes for the masses! I did receive a free trials t-shirt, stating USA Munich Trials 1972, Eugene, Oregon. I treasured that shirt for the next few years.

The day of the race was too warm (70 degrees). They herded the 100 runners into a packed bullpen area next to the track. The trials crowd was cheering loud. Track Town fever! I told a friend, Mark Covert, that it was too warm and that a time of 2:20 would qualify for the team. He said "no way with all these fast runners." Turned out that 2:20 was the 3th place finishing time that made the U.S. team to Munich. (Mark was in third place at 20 miles and ended up sixth.)

The meet official opened the bullpen gate and asked all the runners to head out to the starting line on the track. No one moved. I was standing next to Frank Shorter (eventual 1972 Olympic marathon winner). I was in awe of him! Then we both just silently headed out and the rest of the runners followed. The crowd went wild when we came into sight and I felt like a Roman gladiator going out into the Coliseum! The officials lined us up on the track. I was in row 7 at the rear. Never before had I been in a race with 100 fast runners that started on a track.

The elite 100 runners started out quickly with 3 laps of the 400-meter track before heading out onto the University of Oregon campus. We ran across the Willamette River bridge to the running paths, and I went too fast for the first two miles; due to being tense and nervous. My training prior to the race had been up and down, so I developed a few hot spots on my feet and mental fatigue. I dropped out at 13 miles.

Then I got a ride back to Hayward Field in the race "sag wagon." I was embarrassed, as it was my first DNF (did not finish) in any race. We picked up a few more runners. As it turned out, 33 out of 100 starters DNF'd the race. I entered the Hayward Field east stadium stands and sat down to watch the featured 5,000-meter race. I heard someone call my name. It was my old high school cross country coach Kevin Calandi. I had not seen him in five years. He was happy to see me and consoled me that I had come a long way from Riordan High School to the Olympic Trials, and I felt better.

We watched together as "Pre" (Steve Prefontaine) jogged out to the track. He took off his top t-shirt and the one remaining read "Stop Pre" embossed over a red stop sign (created by Gerry Lindgren, who had introduced it in a previous competition against Prefontaine). The crowd went wild. Prefontaine was battling "old man" George Young, who was all of 32 years old. Pre had to run an American 5,000 meter record of 13:22:8 to beat Young's PB of 13:29. It was an exciting race.

The next day, I headed back to San Francisco to get on with the rest of my life. I had come a long way from being an average high school runner (4:43 mile/9:59 2-mile) to the Olympic Trials. Eugene continues to hold a special place in my heart.

I tried to qualify for the Olympic Trials Marathon in 1976 and 1980. (Trials fever every four years.) I came fairly close in 1980. The marathon effort earned me a new nickname, "The Rocket." That is another story for another day.

"MAD DOG" BILL SCOBEY THWARTED BY INJURY

Bill Scobey, a 2:15.21 marathoner and one of the favorites to make the Olympic team, was sidelined by injuries and unable to compete in the trials. Highlights while running for Humboldt State (1969-72) follow:

Photo 8-3

Enrolled at Humboldt State in 1969 following his U.S. Army service

NCAA College Division 3-mile champion in 1969

Personal Bests:
880 (1:52.6), mile (4:03.2), 2-mile (8:48.2), 3-mile (13:38.2), 6-mile (28:42.2), marathon (2:15.21)

Bill Scobey leading Mark Covert in the 1971 PA-AAU one-hour run. He took second to Bill Clark in this race. (*Nor-Cal Running Review*, February 1973)

Darling provided some background material about Army veteran-FWC competitors, and the 1971 NCAA College Division National Track Championships:

> Bill Scobey, Gary Tuttle and Kim Ellison all got drafted and did two years in the U.S. Army. All were from SoCal [Southern California]. They were national-class runners. In fact I let Gary Tuttle stay in my room at Sacramento State during the 1971 NCAA D2 track championship! Burleson would of "blown a gasket" if he had found out. I had the fourth fastest 6-mile time and had a shot at top six placing for All-American status. But a serious chest cold hindered me and I placed 13th in 30:50.

9

1972 Cross Country Season

Photo 9-1

Pat Stordahl was selected as the CSU Chico Coaches' Athlete of the Week, following his individual win in the opening meet of the Cross Country season. (In 1972, Chico State College became California State University, Chico.) *Wildcat*, October 10, 1972

Chico State University 1972 Men's Cross Country Team		
John Aldridge	Neil Glenesk	Mark Shuman
Tom Brown	Bob King	Eddie Silva
Dan Chapman	Mike Leonard	Pat Stordahl
Pat Finn	Scott McVey	Junior Torres
Mike Fornaciari	Jim Price	Dave Wood

The 1971 Cross Country 'Cats opened their season at 11 A.M. on a Saturday morning, in a home meet against San Francisco State's Golden Gator squad. Spectators were advised that the best location to watch the 5-mile race in upper Bidwell Park, was on a hillside directly below the Easter Cross.[1]

When the competition was over, Chico runners had astoundingly swept the top nine places in beating the university by the bay, 15-50. Senior Pat Stordahl, defending FWC three-mile champion, led the assault in record time, 24:27. Eddie Silva, former Watsonville High School great, finished second, followed by Tom Brown, Neil Glenesk and Mike Fornaciari, third through fifth, respectively. Coach Burleson had special praise for Freshmen Pat Finn and Mark Shuman.[2]

Photo 9-2

Chico State Wildcats in a cross country race.
Left to right: Mike Leonard, Mike Fornaciari, Pat Finn, and Scott McVey.
Courtesy of Pat Finn

Photo 9-3

Photo 9-4

Left: Pat Stordahl racing to victory in the 1972 meet against San Francisco State.
Right: Watsonville High's Eddie Silva (wearing a West Valley Track Club singlet) competing in the PA-AAU 20km Championships in 1970.
Wildcat, October 6, 1972, and *West Valley Newsletter*, March 1970

In 1969, Watsonville High's Eddie Silva had won the Nor Cal USTFF/T&FN two- and three-mile postal races on the track. "Postal" meant that meet results would be posted (mailed) to *Track and Field News* magazine. Going into the last lap of the three-mile race, Silva trailed by about 15 yards, but put on a good kick to win in 14:47.2.[3]

CHICO STATE INVITATIONAL

In the Chico 11th Annual Invitational, Humboldt's Steve Mead won the contest in 23:40, shattering the course record of 24:21, which six other runners also dipped under. However, the biggest surprise to many people was Eddie Silva finishing second and leading the Wildcats to a 35-42 upset victory over favorite UC Berkeley. Pat Stordahl and Tom Brown took the fifth and sixth positions, Mark Shuman came in ninth, and Neil Glenesk, thirteenth. Shuman, a freshman, earned special praise from Burleson.[4]

During the race, there were more than 100 spectators at the creek crossing out on the course, suggesting that this was becoming the favorite viewing spot for observers.[5]

The following week, the 'Cats team planned to split with one squad going to the Jefferson Days run in Ashland, Oregon, and another to the Sacramento State Invitational—to allow more runners the chance to compete.[6]

CONFERENCE DUAL MEET

In late October, led by Eddie Silva with a time of 23:43, Chico raced to an easy victory over a weak Sacramento Hornets squad. Pat Stordahl was second in 23:57, and Bob King, Tom Brown, and Dan Chapman placed fourth, seventh, and eighth, respectively, for the 'Cats.[7]

FAR WESTERN CONFERENCE CHAMPIONSHIPS

> *"I honestly don't know who will run for us. I doubt if we have seven healthy competitors." The problem seems to be injuries in some cases and a virus cold or flu in others.*
>
> —*Wildcat*, November 2, 1972 article quoting Coach Burleson's response to a question about the expected composition of Chico's 7-man team at the Conference Championships, and assessment by the interviewer of the reason the cross country team was not then at full strength.

In late season, on the eve of the Conference Championship, the Chico State Cross Country Team was not at full strength owing to injuries and sickness, leaving Coach Burleson in a quandary. Should he run top performers who might be slowed by ailments but who, if they could perform at their best, would most help the team? Or should he select replacments who were neither sick nor injured? He had the fifteen individuals listed at the chapter's head from which to choose.[8]

UC Davis and Humboldt State were considered to be the toughest teams in the FWC, and the favorites to take home team honors. Competing for individual honors were Humboldt's Chuck Smead and Ron Elijah; UC Davis' "Peanut" Harms, John Sheehan, and Bill Hansen; Jerry Metcalf of Hayward; and perhaps any of the seven Chico runners that toed the line on Saturday morning.[9]

When the championship race was completed on Sacramento State's course and team scores were calculated, UC Davis came out ahead, with Humboldt and Chico State in second and third place. Significantly, six Wildcats qualified for the National Championships by finishing in the top twenty-five spots. Humboldt's Chuck Smead was the race winner. Mark Shuman led the 'Cats with a fifth place finish, trailed by teammates Tom Brown in 12th; Pat Stordahl, 15th; Bob King, 19th; Neil Glenesk, 20th; and Eddie Silva 22nd.[10]

NCAA CHAMPIONSHIPS AT WHEATON, ILLINOIS

The Chico State Finance Board declined to provide funds to send the harriers to the Nationals. Undaunted, but likely with very meager means, Tom Brown, Pat Stordahl, Eddie Silva, Neil Glenesk, and Bob King left Chico on a Wednesday bound for the NCAA College Division Championships at Wheaton, Illinois. They paid their own way.[11]

On Saturday, racing under overcast skies, but in balmy (for that time of year) 48 degree weather with a light breeze, the Wildcats finished 15th out of 59 schools. "Top 'Cat" Bob King crossed the line in 36th place; followed by Pat Stordahl, 75th; Tom Brown, 87th; Neil Glenesk, 104th; and Eddie Silva (ill that day) 296th.

DOOBIE BROTHERS PLAY AT CHICO STATE

The Doobie Brothers are actually not related, except in their music. Tom Johnston (lead singer, writer, guitarist, pianist and harp player), John Hartman (drummer), Pat Simmons (writer, singer and guitarist), Tirian Porter (bassist) and Michael Hossack (drummer) comprise what is the Doobies.

Living in the San Jose area, the group has developed into a hot live band.

—*Wildcat*, October 17, 1972.

Elvin Bishop and the Doobie Brothers put on a great show last Wednesday night, Oct. 18, to an enthusiastic crowd in the North gym. The Doobie Brothers have added a new guitar player since their last visit to Chico. They started off the show with some fine music, which included their current hit single "Listen to the Music," and another popular song "Jesus is just all right."

The crowd warmed up slowly, which is typical of a lazy Chico crowd, but by the end of the Doobie Brothers' set, many people were enthusiastic.

—*Wildcat*, October 29, 1972.

Photo 9-5

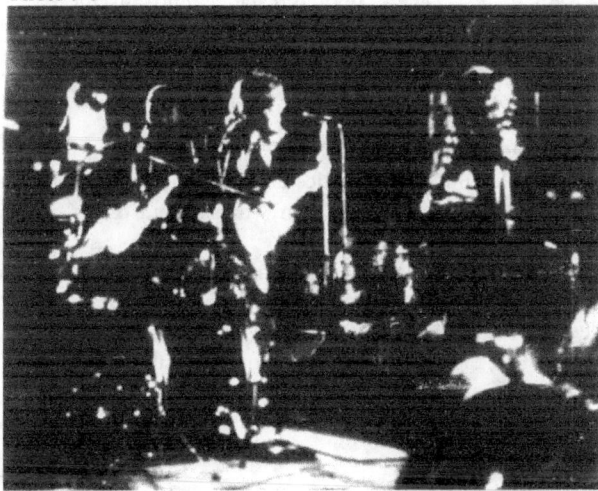

The Doobie Brothers in concert at Chico State, October 18, 1972. *Wildcat*, October 26, 1972

During the 1972 cross country season, the Doobie Brothers band played a concert at Chico State on October 18th. The rock band from San

Jose, which had started out in 1969 as a northern California bar band, had released its debut album, self-titled "The Doobie Brothers (1971)," the previous year. Although the album didn't chart, it launched the beginning of a 12-year streak in which The Doobies released ten albums:

- The Doobie Brothers (1971)
- Toulouse Street (1972)
- The Captain And Me (1973)
- What Were Once Vices Are Now Habits (1974)
- Stampede (1975)
- Takin' It To The Streets (1976)
- Livin' On The Fault Line (1977)
- Minute By Minute (1978)
- One Step Closer (1980)
- Farewell Tour (1983)[12]

The rock band was then in its infancy, relatively speaking, but its members liked Chico, and Chico audiences liked their music. A group of Chico State women runners had occasion to enjoy their music the afternoon before the concert as recently discribed by Laura de Ghetaldi:

> I remember coming in from a warmup distance run with Merill Cray and Sandy Wiseman. We were middle-distance and distance runners on Chico's track team. We entered onto the track and, there was a large stage set up with a group practicing for that night's Pioneer Week concert.
>
> We were not sure who they were yet until . . .we heard "Listen to the Music. We had fallen into their practice unknowingly providing the best "Fartlek" training I ever had in all my years on our track.
>
> Each time, as we rounded to their end of the track where the stage set-up was, we would give thumbs up and scream "LOUDER." They responded. The lead singer and guitarist (who I later found out was Tom Johnston) signaled the tech person to up the sound. They responded to our yells all six times. I am sure their music was heard in the inside of the Physical Education building and possibly across most of the campus.[13]

Years later, de Ghetaldi formally met Tom Johnston in Del Mar, a community north of San Diego, when he approached her and initiated a conversation. She explained:

I was in a parking lot in Del Mar, California. It was a very hot summer day. I was sitting in my car with the door opened finishing up a letter to be sent off. I had my leg crossed somewhat out the driver side door.

I noticed a new red Mustang convertible with the top down. I saw the driver looking at the tattoo above my ankle. He kindly asked, "Do you mind telling me about the story behind the fawn tattoo above your ankle. I was a bit taken aback, and a bit shy. Previously I had been a wildlife rehabilitator for the Colorado Division of Wildlife. The tattoo represented my last fawn to be released back into the wild before I left teaching at the University of Colorado, Boulder to begin a Kinesiology Degree program at the newly built California State University of San Marcos.

Here he was in this flashy new car, and I did not know who he was. I decided to tell him the story behind it. He was touched to know what I had been doing with deer, fawns, foxes, and other wildlife.

I asked him if he lived in Del Mar. He said no that he was here from Hawaii with his horses. He had them flown out to race at the Del Mar Racetracks. I asked if he did that for a living and he said no. I am in a band.

At this point I thought, okay, now I felt something was unique about his looks. He seemed familiar to me! I asked, "What band?" He replied, "The Doobie Brothers." It was Tom Johnston. Literally 39 years later, we met again.

I screamed "Chico State Pioneer Week-70s on the Track!" He smiled a great grin and said it was one of the best venues they had played at in the early 70s. He always remembered Pioneer Week and Chico State.

I then said, "Well I was running with a few other women training on the track the afternoon you were practicing. And we kept screaming 'louder' each time we rounded the track." He laughed and said, "Well then you must have been with those 2 other runners with long legs and long ponytails." He said he never forgot the fun they had watching us as we ran, and played "Listen to the Music." I have always loved that song to this day!

He then asked if I had a piece of paper and a pen. I did and he wrote and signed a beautiful prose about his wood nymph in the forest surrounded by deer and other wildlife. I still have that piece of paper. It could have been a song.[14]

10

1973 "Track Cats" Win FWC Championship

Wildcat Track & Field

Chico State University 1973 Men's Track Team Distance / Middle-Distance Runners	
Tom Brown	Eddie Silva
Mike Fornaciari	Pat Stordahl
Scott McVey	Tom Tremaine
Jim Price	Jack West
Mark Shuman	Dave Wood

In early March, Chico State's 1973 Track Team travelled to Boise, Idaho, and easily surpassed Boise State 91-54 in a non-conference dual meet. Wildcat Jack West won both the mile (4:29) and the 880-yard run (2:05.5) in modest times reflecting the prevailing poor weather. Teammates Jim Price and Dave Wood lost to West by a whisker in the mile and 880, respectively. Both clocked the same times as his in their second-place finishes. Steeplechaser Tom Brown (likely enjoying an alternate race in early season without the requirement to traverse hurdles and a then frigid waterjump) won the two-mile with a time of 9:40.0.[1]

Jack West, another gifted runner from Oroville, had arrived at Chico State—like Gene Meyers and Tom Brown before him—from the neighboring town twenty-five miles distant. Starting his higher education at Butte College, West was a teammate of Kim Ellison there, and competitor of Shasta's Jim Price and Mike Leonard who were now teammates at Chico State. West described in *Toe the Mark*, Butte's Cross

Country Team and the arrival of Ellison on campus, who was "dipping his toes" back into running, after returning home from Vietnam:

> The team was good from the start, but not championship material. However, [Coach Karl] Springer had a secret weapon, an older runner who could not begin running with us until the second meet. Springer was from Southern California, and our future star was his idol, since he was a senior when Springer was a sophomore. Springer was so excited about our new runner, that we were sick of this new guy by the time he arrived. After the first meet, Kim Ellison showed up and we were ready to give him hell on the first run. He was heavy and out of shape, but he hung with us on the first long run, and we all became Ellison fans within the first week.
>
> With Kim improving, we were getting to be a good team. We were rated 4th in the league, but considered a dark horse by league organizers. The powerful Shasta team, led by Mike Leonard and Jim Price, were favorites. However, everyone on the Butte team had their best races and we crushed the competition, winning the first Butte College [Golden Valley Conference] League Championship in any sport. I finished in second place and Ellison was third. We took second in the [California] Small Junior College Championships the following week.

Now, in March 1973, Ellison was "dipping his toes" into politics; greater detail about this follows the photographs.

Photo 10-1   Photo 10-2

Left: Jack West winning a race on the track, while competing for Butte College. Right: Fuzzy photograph of Chico State graduate Kim Ellison published in the *Wildcat*. Courtesy of Jack West and *Wildcat*, March 22, 1973 issue

Ellison's reasoning for seeking an Associated Student Body position accompanied his photo in the *Wildcat*; one of the two paragraphs of his "pitch" to voters follows:

While quietly observing several BOD [Associated Student Body office of Director of Athletics] meetings this past semester, I became steadily more disenchanted with the incredible amount of confusion and petty bickering that have been evident in the majority of their meetings. It seems to me that individual dignity and worth have been sacrificed for personal gain. An effective group must be rational in the decision-making process; to act otherwise is uncivilized and not befitting the leaders who are in charge of a million-dollar corporation.[2]

When the votes were tallied, Ellison found that he had finished in second place. Having endeavored unsuccessfully to gain a position to champion athletes concerns, he pursued a career teaching and coaching.

Following this foray off course, we return to the 1973 track season. The 'Cats were next scheduled for an FWC dual meet the following Saturday at San Francisco State.

THREE-WAY MEET AT SAN FRANCISCO

Chico State found, upon arrival at San Francisco State's stadium, the addition of tough Cal State Northridge from Southern California (formerly San Fernando Valley State) and a three-way meet. Northridge won eleven events in edging Chico 92-89, with SF State trailing with 21 points. The Wildcats managed eight firsts, two by its distance-running contingent. Jim Price and Jack West tied for first in the mile with identical times of 4:25.9, and Chico swept the first three places in the two-mile with Eddie Silva (9:33.8), Pat Stordahl (9:39.7) and Mark Shuman (9:39.8).[3]

UNIVERSITY OF NEVADA AT HOME

Mid-season, Chico State hosted the University of Nevada at University Stadium in what was anticipated to be the best dual meet of the year. Nevada was loaded, with among its ranks: Jamaican sprinter Deamon Felson, English miler Peter Duffy, Columbian distance runner Domingo Tibaduiza, and Swedish javelin thrower Djorn Koch.[4]

The 'Cats' distance runners faced a daunting task: miler Jack West (whose best that season was 4:12) would challenge Duffy; steeplechaser Tom Brown (9:12.7) would go up against Rich Trachok; Eddie Silva would race whoever lined up against him (likely Tibaduiza); and middle-distance runners Scott McVey and Tom Tremaine against their competition. It was believed the 'Cats would have to gain lots of lesser points with their depth, if they were to upset Nevada in the team scoring. In the end, Nevada narrowly won 81-72.[5]

In the distance events, entries differed from what was expected. Tom Brown won the steeplechase in 9:03.9, with teammate Mike Fornaciari (9:47.2) in second place. Duffy (4:06.1) and Tibaduiza (4:12.8) finished ahead of Eddie Silva (4:13.4) in the mile; and also went one-two against Pat Stordahl in the 3-mile (14:27.7, 14:27.9, and 14:41.1, respectively). Dave Wood was second in the 880 with a time of 1:56.9.[6]

EDDIE SILVA

Adelino ("Eddie") Silva, to whom readers were introduced to in the last chapter, arrived at Chico State University in autumn 1972 via Watsonville High School and Cabrillo College. Six years earlier in 1966, he'd received the Northern California Freshman Cross Country Athlete of the Year award, and was ranked high in USTFF/*Track & Field News*-sponsored postal competition nationally during his senior year at both two and three miles.[7]

Photo 10-3

Personal Bests in 1973

1970
880-yard Race: 2:00.0

1972
20 Miles (Roads): 1:48.25

1973
Mile: 4:13.4
"Devil" Mile: 4:18.2
2-Mile: 9:00.7
3-Mile: 14:12.0

Eddie Silva competing in the District 20K Championships in 1972.
Nor-Cal Running Review May-June 1973

Between Chico's 1972 Cross Country season and 1973 Outdoor Track Season, Eddie competed in the *San Francisco Examiner* "Devil-Take-the-Hindmost" Mile on an indoor track. Competing for the 'Cats only as an alternate, he ran away from the field with a time of 4:18.2, followed by teammates Tom Brown (4:19.0) and Bob King (4:20.2).[8]

Because of race rules, spectators witnessed the excitement of a survival of the fittest contest, instead of a typical "tactical kickers race." In the "Devil Mile," competitors had to negotiate tight turns while circling the small track eleven times. Additionally, many of the runners could not finish the race because, at the conclusion of each of the later laps, the trailing competitor had to step off the track.

During the 1970s, a whole parade of Wildcats—Kim Ellison, Bob Darling, Eddie Silva, Tom Brown, Bob King, Jim Price, Toni Ruggle, etc.—qualified for and participated in the Devil Mile. Darling took part in the race in 1972 won by Ellison, and he recently described the process to get into it, and his experience running "on the boards:"

> You had to qualify in a mile race at a designated College of San Mateo All-Comers meet. They took the top 12 finishers. In 1972, I was the last qualifier (12th) with my PR [personal record] mile time of 4:23. The indoor track meet was run on a 160-yard banked wooden track (11 laps for one mile).
>
> I lived in the southeast part of San Francisco, only 1 ½ miles from the Cow Palace. Not being a miler and never having run indoors before, I jogged over there early, so as to get a bit of practice on the wooden track. They let me put on my spikes and run 1 lap before I was told it was time to clear the track.
>
> I knew that I was the slowest runner, but was determined not to be eliminated first! They let all runners complete 3 laps, before the last place person was eliminated by a dude dressed up in a Devil costume holding a fake pitch fork. After each succeeding lap, he judged who was to be eliminated. By the gun [final] lap, eight guys had been sent off the track. It was a pure carnival entertainment event.
>
> After two laps I was behind by a few yards. I had to go into an all-out kick to catch the runner in front of me. I succeeded, but was now in last place again. I had to catch my breath in 10 seconds before another all-out sprint. I did this for the next 8 laps, before the Devil tapped me and I was eliminated. So, I was able to outsprint seven faster runners on pure adrenaline and entertain the crowd! After the meet I jogged home with a great experience.

During this season to date, Eddie's most satisfying achievement had come at the Woody Wilson Relays where he clocked a 9:00.7 in the two-mile. In this race, he raced to a win against a strong field that included Humboldt's Chuck Smead and Ron Elijah, UC Davis' John Sheehan, and John Caldwell of the University of the Pacific.[9]

NARROW VICTORY OVER HUMBOLDT STATE

In the first week in May, the Chico State Track Team, coming from behind in the final events, pulled out a narrow 87-85 victory over Humboldt State. A Wildcat 1-2-3 sweep in the 880-yard run, plus a second place finish by Mark Shuman in the three-mile provided the margin. The 'Jacks scored a lot of points in other distance events. Early in the meet, Humboldt's Conrad Lowry, with a modest time of 32:55.5, led a sweep in the six-mile. The Wildcats had no entries in this event. In what was expected to be a close match-up, Tom Brown, Wildcat steeplechaser and, to that point, the nation's best in the event with a time of 9:03.2, fell early in the race while going over a barrier. Injured, he had to withdraw. The Lumberjack's Ron Elijah led a team sweep of the event with a winning time of 9:01.1.[10]

WEST COAST RELAYS

A week before the conference championship, a group of Wildcats competed in the West Coast Relays at Fresno in the shot put, discus, three-mile run, steeplechase, pole vault, and high jump. The best performance for Chico was Tom Brown's third place finish in the steeplechase (9:14.0) behind two former Olympians. Mark Shuman was fifth in the three-mile with a time of 14:41.0.[11]

WILDCATS WIN CONFERENCE TITLE

Two weeks later, Chico State, coming from behind on the last night of the competition, won their first FWC Track and Field Championship since 1958. Final team scoring was Chico State 181, UC Davis 140, Humboldt State 123, Hayward State 106, Sacramento State 51, San Francisco State 45, and Sonoma State 1.[12]

Although the Wildcats had six individual winners, the bulk of the team scoring resulted from a well-balanced team effort.[13]

In the six-mile race. Pat Stordahl (30.35.0) and Mark Shuman (30:36.0) finished 5th and 6th. Lumberjacks Chuck Smead and Ron Elijah tied for 1st with a time of 29.52.2. Humboldt State also took first and second places in the steeplechase, with Dan Mullens winning the race in 9:08.0 trailed by Bob McGuire (9:11.0). Tom Brown clocked 9:20.9 to finish fourth.[14]

Hayward's star Willie Eashman won both the mile (4:13.2) and the 880-yard run (1:53.7), but Wildcats picked up important points in these races as well as earlier ones. Jack West (4:19.6) finished 4th in the mile. In the 880, Dave Wood (1:54.0) and Scott McVey (1:54.2)—on the heels of Eashman—came in second and third.[15]

In the three-mile won by Humboldt's Ron Elijah (14:05.4), 'Cats Eddie Silva (14:20.4), Pat Stordahl (14:23.0), and Mark Shuman (14:35.6) garnered third-, fourth-, and sixth-place finishes.[16]

NCAA NATIONAL CHAMPIONSHIPS – TOM BROWN EARNS ALL-AMERICAN HONORS

Six members of Chico State's Far Western Conference Championship Track and Field Team competed in the NCAA College Division Championships at Crawfordsville, Indiana. Making the trip to host Wabash College were shot putter Randy Watt, steeplechaser Tom Brown, pole vaulter Mark Jones, hammer thrower Terry Franson, high jumper Paul Sullivan, and discus thrower Bob Yourek.[17]

The meet was held June 1st and 2nd, with both days sunny and warm. The top six finishers in each event qualified for the subsequent University Division Championships if they met the standard.

Randy Watts (58' ½") and Bob Yourek (167' 8") were both third in their specialites, the shot put and discus throw, respectively. On the biggest stage, Tom Brown from Oroville, and only a university sophomore, earned All-American honors by finishing sixth in the steeplechase with a time of 9:18.5.[18]

**Chico State University
1973 Women's Track Team**

Distance / Middle-Distance Runners
Lauri de Ghetaldi   Darlene Wallach   Sandy Wiseman

National Championships: May 11-12, Hayward, California

While doing an 8-mile run through Bidwell Park, there was an intersection between the university and the park that we always had to navigate. On this particularly drizzly day, we were returning and had picked up our pace for the last mile, running hard, so we decided to cross the street before we got to the intersection so as not to have to stop and wait for the light.

A policeman saw us, pulled us over and told us to get in the back seat while he wrote us a ticket for jaywalking. As you can imagine, we were sweaty and breathing hard so ended up steaming up his whole car. He was flipping through pages looking for the code to write a ticket. He finally got so flustered that he told

> *us we could go but next time to make sure no cops were around when we ran across the street.*
>
> —Sandy Wiseman recalling a training run with teammates.[19]

In early April 1973, the Chico State Women's Track Team easily beat five competitor colleges in a meet hosted by Humboldt State. Chico scored 137 points, with athletes placing at least third in all events except for the javelin. UC Davis (70) was second in team standings. Wildcat Darlene Wallach easily won the two-mile run with a time of 12:47.[20]

LADY 'CATS WIN NCIAC CHAMPIONSHIPS

> *CSU's victory was not unexpected. Track manager and runner Laura de Ghetaldi predicted last week that Chico would win by 50 points. Her prediction wasn't too far off.*
>
> —*Chico Enterprise-Record* article titled "CSU Women Top NCIAC Trackfest" (no date on clipped article).

Photo 10-4

L-R: Laurie de Ghetaldi; up top, assistant coach Betty Best; below her, head coach Deanne Carlsen; to Carlsen's left is Sandy Wiseman; and below her, Darlene Wallach. The women are timing other runners at the Chico State track, in preparation for the Nationals, following the preceding NCIAC Championships.
Courtesy of Laura de Ghetaldi

The Chico Women's Track Team easily bested UC Davis at the Northern California Intercollegiate Athletic Conference Championships (NCIAC) 123-65 to take team honors. Hayward was third with 52 points, and Humboldt fourth with 39 points. Lady 'Cat Darlene Wallach won the two-mile run in a time of 13:06.0.[21]

These championships were the last chance for runners to obtain qualifying times to compete in the National Championships. Over the course of the season, seventeen Lady 'Cats had qualified, and they would comprise the largest team to ever represent Chico at the Nationals, which would be held at Hayward. This site didn't excite many of the athletes. As Laura de Ghetaldi recalls, "We had qualified for the Nationals, and we were going to Hayward? We drove there."[22]

AIAW CHAMPIONSHIPS

Photo 10-5

T-shirt from the 1973 National AIAW Track & Field Championships.
Courtesy of Laura de Ghetaldi

In May at the National Championships in Hayward, Texas Women's University garnered top honors, with Hayward second, Cal State Los Angeles third, and Chico State in the top ten teams. The Lady 'Cats' best performance was by the 440-relay team, which finished fourth with a time of 49.9, after being slowed by a bad handoff. In the 880-yard run, won by Nancy Mullin of Sacramento State in 2:11, Sandy Wiseman finished ninth with a time of 2:19.[2]

Photo 10-6

440-relay team members, top row left to right: Linda Wong, Sandy Wiseman; bottom row L-R: Regina Robinson, Michelle Devol.
Courtesy of Laura de Ghetaldi

11

Harriers Sixth at Nationals – Shuman an All-American

Chico State University 1973 Men's Cross Country Team		
Tom Brown	Calvin Lantrip	Mark Shuman
Pat Finn	Scott McVey	Rich Smith
Mike Fornaciari	Jim Price	Jack West
Greg Griffin	Toni Ruggle	Dave Wood

> *We're not in very good shape at this point. Our top runner of last year, Mark Shuman, who finished fifth in the conference cross-country finals, has a long way to go to come up to last season's condition.*
>
> —Coach Burleson being cautious concerning team prospects prior to a pre-season competition by some Wildcats, a 10-mile race at Lake Wildwood, which lay 70 miles southeast of Chico, and 11 miles due west of Grass Valley, California.[1]

Roadracing was extremely popular in the 1970s, and these competitions offered high school, college, open-category runners—and anyone else who wanted to take part—opportunities to race on roads or trails. On September 15th, Chico State's Tom Brown and Greg Griffin eclipsed Pat Stordahl's 1972 course record by 16 seconds as they tied for first at the Gold Spike Track Club's Lake Wildwood run, clocking 56:08 over the very scenic course. Pat Finn in third place (56:45) was three minutes ahead of the next finisher.[2]

Two weeks later, a full 'Cat team with 21 points was victorious against Fresno Pacific (45), Hayward (67), and Stanislaus (94) at a meet hosted by Hayward. Greg Griffin won the race in leading a 1-2-3-4-11 team effort. He was followed by Tom Brown, Pat Finn, and freshmen Toni Ruggle and Calvin Lantrip.[3]

Ruggle and Lantrip were the fourth and fifth runners in recent years to make the "short hop" from Oroville to Chico State. However, unlike Meyers, Brown, West, and now Lantrip (all ex-Oroville High School Tigers), Ruggle was a former Thunderbird from Oroville High's crosstown rival, Las Plumas High School. The two new Wildcat accessions had been the Northern Section's top prep miler and 2-miler, respectively. The Northern Section (commonly called the North Section), begins to the north-northwest of Sacramento, and extends to the Oregon border minus the northern coastal region.

Photo 11-1

Calvin Lantrip winning the 2-mile race in 9:32.9, on a slow dirt track at the 1972 Northern Section Sub-Section Championships, shattering the old Oroville High School record of 9:49.6 set two years earlier by Jack West.
Courtesy of Calvin Lantrip

THE TRACK HOUSE AND SUNDAY MORNING RUNS

That fall, newly-minted Chico State freshmen Lantrip and Ruggle were roommates at the "track house." Back in those days, some owners of historic two-story homes, and also more modest dwellings in student areas around the campus, would endeavor to get as much rent money as possible. This was done by putting up partitions inside of rooms, to make smaller rooms.

The "track house" was one such domicile and, despite its moniker, it housed members of both the track and soccer teams. Sometimes visiting teams, having completed competition with the Wildcats, would "party" at the house on Saturday night, then stay over before departing on Sunday. Distance runners in general, including those of Chico State, traditionally do long runs on Sunday. Sunday mornings would find the common area inside the front door littered with empty beer cans. At some point the Wildcat distance-runner occupants would assemble outside, and start off on their run.

These long runs were either to the nearby ridge community of Paradise via an ascent of Honey Run Road, about 16 miles, or a longer, approximately 23-mile run, to Magalia, a community farther up the ridge. At run's end, the Wildcats would find Coach Burleson waiting in his red pickup truck and pile into the back of it. (No one was particularly concerned about seatbelts back then, and parents routinely had kids ride in truck beds.) Errant runners that did not make it to the finish point by the appointed time were on their own, their ride having departed.

PREVIOUS INTERACTION WITH OLDER RUNNERS

The former Thunderbird and Tiger were new CSU Chico students, but well-accustomed to their now teammates. During their senior year in high school (1972-73), Ruggle and Lantrip travelled to Chico every day after school to train with the Chico State distance runners. Kim Ellison recounted how this came about. In 1972, Las Plumas Track Coach Norm MacKenzie contacted him, told him that there were two outstanding distance runners from Oroville with abilities well beyond those of their teammates, and asked if it was possible for them to train with the Wildcats. Kim replied in the affirmative, "Sure, they're welcome to join us."

CHICO STATE CROSS COUNTRY INVITATIONAL

On Saturday, October 6th, the Wildcats hosted Chico's annual 5-mile race in Bidwell Park, which began at 11 A.M. on the Bidwell Park Golf Course. UC Berkeley was the favorite in team competition, and bested second-place Humboldt State 26-37, but the Jacks put up a good fight. UC Berkeley's Duffey won the race in 24:36, and placed six runners in the top ten finishers (1-3-5-8-9-10). Impressively, Humboldt (2-4-6-12) put four in the top twelve. A Southern Oregon runner finished seventh, and Chico's Mark Shuman, eleventh in 25:35.[4]

SACRAMENTO STATE INVITATIONAL

One week later, on October 13th, Chico State (32) squeaked out a win over a West Valley Track Club squad (40) at the Sacramento State Invitational. West Valley's Jim Nuccio won the race in 24:52. Two places back in third place, Jim Price (25:22) led the 'Cats, followed by teammates, Scott McVey (4th 25:30), Dave Wood (6th 25:38), Mike Fornaciari (9th 25:46), Jack West (10th 26:05), and Eddie Silva (12th 26:10). Based on their unimpressive scores, Stanford (122) and UC Berkeley (124) were resting or running their top athletes elsewhere.[5]

Photo 11-2

At right: Jim Nuccio, the winner in this race, battling UC Davis' "Peanut" Harms in a different race. In April 1972, Dwayne "Peanut" Harms had broken his school's mile record with a time of 4:07.1, in finishing behind Kim Ellison's 4:01.4.
Nor-Cal Running Review, October-November 1973

WILDCATS WIN CONFERENCE CHAMPIONSHIP – "GOAT POWER" CREDITED FOR HARRIER TITLE

Photo 11-3

Wildcat Greg Griffin leading teammates Tom Brown and Jim Price at the FWC Championships.
Wildcat, November 8, 1973

Throughout the season, Coach Larry Burleson had changed up the composition of the team that he ran against other conference opponents in dual meets, never putting his best seven runners on the line in any of these competitions. As a result, on November 3rd, Chico entered the Far Western Conference Championship—held at Coyote Hills Regional Park overlooking the San Francisco Bay—as a dark horse. Humboldt State University was expected to win, with the biggest challenge coming from University of California at Davis (UCD).

In an upset victory, the Chico State Wildcats nosed out the Davis Aggies, 46-48, for the team victory. Sacramento State's Kevin Furey finished first over the 5-mile course, setting a course record of 25:05 in doing so. Behind him came four Wildcats in the top ten spots and three others in the next eleven. Calvin Lantrip, the team's seventh man, finished twenty-first in the race. The point totals of the other schools were: Humboldt, 59; Sacramento, 108; Sonoma, 135; Hayward, 164; and San Francisco, 178.

Top Finishers at the 1973 Far Western Conference Championships

#	Name	School	#	Name	School
1	Kevin Furey	Sacramento	12	Hersh Jenkins	Humboldt
2	Dwayne Harms	UCD	13	Mark Elias	Humboldt
3	Chuck Smead	Humboldt	14	Anthony Reynoso	UCD
4	Mark Shuman	Chico	15	Conrad Lowry	Humboldt
5	John Sheehan	UCD	16	Steve Owen	Humboldt
6	Dave Anderson	Hayward	17	Pat Finn	Chico
7	Greg Griffin	Chico	18	Donn Wells	Davis
8	Jim Price	Chico	19	Toni Ruggle	Chico
9	Angelo Martinez	UCD	20	Bob Bunwell	Sonoma
10	Tom Brown	Chico	21	Calvin Lantrip	Chico
11	Pete Flores	Sacramento	22	Michael McGrath	Davis

Particularly gratifying for sports fans in Oroville, only twenty-five miles from Chico, was the fact that three members of the team—Tom Brown, Toni Ruggle, and Calvin Lantrip—were natives. Toni recently described the conference race, including ten extra miles devoted to the Wildcats pre-race warm up, and post-race warm down.

> Coach Burleson dropped us off five miles out from the course near Fremont for our warm up. Other teams were driving past us as we ran to the course. I can only imagine what they were thinking. That's right, all races included a five-mile warm up. Burleson's plan for the conference meet was well thought out. In order to get our team to Nationals we needed to win the conference meet.

Because he knew the course was very hilly, he trained us all season with lots of runs in the areas outside of Chico. Runs would start from Chico State and either go up to Cohasset, or up to Paradise via Butte Creek Canyon and Honey Run Road, or continue through Butte Creek Canyon up past Centerville to Helltown. Additionally, we would run weekly hill charges on the Vilas dirt road in the town of Cohasset. We were given the name "The Goats" by Burley. We were ready for any hills put before us. (Another group of Wildcats, who were particularly good on flat courses, were termed "The Greyhounds.")

Race day conditions were cool and sunny that day. Coach's instructions were very explicit. Run together as a team for the first mile plus on the flat area of the hilly Coyote Park course. When we hit the first hill, we were to make our move up and through the hills. We did just that, passing runners from other teams along the way. The road to the finish line was relatively flat. Everyone was letting it "all hang out" (70s slang).

After the race concluded it took several minutes to tabulate the results (This was the 1970s with no chip timing). Everyone waited anxiously and then the results came over the bullhorn that Chico State was the winner with 46 points followed by Davis and Humboldt. We all went crazy. Then Burley directed us to hike up a steep hill above the finish line, where our picture was taken while we celebrated. After receiving our award our day wasn't done yet as we had to retrace our warmup steps with a 5-mile warm down as other teams drove past us. All in all, it was an amazing day that our team will never forget.

Photo 11-4

Chico State 1973 Far Western Conference champion team members. L-R in back: Mark Shuman, Greg Griffin, Tom Brown, Calvin Lantrip, Toni Ruggle, Jim Price. In front, Coach Larry Burleson and Pat Finn. Courtesy of Toni Ruggle

By virtue of their team win, the Wildcats qualified to compete in the NCAA Division II National Championships the following Saturday, November 10th, in Wheaton, Illinois. The top ten finishers in the conference championship race, excluding Wildcats, earned the right to also make the trip to Illinois.

NATIONAL CHAMPIONSHIPS

The NCAA II Championship Meet was hosted by Wheaton College on November 10th in Wheaton, Illinois. Not unexpected at that time of year, it was cold, 30 degrees. The sky was clear with only a hint of wind from the northwest. One hundred ninety-four competitors completed the race, with many in the front finishing seconds apart from one another. Gary Bentley of South Dakota State University was the individual winner with a time of 23:49. Mark Shuman, the top Wildcat, clocked in at 24:50—finishing 23rd and earning All-American honors.

Photo 11-5

Wildcat Mark Shuman raced to a 23rd place finish at the 1973 NCAA Division II Cross Country Championships. He led Chico State to a sixth-place team finish and individually earned All-American honors.
Wildcat, November 13, 1973

The finishes of the other Wildcats were: 50th, Jim Price (25:16); 55th, Toni Ruggle (25:18); 58th, Tom Brown (25:20); 59th, Pat Finn (25:21); 81st, Greg Griffin (25:40); and 138th, Calvin Lantrip (26:59). Five of the 'Cats came across the line within 24 seconds of one another. The top twenty-five individuals in the race made All-American. Only 26 seconds separated college freshman Toni Ruggle (55th) from this honor. Less than half a minute faster, and he would have crossed the finish line one second ahead of Ron Peters in 25th from the University of Northern Iowa.

VERY SPECIAL TEAM
The 1973 'Cats were a very special team, with All-Americans Mark Shuman (Cross Country) and Tom Brown (the steeplechase in Track & Field) among its members. It wasn't until 1999 that another Wildcat team equaled the 1973 sixth-place team finish at the Nationals, and 2002 when it was bested with a fifth-place finish. Moreover, after Shuman, the Chico State Men's Cross Country program did not boast another All-American until two decades later when Wildcat Eric Ricketts earned these honors in 1995. Jill Symons garnered All-American honors as a Lady Wildcat Cross Country team member in 1979.

RUGGLE WILL HAVE LONG RUN AS A WILDCAT
Following the 1973 cross country season, Toni Ruggle injured his quadricep just prior to the 1974 track season and, because he could not compete, it became a "redshirt season." This meant that 1974 did not count against his four years of athletic eligibility in this sport; 1975 would be his freshman track and field season, and 1978 his senior one.

12

1974 Track Season

**Chico State University
1974 Men's Track Team
Distance / Middle-Distance Runners**

Tom Brown   Jim Price
Dennis Butler   Corbin Scott
Burt Hume   Jack West
Calvin Lantrip

Early in the 1974 season, Chico State's trackmen had little difficulty on Saturday, March 16, in defeating host Humboldt State by more than 10 points. Their next meet was against Southwestern Oregon Community College, Coos Bay, Oregon, on Friday, March 22, at University Field.[1]

In Far Western Conference action on April 13th, Chico State (118 points) easily prevailed against a pair of opponents: Sacramento State (78) and Sonoma State (12). Tom Brown ran the six-mile as a "warm-up," then came back to win the 3,000-meter steeplechase with a time of 9:26.0 Also winning for the Wildcats were Jim Price (4:25.9) in the mile, and Calvin Lantrip (33:44.2) in the six-mile.[2]

In a later meet on April 27th, Chico State did not have the depth to win against Hayward owing to injuries, and finished second in team competition—but took most of the firsts in all events except the 100-yard dash and the 220. One exception was the 880-yard run in which Wildcats Dennis Butler (1:56), Corbin Scott (1:56.3) and Tom Brown (1:57.4) swept the first three places. In the mile, Jim Price (4:19) and Burt Hume (4:30) finished first and third, respectively.[3]

On May 4th, the 'Cats won an exciting dual meet 88-84 against UC Davis at home. Chico edged Davis in a meet in which two new Chico school records were set. Tom Brown raced to a time of 8:55.7 in the steeplechase to break the old mark of 9:02.7, and Stan Urmann leaped 24'3" to break the old standard of 23'11" in the long jump.[4]

Photo 12-1

Center: Jim Price, circa 1974. Teammate Jack West is running inside of him in lane 1, and Toni Ruggle, just outside of Price.
Courtesy of Jack West

TRACK AND FIELD STARS, BUT...

> *The five outstanding specialists mentioned earlier start with Tom Brown, steeplechaser, who has by far the fastest time in that event in the nation this year among NCAA Division II steeplechasers.*
>
> *Second come Burleson's spectacular pair of long jumpers, Stan Urmann, who is tops in the nation right now; and Tony Colborn.*
>
> *Next, Bob Yourek ranks Number One in the discus across the land, Division II once again, and he's been here before.*
>
> *Last, only in this line-up, strides Ken Mossbacker. He's the decathlon man who has the highest score in his event after the last national rating.*
>
> —*Wildcat*, May 9, 1974.

In mid-May, on the eve of the Far Western Conference Championships, Coach Burleson was concerned about Chico State's prospects. The five individuals highlighted in the quoted material were expected to do well in their events, but Burleson recognized "there isn't much depth behind them." The three-day championships were to take place Thursday-Saturday at Laney College in Oakland. Hayward State was the host but since its track was being overhauled, the meet was to be moved to the nearby junior college.[5]

FAR WESTERN CONFERENCE CHAMPIONSHIPS

Track Team Loses by One Point

In a remarkable performance, Chuck Smead of Humboldt State won all three distance events: the mile (4:15.7), 3-mile (14:06.6), and 6-mile (time not known). Wildcat Tom Brown raced to victory in the 3,000-meter steeplechase with a time of 9:01. Brown was a great runner and he was tough. Chico State also had three other Conference champions:
- Stan Urmann in the long jump (24' 8½")
- Dave Faeth in the 440-yard intermediate-hurdles (54.0)
- Mark Jones in the pole vault (15' 0")

At completion of the meet, the final tally of results revealed that Sacramento State had narrowly beaten Chico State 125-124 for the team title. Next came Humboldt State (106) in third place, followed by San Francisco State (104), Hayward State (103), and Sonoma State with four points. A fifth place finish by Sacramento high-jumper John Cox, who leaped 6'8", gave the Hornets the team victory.[6]

1974 NCAA DIVISION II CHAMPIONSHIPS
The NCAA Division II and III Championships were hosted by Eastern Illinois University, May 27th through 31st and June 1st, in Lincoln Stadium at Charleston, Illinois. Competing in the steeplechase, Tom Brown finished fourth with a time of 9:06.6, earning All-American honors for a second time in this event. (The top six in each event achieved this laudable recognition.)

Photo 12-2

Tom Brown clearing a steeplechase barrier.
Chico Enterprise-Record photograph

Brown had become an All-American in the steeplechase for the first time a year earlier at the 1973 National Championships, May 31st-June 2nd, at Wabash College, Crawfordsville, Indiana. In that competition he finished sixth with a time of 9:18.5.

Tom Brown was the only two-time All-American among Chico State Wildcat distance runners in the 1970s. (Gene Meyers was an All-American in 1969 and 1971.)

CALVIN LANTRIP

A low point of the 1974 Season was the loss of Calvin Lantrip to injuries. These ailments and other responsibilities during Calvin's freshman year of track at Chico State ended his competitive running career. Previously, while attending Oroville High School, he'd had a storied prep career, albeit one also accompanied by injuries. He did, however, go on to be a member of the 1973 Chico State Cross Country Team which placed sixth at the NCAA II Cross Country Championships.

> **Chico State University
> 1974 Women's Track Team**
>
> **Distance / Middle-Distance Runners**
>
> Merill Cray   Darlene Wallach
> Laurie de Ghetaldi   Sandy Wiseman
> Stacy Sudduth
>
> **National Championships: May 17-18, Denton, Texas**

After watching Merill Cray hold a fast lead against an experienced Davis girl, Coach Meyers believes the junior from Lake Arrowhead [an unincorporated community in the San Bernardino Mountains of San Bernardino County, California] will break twelve minutes [in the two-mile] easily in the future.

—*Wildcat*, April 18, 1974.

The Chico Women's Track Team made a strong start to its 1974 season by winning a home meet at Chico, followed by one at Humboldt State the weekend of Easter vacation. Competition for the two meets included UC Davis, UC Berkeley, Hayward State, and Humboldt State. At Chico, rookies Stacy Sudduth won the mile with a time of 5:41 and Merill Cray the two-mile in 12:12, and they were repeat winners at Humboldt with slightly slower times.[7]

In their next competition, the Lady 'Cats won the Women's Division of the Woody Wilson Relays for the second straight year. The defending Northern California Intercollegiate Athletic Conference (NCIAC) champions accumulated 41 points to Hayward's 39. UC Davis followed with 30, UC Berkeley with 19, and Sonoma State, one point. Chico's Sandy Wiseman finished second in the mile race with a school record time of 5:22.8.[8]

On April 27th, the Chico State Lady 'Cats tallied 178 points to easily win the Chico Invitational track meet at University Field. Their closest competitor was UC Davis with 106 points; followed by Hayward State, 66; Humboldt State, 52; and UC Berkeley, 50 (fairly evenly matched in depth); then Shasta Junior College's smaller squad with 12 points.[9]

Several Chico runners met the qualifying standards in this meet to compete in the National Championships, May 17-18 at Denton, Texas. Chico State's 440 relay team—Bonnie Albrecht, Vanita Walters, Michelle Devol and Renda Cary—blazed to the third fastest time in the nation in completing a lap of the oval in 49.0. Cary and Walters also earned a trip to the Nationals in the 100-yard and 200-meter sprints. Both clocked 11.3 in the short sprint, with Cary edging Walters at the tape. Walters won the 200 in 26.2, and Cary was third with a 26.6.[10]

Sandy Wiseman raced to first in the 800-meter run. Her 2:19.1 set a new school record, and qualified for the Nationals. Lynn McClintock also qualified for Denton with a 15.8 in the 100-meter hurdles.[11]

LADY 'CATS CONFERENCE CHAMPIONS

> WOMEN'S TRACK RAFFLE: Chico State's women's track team is raffling off a pair of new cross-country skis, Addidas running shoes, Oh Shirt! tee-shirts and free bananna splits from Baskin Robbins in hopes of raising money to go to the nationals in Denton, Texas. Tckets, which cost 50 cents, can be purchased from members of the track team.

Wildcat, March 7, 1974.

In early May, in the conference championships at UC Davis, the Lady 'Cats tallied 89 points to retain their NCIAC title. Runner-up Davis had 60 points, followed by Hayward State with 51, and Berkeley in fourth with 29 points. Chico gained most of its points in the sprints. Merill Cray set a new school record in the two-mile with a time of 11:36, while finishing second in the race. Sandy Wiseman was second in the 880-yard run with a time of 2:22.6. Over the season, Chico State qualified several competitors for the National Championships, hosted by Texas Women's University in Denton, Texas.[12]

1974 AIAW NATIONAL CHAMPIONSHIPS

By 1974, what had begun in 1970 as a small idea at Urbana, Illinois—the inaugural DGWS (Division for Girls' and Women's Sports) National Championships—had developed into a full-fledged track and field classic. The 1974 AIAW (Association for Intercollegiate Athletics for Women) National Collegiate T&F Championships were staged at the defending Texas Women's University campus. The DGWS designation had changed to AIAW the preceding year, and at this year's venue, 84 colleges and universities took part.

Photo 12-3

Photo 12-4

Left: T-shirt from the National Championships.
Right: Sandy Wiseman's adidas spikes, spike key, and a patch from the meet.
Courtesy of Laura de Ghetaldi and Sandy Wiseman

In the two-day, May 17-18, Championships at Denton, Texas, Chico State's 440-yard relay team finished fifth in the Finals with a time of 48.7. None of the Lady 'Cats advanced from their heats in individual events. High jumper Jan Basich was eliminated at a height of 5'0". As shown in the table, the times for the athletes in the 220-yard dash and 100-meter hurdles were wind-aided (w).

Event	Name(s)	Level	Place	Time/Mark
440-yard relay	Albrecht-Walters-Devol-Carey	final	5th	48.7
220-yard dash	Vanita Walter	heats	4th	26.5w
	Renda Cary	heats	3rd	27.0w
	Michelle Devol	heats	3rd	27.5w
100-meter hurdles	Lynn McClintock	heats	7th	16.2w
880-yard run	Sandy Wiseman	heats	4th	2:20.0
High jump	Jan Basich	heats	none	none

Final Team Standings

1-Prairie View A&M (84), 2-UCLA (68), 3-TWU (47), 4-Cal State-LA (36), 5-Iowa State (29), 6-Chicago State (26), 7-Colorado State (25), 8-Seattle Pacific (23), 9-Kansas State (20), 10-Flathead Valley CC (18), 11-Cal State Fresno (16), 12-Baylor (14), 13-Illinois State (12), 14-Cal State Hayward (10), 15-Temple, 16-Univ. of Kansas (8), 17-Washington State, 18-Central Missouri, 19-Graceland, 20-Univ. of Hawaii, 21-BYU (6), 22-Grambling, 23-San Diego State, 24-Oklahoma State, 25-Michigan State, 26-Univ. of Minn, 27-Seattle Univ, 28-Univ. of Washington, 29-Tabor (4), 30-Univ. of Mont, 31-Central Washington, 32-Kearney, 33-Cal State Chico (2), 34-Dawson, 35-UC Davis, 36-Rutgers, 37-Southern Connecticut, 38-Univ, of Oregon, 39-UC Berkeley, 40-Michigan State (1)

Photo 12-5

Sandy Wiseman and Merill Cray outside the Samoa Cookhouse, a favorite eatery of Chico State Cross Country and Track teams when in the Arcata area for meets hosted by Humboldt State.
Courtesy of Laura de Ghetaldi

13

1974 Cross Country Season

Photo 13-1

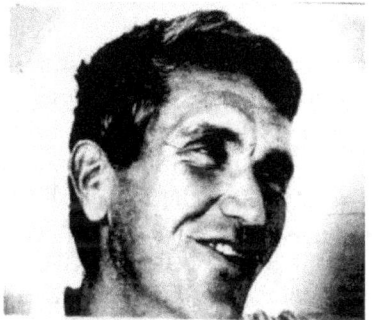

Chico State Head Coach Larry Burleson.
Wildcat, October 15, 1974

>   *WC: You played pro-football for the Green Bay Packers in 1960-61. Describe your experience in the NFL.*
>   Burleson: *Well, all I did was play on the suicide teams covering kicks, punts and that stuff.*
>   *WC: How did you get switched from football to track?*
>   Burleson: *We were involved in track and field at school. I had a brother [Dyrol Burleson] who was an outstanding track athlete who ran for the University of Oregon and was America's top miler for about 12 years and ran on two Olympic teams in the 1500 meters.*
>   *WC: How has your pro-football experience influenced your coaching philosophy? Is it similar to Lombardi's "Winning isn't everything, it's the only thing"?*
>   Burleson: *No, hardly. After getting out of football, my coaching philosophy is completely different from that of football. Winning is the ultimate aim, but in football or team-type sports activities, you have to win week-in and week-out. In track and field, it's not so important that you win week-in and week-out. It's more important for the athlete to succeed in the end. So our philosophy is "the ultimate end is the ultimate success," and that's what we strive for.*
>
>   —*Wildcat*, October 15, 1974 article titled "Coach Larry Burleson talks jogging," in which he answered questions posed by the interviewer about his background and related topics.[1]

Chico State University 1974 Men's Cross Country Team

Tom Brown	Ken Loene	Toni Ruggle
Pat Finn	George Rogers	Tony Webb
Greg Griffin	Corbin Scott	
	Tim Stone	

On September 14th, Chico State's 1974 Cross Country Team travelled north to the city of Albany, in the heart of Oregon's Willamette Valley, to compete in an invitational hosted by Linn-Benton Community College, a low-key precursor to the regular season.[2]

Three weeks later, the Wildcats—defending conference champions and sixth in the Nationals the previous year—opened their season on October 5th by hosting the Chico Invitational Meet. Coach Burleson was optimistic about his team's prospects, believing that it was probably stronger than last year, despite there being only five returning runners. He described in an interview with a *Wildcat* reporter, the runners' high-volume training. "The team works hard, running at least 20 miles a day." Two of the new team members were Tony Webb and George Rogers, who had been "red-shirted" the previous year. This term meant that they trained, but didn't compete with the team, and this interaction didn't count against their four years of college athletic eligibility.[3]

The Wildcats won their own invitational as six team members finished in the top ten. San Jose State's Mark Genet was first with an impressive time of 23:25 on the course in upper Bidwell Park. Behind him were Chico's Tom Brown (2nd) and Pat Finn (3rd), and close on their heels, four more 'Cats—Greg Griffin, Toni Ruggle, Tim Stone, and Corbin Scott in fifth, seventh, eighth, and ninth place, respectively. Behind Chico State (25 points) in the college division team competition were San Jose State (32), and Southern Oregon with 72 points.[4]

Following this meet came the Aggie Invitational on October 13th at Davis. The UC Davis 'A' team easily won the meet with 37 points. Team scores for the other seven scoring schools were Humboldt State (67), Fresno Pacific (100), San Jose State (114), UC Davis 'B' team, Chico State (141), Stanislaus State (170), San Francisco State (224), and Hayward State (278). Steve Brooks with a time of 24:42.8, was the race winner. Chico's next competition was a dual meet against Hayward State at Hayward, a week later.[5]

MEET AGAINST UC DAVIS AT HOME

> *"The first three miles of the race were clocked in a very fast 14:14. By that time, we were out of it. Tell them it was the coach. First, Burleson selected the wrong course, and second, Burleson didn't train his team right."*
>
> —Coach Larry Burleson speaking of himself in the third person about Chico State's loss to UC Davis, in a Chico-hosted Cross Country meet in lower Bidwell Park.[6]

On Saturday, November 2nd, the Chico State Wildcats hosted a dual meet against the UC Davis Aggies in Bidwell Park. In a hospitable act, Coach Burleson chose to run the race on a section of flatter, faster lower Bidwell Park, instead of Chico's normal, more-hilly course in the upper park. This was a mistake, as the quoted material suggests. Elaborating on what he meant by not training his team right, Burleson explained that the Wildcats had been doing long-distance training, while Davis had concentrated on speed work for some time.[7]

Under ideal conditions for them, the Aggies collectively sped away from the 'Cats in the 5.2-mile race. Davis' Matt Yeo and Jox Taxiera finished first and second in 24:26 and 24:43 respectively. Wildcat Tom Brown was third, and Pat Finn and Greg Griffin seventh and eighth. However, the Aggies third, fourth, and fifth team finishers came in ahead of Chico's fourth and fifth harriers, and that was that.[8]

FINAL DUAL MEET AT SAN FRANCISCO

On November 2nd, the Wildcats travelled to San Francisco for their final dual meet of the season against the San Francisco State Gators.

FAR WESTERN CONFERENCE MEET

The Conference Championship Meet was contested on Saturday, November 9th, at Arcata; hosted by Humboldt State on their 5.2-mile course at Patrick's Point. The course, 2.5 miles of asphalt and 2.7 miles of trails, was fairly flat with a few hills. The meet favorite was Humboldt State.[9]

Humboldt with 29 points emerged as the team winner in the race, held in a driving rain which created a muddy surface over much of the course. Davis was second with 37 points, and Chico third with 61, followed by Sacramento State (110), San Francisco State (148), and Hayward State (168).[10]

The individual winner was Matt Yeo from UC Davis in a time of 26:33. Chico's top five team finishers were Tom Brown (7th, 26:58), Pat Finn (11th, 27:08), Greg Griffin (12th, 27:16), Toni Ruggle (15th, 27:25), and Tim Stone (18th, 27:29).[11]

1974 NATIONAL CHAMPIONSHIPS

Humboldt State and UC Davis sent teams to the 1974 NCAA II Cross Country Championships, held on November 16th at the Grandview Municipal Golf Course in Springfield, Missouri. At this meet, won by Southwest Missouri State University with 112 points, Humboldt (224) was seventh, and Davis (344) fourteenth in the team standings.[12]

14

1975 "Track Cats"

Chico State University 1975 Men's Track Team Distance / Middle-Distance Runners	
Tom Brown	Mike Pick
Dennis Butler	Toni Ruggle
Greg Griffin	Tim Stone

On March 15th, the Wildcat Men's and Women's Track teams travelled to Davis for their first meet of the year. In an earlier practice meet at Corvallis, hosted by Oregon State University, steeplechaser Tom Brown was named the outstanding runner at the Stater's Preview Track Meet. At the end of the preceding 1974 track season, Brown placed fourth in the NCAA II Nationals (9:06.6) and twelfth at the DI (University) Championship Meet in the steeplechase. The latter race was won by Doug Brown of the University of Tennessee, Knoxville, in 8:35.94.[1]

In an ensuing non-scoring meet with Puget Sound, Southwestern Oregon Community College, and Southern Oregon College, Chico captured first place finishes in all but four of the events. In the middle-distance/distance events, Mike Pick won the 880 and Tom Brown the mile. On Saturday, March 29, the Wildcats drubbed the Humboldt 'Jacks 115-45 in a conference dual meet. Chico's next competition was the following Saturday, April 5, against University of Nevada, Reno. Nevada had not lost a dual meet in three years.[2]

NEVADA RENO AND SAN FRANCISCO STATE

A strong Nevada team, relying on its distance events strength and two Olympic competitors, prevailed over the Chico trackmen 81-70. A win by Tom Brown in the steeplechase prevented a complete rout by the Wolf Pack in the middle-distance and distance races.[3]

A week later on April 12th, the Chico men's track squad toppled the San Francisco State Gators in a conference meet. The final tally was

92-62. Again, Tom Brown was impressive; leading the 'Cats distance runners with a win in the mile and a second place in the three-mile.[4]

WOODY WILSON RELAYS AND SUBSEQUENT MEET AGAINST SACRAMENTO STATE

At the Woody Wilson Relays, April 19, Chico won the Distance Medley Relay with a time of 10:17.8, over a Humboldt quartet in second (10:19.0). Tim Stone, Toni Ruggle, and Dennis Butler ran three legs of this relay. In a fiercely contested 3,000-meter steeplechase, Tom Brown placed third in the race with a time of 9:13.9; behind Humboldt's Barry Anderson (9:12.8), and Davis' Michael McGrath (9:13.0).[5]

In a meet against Sacramento State later in April, the Wildcats came out on top with an 89-72 win. Tom Brown easily won the steeplechase with a 9:26.6 clocking, and Greg Griffin finished first in the three-mile, in a relatively easy 14:56.2 effort.[6]

FAR WESTERN CONFERENCE CHAMPIONSHIPS

Humboldt State hosted the 1975 Far Western Conference (FWC) Track & Field Championships, May 15th-17th, at Arcata, California. In the team competition, Cal State Hayward came out on top with 142 points, followed by Chico State (126), UC Davis (117), Sacramento State (112), Humboldt State (83), and San Francisco State (68).[7]

Tom Brown led Chico's middle-distance and distance runners with a second-place finish in the steeplechase, followed by Dennis Butler (3rd) in the 880 and Toni Ruggle (3rd) in the mile. Tim Stone, a transfer from Yuba College, finished behind Ruggle in the mile, and Greg Griffin garnered a sixth-place finish in the 3-mile race.[8]

Middle-Distance and Distance Races

Event	Name	Place	Mark
880-yard run	Dennis Butler	3rd	1:55.2
mile	Toni Ruggle	3rd	4:13.1
mile	Tim Stone	4th	4:15.8
3,000-meter steeplechase	Tom Brown	2nd	9:09.9
3-mile run	Greg Griffin	6th	14:19.0

The results of top Wildcats in other track & field events gave proof of the strength of the team, and foreshadowed great success in the forthcoming National Championship Meet.

Hurdles, Dashes, and Team Relays

120-yard high-hurdles	Mike Stokes	1st	14.8
440-yard intermediate-hurdles	Mike Stokes	2nd	54.7
440-yard dash	Steve Porter	3rd	48.6
mile relay	Chico State	4th	3:18.7

Jumps

high jump	Paul Sullivan	3rd	6' 6"
long jump	Stan Urmann	1st	23' 11"
long jump	Carl Knox	2nd	22' 11¾"
triple jump	Herman Blake	2nd	48' 1¼"

Throws and Decathlon

discus throw	Steve Frankienich	1st	169' 0"
javelin throw	Doug Ladd	3rd	211' 4"
decathlon	Bob Myers	2nd	6,319 points[9]

NCAA DIVISION III CHAMPIONSHIPS

In 1975, Chico State and Humboldt State competed in the NCAA III Championships; during the remainder of the decade, the Wildcats were in Division II. In team competition at the National Championships held at Baldwin-Wallace College in Berea, Ohio, the 'Cats were third overall of the sixty-two schools participating in the meet.

Wildcats, who had finished in the top three places in their events at the FWC Championships, were named to the All-Conference team, and qualified for the Nationals if they had met the standard. These included Toni Ruggle in the mile and Tom Brown in the steeplechase. In his heat at the Nationals, Ruggle ran 4:13 in his marque event, but missed qualifying for the Final by one spot.

Chico's third place in the team competition resulted from points accumulated by five Wildcats in throwing and jumping events and the decathlon. All five of these individuals made All-American and two were National Champions.

Chico State Track & Field All-Americans

Name	Place	Event	Mark
Steve Frankienich	1st	discus throw	164' 0"
Stan Urmann	1st	long jump	24' 3"
Doug Ladd	3rd	javelin throw	220' 10"
Bob Myers	5th	decathlon	6,404 points
Herman Blake	6th	triple jump	47' 6¾"

> **Chico State University**
> **1975 Women's Track Team**
>
> **Distance / Middle-Distance Runners**
> Laurie de Ghetaldi   Stacy Fitzgerald   Merill Cray
>
> **National Championships: May 16-17, Corvallis, Oregon**

One good side-effect of the women's track program in the USA can be noted in the list of college coaches for now we are beginning to find former athletes taking over in the coaching side. Among these are Deanne Carlsen at Cal State Chico.

—*Women's Track & Field World*, June 1974, Vol. 8, No. 6.

Her main philosophy on training and coaching is "quality over quantity." She realistically assesses her runner's chances individually and encourages them to try for high but not impossible goals.

They're [workouts] not exactly tame, but: "I don't want people dragging themselves off the track day after day.... Once in a while, yes: I'll give them a very strenuous workout, but instead of fatigue and a negative attitude, I want them to leave the workout pleasantly tired, willing to come back the next day, rarin' to go."

—Article in the *Wildcat* in which Chico State Women's varsity track coach Deanne Carlsen describes her general training and workout philosophy.[10]

As a new track season broke in 1975, Women's Coach Deanne Carlsen had high hopes for the year. The Chico State Women's Track Team had taken the Northern California Intercollegiate Athletic Conference (NCIAC) title the last three years, and fifty-five women were turning out for track this year. Carlsen, a Pleasant Valley High School graduate and international-caliber athlete, had placed fourth in the 100-meter hurdles at the 1973 U.S. National Championships at Irvine, California, with a wind-aided time of 13.9.[11]

On April 12th, the Lady 'Cats easily won the invitational they hosted at Chico State. The final team totals were Chico 74, Hayward 52, Berkeley 42, and Humboldt 13. DeAnza, Butte, and Shasta Junior Colleges also competed. In the distance events, Laurie de Ghetaldi ran a 5:38 for her first mile race of the season, and Stacy Fitzgerald 5:50.3

for third and fourth places in that event. Merill Cray clocked 11:46 for second place in the two-mile. Chico State's next competition would come the following Saturday at the Picnic Day Meet (Woody Wilson Relays) in Davis.[12]

The Lady 'Cats indeed had a picnic that Saturday at Davis; they won the relays meet, with host UC Davis not far behind with 31 points. Hayward State was third with 26, and UC Berkeley finished in fourth.[13]

MEET AT HAYWARD

The Chico State Women's Track Team continued their winning streak in a meet at Hayward on Friday, April 25, characterized by cold winds. In the mile-race, Laurie de Ghetaldi and Stacy Fitzgerald finished first and second to contribute distance points. The final team points were: Chico 101, Davis 60, and Hayward 58.[14]

The following Saturday, Hayward would again be host for the final meet in which the Lady 'Cats would compete against Davis, Hayward, Humboldt, Berkeley, and Sacramento for the conference title.[15]

NCIAC CONFERENCE CHAMPIONSHIPS

Photo 14-1

Laurie de Ghetaldi leading her race.
Wildcat, May 6, 1975

AIAW NATIONALS, MAY 16-17, CORVALLIS

Photo 14-2

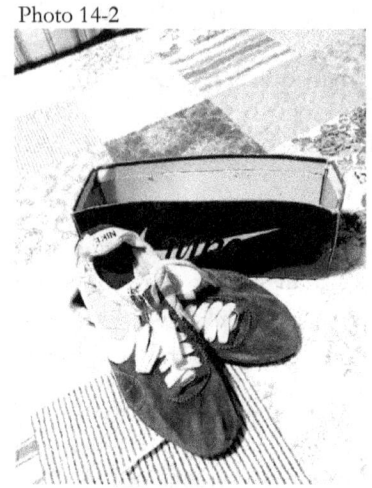

Photo 14-3

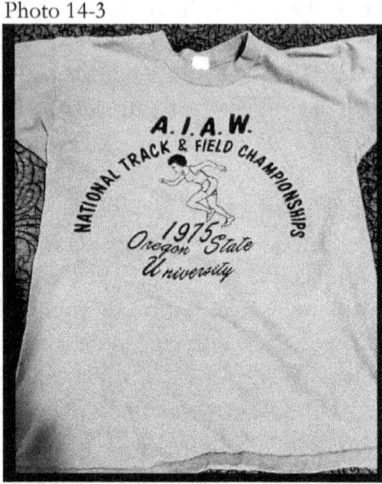

Left: Laurie de Ghetaldi's yellow and blue track spikes she wore at the Nationals.
Right: T-shirt from the National Championships.
Courtesy of Laura de Ghetaldi

Photo 14-4

Waiting in the shade to race at Oregon State University.
L-R: Jan Basich, goofball Laurie de Ghetaldi, unidentified
athlete, Vanita Walters, Renda Cary, and Merill Cray.
Courtesy of Laura de Ghetaldi

At the 1975 AIAW National Championships held May 16th and 17th, at Oregon State University in Corvallis, Oregon, Wildcat sprinter Veronica Harris blazed to an 11.18 win in the 100-meter dash. By this effort, she earned All-American honors and placed Chico State University eleventh in team standings.

Final Team Standings

1. UCLA (89); 2. Prairie View (71); 3. Texas Women's University (29); 4. Colorado State (27); 5. Michigan State (27); 6. Oregon College of Education (23); 7. Oregon State (20); 8. Iowa St. (20); 9. Oregon University; 10. Flathead Valley; 11. Chico State; 12. Kansas State; 13. Seattle Pacific; 14. Colorado; 15. Baylor; 16. Central Washington; 17. Southern California; 18. Cal. State Long Beach.

15

No Wildcat Cross Country in 1975

> *It's [the loss of cross country] detrimental to the development of the distance program at Chico. It also hurts the performance level of track. The decision [to drop cross country] wasn't the wisest decision, but I guess it's the only alternative at this time.*
>
> —Head Cross Country and Track Coach Larry Burleson commenting on a decision by the Chico State Athletic Department to cut four sports—cross country, water polo, boxing, and fencing— as nationwide inflation caused tight funding in the department.[1]

Chico State University 1975 "Club Chico" Distance Runners (Coach Randy Watt)		
Wayne Barth	Charlie Griffin	Mark Shuman
Stan Edwards	Gary Kohl	Tim Stone
Neil Glenesk	Kent Mulkey	Roger Stordahl
Greg Griffin	George Rodgers	Tony Webb
	Toni Ruggle	

CSUC LOSES FOUR SPORTS / HARRIERS PRESS ON

High inflation in the 1970s caused "belt tightening" all across the nation, including within the Athletic Department at Chico State. In 1975, Wildcat funding for four "lesser sports," including cross country, was eliminated. As explained by PE department head Dick Marshall, "We couldn't make ends meet." Justification to eliminate cross country was based in part on rationale that "track was still available for long distance runners."[2]

Coach Burleson emphasized—to no avail—that track would suffer because races run by cross country competitors (half-mile, mile, 3-mile, 6-mile, steeplechase) made up one-quarter of the track program. After the announcement concerning cross country was made, several recruits he thought he had obtained decided to attend college elsewhere.[3]

Despite losing its funding, the Chico State Cross Country Team kept active in autumn 1975, training and competing. On Saturday,

October 11th, the harriers took part in the UC Davis Invitational, finishing seventh out of twelve teams. Davis won the race with 43 points, followed closely by Fresno State and San Jose State.[4]

The Wildcats, running under the name of "Club Chico," were led by Tim Stone who clocked 25:36 over the 5-mile-plus course to finish in 22nd place. He was followed by Tony Webb (30th), Toni Ruggle (33rd), Wayne Barth (50th), George Rodgers (51st), and Mark Shuman (64th). The 'Cats were at a slight disadvantage owing to the absence of their third runner, Kent Mulkey.[5]

STRONG FINISH FOR CLUB CHICO HARRIERS

Closing out its season, Club Chico finished third at the PA-AAU Cross Country Championships, held November 15th at Crystal Springs in Belmont—one of the toughest courses in northern California. The race, involving 142 runners, was won by a strong University of Nevada, Reno team. Tim Stone finished first for Chico in 19th place, completing the hilly course in a time of 33:56. Greg Griffin was 23rd (34:10), Tony Webb 31st (35:02), Mark Shuman 33rd (35:07), and Tony Ruggle 38th (35:30). Ruggle rounded out Club Chico's top five scoring members. Shuman, an All-American in the 1973 Cross Country season, had been hampered by hip injuries. (All-American and ex-Wildcat Bob Darling was also in this race. Running for the Excelsior Track Club, he finished in 30th place with a time of 34:56.)[6]

Roger Stordahl—a Sacramento City JC transfer who had run the steeplechase the previous year—was Chico's sixth (40th overall) man in 35:40. Another veteran steeplechaser, George Rogers, was Chico's seventh man (41st overall). Behind him came other Club Chico runners: sophomore Charlie Griffin (43rd); Wayne Barth (44th), making a comeback after a year layoff; freshmen Stan Edwards (50th) and Gary Kohl (54th), both from Coronado High in San Diego; and Neil Glenesk (58th). Coach Randy Watt observed, "Everyone ran a super race."[7]

Former Wildcat Randy Watt had played on one of the most successful football teams in Chico State history as a member of the 1971 Camellia Bowl Team. In track, he was an All-American in the shot put in 1973, ranked third in the nation, Division II, and 26th overall in the United States. His school record of 58' 7" stood for 33 years, until surpassed by one inch in 2006. As of this writing, Watt is number two on Chico State's Top-10 list, behind Brendan Page's 2006 mark.[8]

1976 Track Season

**Chico State University
1976 Men's Track Team
Distance / Middle-Distance Runners**

Charlie Griffin	Toni Ruggle
Greg Griffin	Karl Schaechterle
Dave Mills	Mark Shuman
Kent Mulkey	Tim Stone

Wildcat Track & Field

The highlight of the 1976 Track & Field Season among the Chico State distance running corps was Wildcat steeplechaser Karl Schaechterle earning All-American honors at the National Championships.

On March 13, Hayward State dominated the Chico State Men's Track Team in a dual meet at Hayward, outscoring the Wildcats 100-61. Chico only had two individual winners, Steve Frankienich in the discus throw (163'6") and Karl Schaechterle in the steeplechase (9:24.7). Schaechterle was a junior college transfer who had run for legendary Coach Al Baeta at American River College in Sacramento.[1]

At the Sacramento Relays on April 3rd, Chico State distance runners finished third in the four-mile relay (17:11.8), behind winner Nevada, Reno (17:10.4) and the West Valley Track Club (17:11.0), but ahead of Cal-Poly (17:32.6) and UC Davis (17:33.0). The Wildcats' average split of 4:17.9 for each of the four 1-mile legs of the race demonstrated they had been training hard the previous autumn despite Chico State having no cross country program.[2]

WOODY WILSON RELAYS, AND SAC STATE MEET

Throughout the season, Schaechterle progressively improved in his marque event. At the Woody Wilson Relays, hosted by UC Davis on April 17th, he finished second in the 3,000-meter steeplechase with a time of 9:18.2. Wildcats Kent Mulkey (880), Ron Teague (440), Toni

Ruggle (1,320) and Tim Stone (mile) won the distance medley with a time of 10:05.6.[3]

On Saturday, May 3rd, in the Sac State meet, the Wildcats defeated Sacramento State 95-62, with strong showings in the long jump and distances, and a clean sweep in the javelin.[4]

NOR-CAL TRACK EXHIBITION AT CHICO

On Friday, May 7th, a track exhibition featuring Chico State's Men's and Women's Track teams, and stand-out athletes from Chico and other areas of northern California was held at University Stadium. The purpose of the meet was to raise money for travel, lodging, and meals incident to participation in the Nationals in May. Qualified Wildcats were not allocated money for that competition. The entry fee to watch the meet—which was designed to cultivate some track interest in the community, as well as raise money for the Nationals—was one dollar per person.[5]

Featured events at the meet were expected to include Chico ace steeplechaser Karl Schaechterle against his toughest competition of the year. Ron Elijah (formerly of Humboldt State and a sub-nine-minute two miler) and Gordon Innes (ex-UCLA star and now a runner at Humboldt, who had run well under nine minutes) were to be there. In other distance events, there would be a men's mile, with Kim Ellison, who had set the school record of 4:01 four years earlier, matched up against Chico's Tim Stone and Toni Ruggle. Three other mile races would also be run: a women's mile, a celebrity mile in which sports broadcasters would compete, and a senior men's mile featuring the mostly over-40-crowd of the Chico Running Club.[6]

Under warm twilight conditions, the competition was staged. As expected, the meet was dominated by Chico Men's and Women's Track Team athletes. Schaechterle won the steeplechase with a clocking of 9:21.0, and All-American Mark Shuman the six-mile race (30:15). In the featured mile race, Tim Stone raced to victory in 4:12.9. Wildcat Kathy Sullivan took the women's mile (5:53.0) and teammate Lisa Foy triumphed in the 880-yard run (2:23.0). In the celebrity mile, reporter Scott Mowry of the *Enterprise-Record* won in 5:35.1, and in the senior men's mile, Walt Schafer easily prevailed with a time of 4:36.3.[7]

Before continuing on with the subject of the 1976 Wildcat track and field season, it's worthwhile to devote a couple of pages to the formation of the Chico Running Club, and a visit to Chico by New Zealander and Olympic champion Peter Snell. This material is extracted from a chapter in my book *Toe the Mark*, devoted to the subject.

CREATION OF THE CHICO RUNNING CLUB AND ASSOCIATED VISIT OF OLYMPIC CHAMPION PETER SNELL TO CHICO

The Chico Running Club was formed in summer 1975. At that time, all summer, weekly all-comers evening track meets were held at Chico State, put on by Larry Burleson and Chuck Sheley (Chico High's head cross country and track coach). College and high school athletes, and anyone else who desired, could compete for ribbons against one another at these meets (which took place mostly on very hot nights).

Following one of these meets, Walt Schafer hosted a meeting at his home for anyone interested in attending to discuss forming a local running club. Several individuals showed up—Chuck Sheley, Don Richey, Frank Burk, Larry Dion, Jim Remillard, Mike Andrews, and Suzie Alexander—becoming collectively, along with Walt, the founders of the club. At this gathering, they agreed upon three things:
- They would form a club
- They would find a notable speaker to mark its establishment
- They would host the first Almond Bowl race in November

Photo 16-1

vintage t-shirt

Walt Schafer running the Trail's End Marathon in Seaside, Oregon, 1976; he finished with a very laudable time of 2:37:51—6:01 per mile pace for the 26.2-mile race.

Walt was a Professor of Sociology, who had previously taught at the University of Oregon, and just arrived in Chico to take up a faculty position at Chico State. He was then 36 years old and an accomplished athlete. He had run bests of 4:16 in the mile and 1:54 in the ½-mile at the University of Michigan prior to graduation in 1961; and went on to earn his Master's Degree and PhD in 1962 and 1965, respectively, at the same school. In 1976, Professor Walt Schafer ran both a 2:37:51

marathon and a 4:36.3 mile, demonstrating his considerable talent, fitness and versatility. (As an indication of how good the former time was, in 1972, the qualifying time to participate in the U.S. Olympic Trials Marathon had been two hours and thirty minutes.)

Olympic Champion and World Record Holder New Zealander Peter Snell was the notable speaker for the first gathering of club members and potential club members in September 1975.

First, a little about Snell, whose story is well-known to runners of a particular generation. He was a quarter-finalist in the New Zealand National Junior Tennis Championships when he came to the notice of famed New Zealand Track Coach Arthur Lydiard. Less than a year later, Snell won the Gold Medal for the 800 meters at the Olympic Games in Rome. He was so new to the sport, that announcers of the Olympic Final race, knew nothing about him. Four years later, Snell won Gold Medals for both the 800 meters and 1,500 meters at the Olympic Games in Tokyo.

Snell began his talk in Chico, by saying something to the effect, "In America, when someone introduces me by saying, this is Peter Snell, he won at the Olympics, I can see that I go up in their eyes. In New Zealand, a countryman might say, well, so you can run a little, what else can you do?" He then explained how he happened to be with us that night. Following his athletic career, he had accepted a position as a spokesperson for the Reynolds Tobacco Company, but came to feel bad about this choice, partially because both of his parents had been educators. So, he had come to the United States to pursue a bachelor's degree in exercise physiology at U.C. Davis.

Walt, learning of this, had called the Department Office at U.C. Davis and asked the person answering the phone if he could speak with Snell, to which the reply was, he is standing right here. (Snell ultimately obtained his Bachelors and Masters degrees at Davis, his PhD at Washington State, and became a scholar at the University of Texas.)

Having agreed to speak, Snell journeyed 100 miles north to Chico, and gave a very inspiring talk to some 175 captivated attendees in the university auditorium. At completion, he invited those interested to show up the following morning at Sycamore Pool (a nearby public swimming area on Big Chico Creek) for a fun run with him. Some 100 people did so and ran a loop in lower Bidwell Park with the champion. Prior to the start of this run, Snell, who was then in his late 30s, took off his sweat pants and it was obvious from his chiseled legs why he was renowned for having a great kick.

FAR WESTERN CONFERENCE CHAMPIONSHIPS

The 1976 Far West Conference Championships were hosted by San Francisco State, May 13th-15th. Cal State Hayward won the team title (189 points), followed by Chico State (133) in second, then UC Davis (120), Sacramento State (86), San Francisco State (57), Humboldt State (51), and Stanislaus State (12).[8]

The best performance among Wildcat middle-distance and distance runners was by Karl Schaechterle who finished second in the 3,000-meter steeplechase with a time of 9:05.0. Tim Stone was third in the 1,500 meters (3:53.6) and teammate Toni Ruggle, fourth. Chico's Kent Mulkey ran 1:53.7 in the 800 meters to finish third, and Charlie Griffin garnered third and fourth place in the 10,000 and 5,000-meter races with times of 31:04.2 and 14:46.8, respectively.[9]

NCAA DIVISION II TRACK & FIELD CHAMPIONSHIPS

At the National Championships, held at Slippery Rock, Pennsylvania, May 25-29, 1976, Karl ran the race of his life, coming from behind to finish third in the steeplechase (8:57). Chico State's Bob Myers was fifth in the decathlon, earning All-American honors for a second year in a row. Tim Stone and Toni Ruggle ran in separate 1,500-meter heats at the meet, and both missed making the Final by one place.

Chico State University
1976 Women's Track Team

Distance / Middle-Distance Runners

| Liz Belyea | Lisa Foy | Kathy Spence |
| Toni Crumbo | Vicki Hobbs | Kathy Sullivan |

National Championships: May 13-15, Manhattan, Kansas

Originally, I was a gymnast and got into track to get back into shape after an injury.

I needed a varsity sport for my PE major. I like the social atmosphere; you get to meet a lot of people. I also like competition, because I'm a very competitive person.

—Reasons given by Michelle Devol and Renda Cary (two senior members of the Chico Women's Track Team) when asked about how they became involved with the track program.[10]

As the 1976 track season began, the Chico State Women's Track Team was under the stewardship of a new coach, Cherrie (Parish) Sherrard. Sherrard, like her predecessor Deanne Carlsen, was a former hurdler and superlative athlete, and also an Olympian. She had competed in the 80-meter hurdles at the 1964 Summer Games in Tokyo, and previously coached at Chico High School. Her son Mike Sherrard—who later played professional football as a wide receiver for the Dallas Cowboys, San Francisco 49ers, New York Giants, and Denver Broncos—was a football/basketball/baseball player at Chico High, but was a sprinter on the track team his senior year there.

An even more legendary figure teaching at Chico High across Warner Avenue from Chico State, was Olympic Gold Medalist Jack Yerman. Then a history teacher, he had, years earlier in 1960, teamed with Earl Young, Glenn Davis, and Otis Davis at the Rome Olympics to win the 4 x 400-meter relay in 3:02.2. It's important to note here that having two Track and Field Olympians in a relatively small community was both very notable and unusual. In 1970, the population of the city proper was 19,580. Over the decade, the number of people living within the city limits grew to 26,716 by 1980.

Photo 16-2   Photo 16-3

At left: Chico State Women's Track Coach Cherrie Sherrard (wearing a track suit), pictured with Trainer Tara Lepp in 1980. Right: Jack Yerman, circa 1962. *The Record 1980*, and the *Star Presidian*, Volume 10, Number 39, p. 7

Coach Sherrard, when asked to assess the 1976 team, observed, "Right now we are strong in the sprints and field events, but our weaknesses are in the distances and the jumping events."[11]

In the first competition of the season, a non-scoring meet against UC Davis, Chico did well in distances, but collected more first places in the sprints. Lady 'Cat distance runners brought in a lot of second- and third-place points. Kathy Spence (2:35) and Toni Crumbo (2:36.4) took 2nd and 3rd in the 880-yard run. In the mile run, Lisa Foy placed second with a time of 5:50.2; and Kathy Sullivan and Liz Belyea placed second and third in the two-mile with times of 12:46.8 and 14:12.7, respectively.[12]

The 'Cats sprinting strength was obvious in a meet on March 27th, when Chico State's Women's Track Team came away with an 80½ point win over DeAnza (63½), and Butte College which placed third with 13 points. A highlight of the meet was the success of Chico's 440 relay team in qualifying for the Nationals to be held in Manhattan, Kansas. Also qualifying were javelin throwers Lorna Brandt and Val Richey, with throws of 132'6" and 121'4", respectively.[13]

However, Lady 'Cat distance runners did a fine job, even with a cool evening breeze. Lisa Foy won the 880-yard dash with a time of 2:32.5, and Vicki Hobbs was fourth in 2:45.5. Kathy Spence finished second in the mile in 6:21.3. In the last distance race, the two-mile, Kathy Sullivan raced to a victory with an outstanding time of 12:18.2.[14]

Photo 16-4

Photo 16-5

At left: Lisa Foy winning the 880-yard run at this meet.
Right: Kathy Sullivan in a cross country race.
Orion, March 30, 1976, and *The Record* 1977

CHICO STATE 'CATS BEST CAL BERKELEY BEARS

On April 5th, amid threatening skies and a chilling wind, the Chico State tracksters prevailed on a Saturday afternoon over a shorthanded UC Berkeley squad. The lopsided point spread could be attributed, at least in part, to the fact that Cal only had one or two entrants in several of the events, and no entrants in a few. In contrast, Chico had three or four competitors in all events. The next test for the Lady 'Cats would come the following Saturday, when they met Hayward State.[15]

LADY 'CATS WIN AGAINST HAYWARD AND DAVIS

Following a win against Hayward State, Coach Sherrard's Lady 'Cats beat their toughest opponent, UC Davis, 120-102, in a dual meet on Saturday, April 24, to close out their season undefeated.[16]

CHICO WOMEN'S TEAM CAPTURES NCIAC CROWN

> *The women's track squad will be hosting a 'taco feed' at the Oasis [Bar & Grill, a college student hangout] on May 5th in an effort to raise money for travel to the Nationals. Serving hours will be from 5-9, tickets are $1 and may be obtained from any member of the women's track team or at the door.*
>
> —*Orion*, May 4, 1976.

On Friday, April 30, 1976, the Chico Women's Track Team won, for the fourth year in a row, the NCIAC Championships held this year at Berkeley. The score was tight; Chico with 75 was just ahead of Davis' 72, and close behind was Cal, in third with 61 points.[17]

Seven members of the Chico team qualified during the season, or at this meet, to participate in the AIAW Championships: Lorna Brandt, Renda Cary, Michelle Devol, Sheila Hamilton, Kathy McQuillan, Cynthia Mik, and Val Richie. Comprising this group were sprinters, a high jumper, and two javelin throwers.[18]

17

1976 Men's and Women's Cross Country

Harriers back, add women runners

After a one year absence, cross country is back at Chico State with one added attraction – women. Men's coach Larry Burleson's team will be joined by a women's team, coached by Cherrie Sherrard, to represent CSU in cross country.

—*Orion*, October 11, 1976.

Photo 17-1

**Chico State University
1976 Men's Cross Country Team**

Charlie Griffin Dave Mills   Mark Shuman
Mark Hulbert Kent Mulkey Tony Webb
Toni Ruggle

1976 Women's Cross Country Team

Agnes Berta Toni O'Halloran Kathy Spence
Lisa Foy   Kathy Sullivan

Returning letterman Toni Ruggle working to regain top form.
Orion, October 11, 1976

On Saturday, October 2nd, Chico's Men's and Women's Cross Country teams participated in the Chico State/Butte College Invitational. The *Orion* (former *Wildcat*) student newspaper termed this competition a "tune up meet." In the first race of their inaugural season, the Lady

'Cats ran strong—led by Lisa Foy (3rd) and Kathy Sullivan (5th), who finished in the top five places. Teammates Toni O'Halloran and Agnes Berta placed 11th and 12th of the twenty-three participants.[1]

Chico's men's team boasted only three returning lettermen, Toni Ruggle, Mark Shuman, and Tony Webb. In the 5.1-mile race at Hooker Oak in Chico, Ruggle finished 14th with a time of 26:01. Chico's next four scoring runners were Kent Mulkey (19th), Tony Webb (22nd), Mark Shuman (23rd), and Dave Mills (26th). Sacramento State won the meet, with Humboldt State 2nd, San Jose State 3rd, Chico State 4th, and the UC Davis 'B' team fifth in the team competition.[2]

The Chico coaches' assessment of team prospects after the meet was that the women's conference was pretty much up for grabs, but that the men would have more of an uphill fight against favorites UC Davis, Stanislaus State, and Humboldt State. Chico's next competition was to be at Stanislaus State on October 16th.[3]

NORTH SECTION MILE CHAMPION A NEW WILDCAT

One of the new freshmen on campus—another Wildcat accession arriving with "running chops"—was Chico High School graduate Kent Pease. Pease (like Toni Ruggle) was a two-time North Section champion in the mile, and Chico High record holder with a 4:19.1.

Photo 17-2

Kent Pease winning the mile at the 1975 North Section Track & Field Championships. *Chico Enterprise-Record* photograph

Well-known in northern California running circles for his ferocious kick, Pease was also an accomplished Cross Country runner, having finished second to teammate Doug Avrit (then a junior) at the 1975 North Section Cross Country Championships.

Photo 17-3

Doug Avrit leading Kent Pease during a race at Lassen High School in Susanville. Chuck Sheley collection

In his senior year, the forthcoming 1977 track season, Avrit broke Pease's Chico High school record with a 4:16.5, and also set a new 2-mile record with a time of 9:11.9. These records stood until 2022, when Mario Giannini ran times of 4:12.1 for the 1,600-meter run (metric mile) and 9:00.5 for the 3,200-meter run.

Kent trained as part of the Wildcat Men's Cross Country Team in autumn 1976, but was hindered by a knee ailment. His injury was undiagnosed, but he believed it was caused from a small cartilage or tendon tear resulting from his playing soccer in high school. Because of this limitation, he did not participate in any cross country races, but recalls some details about team training. On long distance runs, Coach Burleson would occasionally drive behind the pack of runners in his pickup truck, and direct those who couldn't keep up to "hop in the back." There were also Sunday runs up the steep asphalt road leading to Cohasset, a small town located in the Sierra/Cascade foothills just north of Chico. These workouts involved using small "green Xs" spray painted on the road as goals for the runs.[4]

Following the runs on Sunday mornings, Burleson would host the runners at his house for a pancake breakfast.[5]

NOR-CAL WOMEN'S CHAMPIONSHIPS

On October 30th, UC Davis hosted the 1976 Northern California Women's Cross Country Championships, and took top honors with a low score of 51 points. Cal was second with 59, and in third place, Stanford (69), only one point ahead of Chico State (70). DeAnza College finished fifth in the team competition with 96 points.[6]

Stanford's Ann Thrupp easily won the 3-mile race in 17:10, crossing the line well ahead of second- and third-place finishers Tina Anex (UC Davis, 17:30) and Sally Metteer (UC Berkeley, 17:43).[7]

The Lady 'Cats were next to race on Sunday, November 14th, in Folsom, and finish their schedule the following week in Berkeley.[8]

FWC CHAMPIONSHIPS

Photo 17-4

UC Davis' Angelo Martinez (right) on his way to the individual Far Western Conference title, with Bill Britten (Stanislaus State) and Jim Birnbaum (Sacramento State) trailing.
Nor-Cal Running Review, November-December 1976

On November 6, 1976, Chico State hosted the Far Western Conference Championships on its 5.1-mile Hooker Oak course. Prior to the meet, Coach Burleson indicated that he believed the top teams would be Humboldt State, UC Davis, and Sacramento. When Chico's top runner, Mark Shuman, was asked about his race prospects, he declined to predict his finish but was hopeful that it would be in the top 20 places.[9]

Led by Angelo Martinez's win, Davis (31) bested Humboldt (41) by ten points for team honors. Sacramento State (68) was third, Chico (121) fourth, and Stanislaus fifth in the team competition with 132 points.[10]

Mark Shuman (25:51) finished in 12th place, less than one minute behind the individual winner's time of 25:00. Kent Mulkey finished 24th for Chico, followed by a group of 'Cats including Toni Ruggle, Charlie Griffin, Mark Hulbert, and Tony Webb.[11]

WOMEN'S STATE XC CHAMPIONSHIPS

On November 14th, the Chico State Lady 'Cats finished second in the Senior Division of the Women's State Cross Country Championships at Folsom, a city near Sacramento. The West Valley Track Club easily won the competition with 32 points, with Chico State (115), San Jose College (116) and Woodside Striders (118) nearly equal in their point talleys.[12]

The top ten individual finishers are identified in the table. Kathy Spence led Chico's team with an 8th place finish.

Top Ten Women Finishers

#	Name	Time	Club	#	Name	Time	Club
1	Graham	17:48	WVTC	6	Hagerty	19:12	SUND
2	Olrich	17:57	WVTC	7	Brodock	19:24	RRR
3	Heald	18:06	SF	8	Kathy Spence	19:33	CSUC
4	Rouda	18:52	CP	9	DeNoon	19:39	BA
5	Furtado	19:08	WVTC	10	Himmelberger	19:41	WVTC[13]

18

1977 Men and Women "Track Cats"

Chico State University 1977 Men's Track Team Distance / Middle-Distance Runners	
Nelson Cobb	Kent Pease
Charlie Griffin	Toni Ruggle
Mark Hulbert	Lynn Ryan
Tom Keller	Tony Mezzapelle
Dave Mills	Tony Webb

On Saturday, March 5, 1977, the Chico State Wildcats opened their track and field season by hosting the University of Nevada, Reno at home. In distance running action, Chico's Dave Mills and Lynn Ryan tied for first in the 800-meter run with times of 1:55.0, and Nelson Cobb was third in 2:01.5. Kent Pease (3:56.2) and Toni Ruggle (3:59.8) were second and fourth in the 1,500-meter run, and Charlie Griffin (10:00.0) third in the steeplechase. Tony Webb finished fourth in the 5,000 meters with a time of 15:47.8.[1]

Photo 18-1

Charlie Griffin relaxing on the infield at the track.
Courtesy of Laura de Ghetaldi

CHICO BESTS DEFENDING CHAMPION HAYWARD

On Saturday, March 26, Chico State narrowly eked out a win (83-80) over defending FWC Track and Field Champion Hayward State. Shutting out Hayward in the 1,500 and 5,000 meters, the 'Cats accumulated a 35-10 point differential in the distances. Lynn Ryan (3:58.4) won the 1,500 and Toni Ruggle (15:52.1) the 5,000 meters. The 800 meters proved to be the most exciting matchup, as Chico's Kent Mulkey passed Hayward's Dave Nolte coming off the final turn and won by six-tenths of a second in a time of 1:59.0.[2]

Photo 18-2

Wildcats Mark Hulbert, Tony Mezzapelle, and Tony Webb round the second lap of the 10,000-meter run.
Orion, March 30, 1977

DUAL-MEET WIN AGAINST DAVIS AT DAVIS

> *April 9, 1977... Toomey Field at Davis... Track is slighty used, blue skies with puffy clouds; northerly breezes varying between 4-10 mph, 42% relative humidity at 1:15.*
>
> —Header on a printed copy of UC Davis-Chico State dual meet results, describing the conditions at Davis that afternoon.[3]

On April 9th, Chico State narrowly beat UC Davis 88-84 in a dual meet at Davis. Wildcat distance runners did best in the 5,000 meters, in which Tom Keller (15:28.8) and Tony Webb (15:31.7) finished first and second, and non-scoring Dave Mills (16:38.8) in sixth place. Toni Ruggle (4:02.3) and Kent Pease (4:10.2) placed third and fourth in the 1,500 meters, and Ruggle (2:01.3) third behind teammate Lynn Ryan's (1:59.4) second place finish in the 800 meters.[4]

COMPETITION IN OREGON

In mid-April, the men's track squad made the long bus trip north to Ashland, Oregon, to compete against Southern Oregon College. The 'Cats easily outscored the Raiders 112-53. Winners for Chico included Kent Mulkey in the 880, Lynn Ryan in the mile, Tom Keller in the three-mile, and Tony Webb in the six-mile. The following Saturday, the 'Cats would travel to Arcata, for a meet against Humboldt State.[5]

INJURY-RIDDEN WILDCATS BATTLE TO 84-84 TIE WITH SAN FRANCISCO STATE

> *Injuries have slowed the Chico cindermen this season, most notably that to defending conference 200-meter dash champion Charles "C.C." Carter. Carter has been hampered by a pulled groin muscle and has not participated in the last three weeks.*
>
> —*Orion*, May 4, 1977.

Following a win over Humboldt State, Chico suffered its first dual-meet loss in Far Western Conference action, in a 99-68 defeat at the hands of the Sacramento State Hornets.[6]

In a subsequent FWC meet on April 30th with the San Francisco State Gators in the Bay Area, the Wildcats managed only an 84-84 tie. Contested on a gloomy day frequented by occasional showers, an injury-ridden Chico Track squad never really got rolling despite some outstanding individual performances. Kent Mulkey (1:55.8) won the 800 meters, Tony Ruggle (4:05.6) the 1,500 meters, and Tom Keller (15:24.8) the 5,000 meters. Tony Webb finished second in the 25-lap, 10,000-meter run.[7]

FAR WESTERN CONFERENCE CHAMPIONSHIPS

> *Heavily favored Hayward State unleashed their horses on Saturday and any hopes the other FWC schools carried into the meet lasted about as long as Duane Bobick did at the Garden the other night.*

> —*Orion*, May 18, 1977 article titled "Hayward burns up conference."
> In May 1971, Duane Bobick (38–0 record with 32 KOs) fought future heavyweight boxing champion Ken Norton in a prime time network television bout. The fight officially lasted just 58 seconds; trainer Joe Frazier, who had previously sparred with Norton, apparently had advised Bobick not to take the fight.

Chico State hosted the Far Western Conference Track and Field Championships May 12-14, 1977. The 'Cats finished fourth in team competition with 93 points; behind Cal State Hayward (156), UC Davis (101), and Humboldt State (95); and ahead of Stanislaus State (88), Sacramento State (86) and San Francisco State (32).[8]

Photo 18-3   Photo 18-4

At left: Humboldt's Gordon Innes won the 3,000-meter steeplechase and the 5,000-meter run at the FWC meet. At right, leaders in the 10,000-meter race won by Bill Britten of Stanislaus State in a conference record time of 30:31.5.
Nor-Cal Running Review, May-June 1977, and *Orion*, May 18, 1977.

Chico's Steve Porter ran 48.0 to finish third in the 400 meters, and three Wildcat teammates finished in the top five in the 1,500 meters. Behind the race winner, Stanislaus State's Peter (E.P.) Richardson in 3:51.7, came Tom Keller (3:52.5), Lynn Ryan (3:54.0) and Toni Ruggle (3:57.2) in second, fourth and fifth place, respectively. Highlights of the meet for Chico were a Wildcat thrower and a decathlete emerging victorious in their events:

- Brian Smith in the discus throw (156' 1½")
- Bob Myers the decathlon (6,994 points)[9]

NCAA DIVISION II TRACK & FIELD CHAMPIONSHIPS

The Nationals were held at Fargo, North Dakota, May 24th-28th. Bob Myers won the javelin throw with a toss of 243 feet—finishing the meet as both a National Champion and an All-American.

MILER HANGS UP TRACK SPIKES

> *I trained some with the XC team in the fall of 1976, but didn't participate in a race, and was likely limited by my knee problem – trying to allow it to heal which it never did. In the spring of 1977, I ran maybe two 1,500m races but that was it, so hardly even a member of the team.*
>
> *I transferred to Berkeley for academic reasons.... Wasn't able to run for Cal due to my knee, but I wanted to.*
>
> —Kent Pease, retired civil engineer.[10]

Wildcat Kent Pease ran a 3:56.2 1,500 meters on March 5, 1977, in Chico State's season opener with University of Nevada, Reno. That time converts to a 4:15.1 mile, his best. However, the aspirations of the former two-time North Section mile champion were truncated by his knee injury which prevented him from training sufficiently to remain a competitive athlete.

After three semesters at Chico State, Kent transferred to UC Berkeley completing his degree in civil engineering, then on to Cornell on scholarship earning a Master's degree.

1977 Chico State Women's Track and Field

Distance / Middle-Distance Runners

Kelly Butler	Pat Donald	Barbara Sprague
Dolores Diaz	Berni Phillips	Kathy Sullivan

National Championships: May 19-21, Los Angeles

> *Right now it looks as if we have the potential, but not the experience.*
>
> —Coach Cherrie Sherrard, in her second year, noting that over half of the 1977 women's team was new; 22 of the 32-member squad.[11]

The Chico State Lady 'Cats—the previous year's Women's NCIAC Track and Field Champions—had to rebuild for the 1977 season, owing to the graduation of much of the former team. The new squad had been practicing since January, and had competed in a few events at the men's meets. Their first meet came on March 4th against Butte College. Coach Sherrard was pleased with the results. Chico took firsts in every event except the mile run, but she pointed out that Butte's team was extremely small. The Lady 'Cat distance squad was weakened by the loss of sophomore Lisa Foy, who had injured herself after cross country and decided not to compete this season. Sherrard said about Foy's unavailability, "She's a good runner and we could use her experience."[12]

Chico's next competition would come at the Oregon-Cal Berkeley Invitational at Berkeley on March 19th, which would serve the dual purpose of gaining experience and scouting the Lady 'Cats' competition.[13]

OREGON-CALIFORNIA INVITATIONAL TRACK MEET

> *I was pleased with the meet, but UCLA is definitely in a class by themselves.*
>
> —Coach Cherrie Sherrard.[14]

Chico State's "cindergals" were fifth at the annual Oregon-Cal Berkeley invitational track meet, finishing fifth out of the eight competing teams with a total of 48 points. The UCLA track squad overwhelmed the other teams with a total of 180 points to Hayward's 87 points, good for second place. Cal was third (74), Oregon State University, fourth (58), and Chico, fifth (48). The Lady 'Cats finished ahead of UC Davis, Humboldt State, and Sacramento State in the team competition.[15]

Barbara Sprague set a new school record in the mile with her time of 5:29.7, good for third place. Kathy Sullivan placed second in the three-mile run, clocking an 18:53.2.[16]

Following the meet, Sherrard remarked that "our women had a chance to watch and compete against some top competitors." She believed that Hayward would be the 'Cats biggest conference threat, noting, "They came on strong at the meet, but didn't appear to have much depth." This theory would be put to the test on Saturday, March 26th, when Chico travelled to Hayward for a double-dual-meet that also included Cal-Poly San Luis Obispo.[17]

Demonstrating both strength and depth, Chico State beat Hayward 124-85 and outpointed Cal-Poly, 128-76 at the meet. Chico garnered three first-place finishes and a slew of seconds and thirds. One of the wins was by 'Cats distance squad members in the two-mile relay with a time of 11:05.3.[18]

DUAL-MEET WIN AGAINST CAL, FOLLOWED BY SECOND PLACE AT WOODY WILSON RELAYS

Chico State (121) beat Cal (110) on April 15th, at Edwards Stadium located on the UC Berkeley campus. Lady Wildcat Kathy Sullivan won the 5,000m in 19:27.6, and teammate Pat Donald was third in the 1,500m with a time of 5:52.0. Barbara Sprague and Berni Phillips finished third and fifth in the 800m, respectively, with times of 2:25.6 and 2:44.4. The 'Cats distance squad gathered still more points in the 3,000m with fourth- and fifth-place finishes by Kelly Butler (12:48.2) and Dolores Diaz (13:16.6).[19]

Following a day's rest after the Friday meet at Berkeley, Chico State (57) finished second to Hayward (98) on Sunday at the Woody Wilson Relays in Davis. UC Davis was third (54) and the University of Hawaii (51) fourth. Kathy Sullivan clocked 12:05.5 for third-place in the two-mile run, meriting a change to the school record board. Tina Anex from Davis won the race in 11:17.3.[20]

The Lady 'Cats next meet was at home against Humboldt State and Sacramento State on Saturday, April 23, with the starting gun for the first running event going off at 11:30 A.M.[21]

DOUBLE-DUAL-MEET AT UNIVERSITY FIELD

In the double-dual-meet at home, Chico State University's Women's Track Team remained unbeaten in NCIAC action by outscoring Sac State 155-96 and Humboldt State 178-69. The Lady 'Cats swept to firsts in all but three events—two of them were wins by Dolores Diaz in the 3,000m and Kathy Sullivan in the 5,000m.[22]

Photo 18-5

Kathy Sullivan rounding the final turn on her way to a win in the 5,000 meters. *Orion*, April 27, 1977

TRACK MEET AGAINST UC DAVIS AT CHICO

We have to defeat Davis for sole possession of first. If we lose, we tie for first with Davis and San Francisco State.

—Coach Cherrie Sherrard.[23]

Despite three school record-breaking performances, Chico State's Lady 'Cats narrowly lost to the Davis Aggies (124-126) at home on Saturday, April 30th. The loss was the first of the season for Chico and dropped them into a team tie (on the eve of the NCIAC Championships) with UC Davis and San Francisco State. In the 1,500-meter run, Chico State's Barbara Sprague set a school record of 4:56.8 in defeating her Davis opponent by three seconds. Teammate Kathy Sullivan was second in the 5,000-meter run.[24]

The NCIAC Championships were to be hosted by Humboldt State the following Saturday at Arcata.[25]

CHICO LOSES CROWN WITH 3RD PLACE FINISH

Hayward State with 148 points won the championship meet at Arcata on Saturday, May 7th. UC Davis (129) finished second, followed by Chico State (123), Cal Berkeley (115), Sac State, and Humboldt State.[26]

Barbara Sprague and Kathy Sullivan placed fourth in the 880-yard run and three-mile, respectively. Hayward's Diana Stohr won the two-lapper in 2:18.1; Sprague set a new school record with a time of 2:21. Sullivan clocked an 18:32.2 in the three-mile, won by UC Davis' Tina Anex in 16:47.5.[27]

19

1977 Men and Women Harriers

It's only a matter of who survives. Those that survive the grueling 25 mile a day workouts will make this year's cross country team. Even then, it's not that easy. Those that survive will make the team.

—Coach Larry Burleson, *Orion*, September 14, 1977.[1]

Chico State University 1977 Men's Cross Country Team
Coach Larry Burleson, Assistant Coach Gene Meyers

Nelson Cobb	Keith Malain	Toni Ruggle
George Gilbert	Tom Olson	Greg Schultz
Tom Keller	Robert Robertson	Mike Smith
Greg Lathrop		Mike Sophie

CHICO STATE INVITATIONAL

Photo 19-1

Photo 19-2

At left: Start of the Chico Invitational men's race, and right, Wildcat Tom Olson. *Orion*, October 5, 1977

We didn't have two of our top runners and that hurt us a great deal. Hopefully we'll look better this week.

—Assistant Coach Gene Meyers.[2]

On Saturday, October 1st, the Chico State Men's Cross Country Team finished fourth at its own invitational, held at the Hooker Oak Complex. Humboldt State placed five runners in the top 10, and won the meet with a score of 22 points. San Jose State was second (41), UC Davis third (79), and Chico State had 98 points. Tom Olson was Chico's top runner, finishing in 11th place with a time of 26:36. Teammate Mike Smith finished 23rd (27:03); Tom Keller, 32nd (27:25); Nelson Cobb, 42nd (28:50); and Greg Schultz, 45th (31:12).[3]

Chico's top runner, Toni Ruggle, missed the meet due to a hurt calf muscle, and Mike Sophie was out with a cold. Ex-Wildcat and two time All-American, Gene Meyers, was helping guide the team this season. Chico's next meet was the UC Davis Invitational on October 8th, followed by two home meets. The Wildcats would host UC Davis and Hayward State on October 15th and, a week later, Humboldt State on October 22nd.[4]

AGGIE INVITATIONAL AT DAVIS

Fresno State University won the talent-laden invitational at Davis with 48 points. The next five teams were Cal (53), Sac State (80), Stanford (105), Humboldt (108), and UC Davis. There were no Wildcats among the top 30 individual finishers in the race.[5]

CHICO-HOSTED DUAL MEETS

Still missing Toni Ruggle, the Wildcats bowed to both UC Davis (18-40) and Hayward State (24-35) in a double-dual-meet at the Hooker Oak Complex on Saturday, October 8th. Chico's top finisher, Tom Keller, crossed the line in fifth place (26:31). Mike Smith (8th, 26:48) was the Wildcats' second finisher, followed by Tom Olson (12th, 27:16), Greg Shultz (19th, 29:44), George Gilbert (20th, 29:47), Nelson Cobb (21st, 29:59), Robert Robertson (22nd), Keith Malain (24th) and Greg Lathrop in twenty-fifth place.[6]

A week later, the Humboldt Lumberjacks easily bested the Wildcats 20-41 in a meet at Chico. Humboldt's Scott Peters won the 10,000-meter race with a time of 31:33, with Chico's Toni Ruggle coming in second in 32:23. Other Wildcat finishers were Tom Olson (6th), Mike Smith (12th), Mike Sophie (13th), and Nelson Cobb (15th). Questioned by an *Orion* reporter about the meet results, Gene Meyers assessed the team's effort against Humboldt State, then expressed caution about a forthcoming meet against Sacrament State:

> Ran much better than I expected. We're still missing one guy, Tom Keller. But I think we'll be at full strength against Sacramento.
>
> Sacramento is exceptionally strong and they beat Humboldt. Humboldt beat us pretty badly, so you can draw your own conclusions.[7]

MEET AGAINST SAC STATE

On Saturday, October 29th, the Sacramento State Hornets took the top five places—achieving a perfect team score of 15 points—in the dual meet against Chico State at the Hooker Oak Complex. Toni Ruggle, in sixth, was the first Wildcat. Following him across the finish line were teammates Tom Keller (7th), Tom Olson (8th), Mike Smith (9th), Nelson Cobb (13th), and Greg Schultz in fourteenth place.[8]

FAR WESTERN CONFERENCE CHAMPIONSHIPS

The UC Davis-hosted FWC Cross Country Championships were held on Saturday, November 5, 1977. Humboldt State won team honors, followed by Sacramento State in second place, and UC Davis in third. Chico State finished fifth in the team competition.[9]

Toni Ruggle was the top Wildcat finisher in 17th place, followed by teammates Tom Olson (22nd), Mike Sophie (24th), Mike Smith (29th), and Tom Keller in thirty-first place.[10]

1977 LADY 'CATS CROSS COUNTRY SEASON

Cross country as a sport is really growing.

I think we have a good team – as good as last year's. Last year we were inched out of third place in the conference.

—Coach Cherrie Sherrard, *Orion*, October 12th, 1977.

Chico State University 1977 Women's Cross Country Team
Coach Cherrie Sherrard, Assistant Coach Mike Porter

Michele Aubuchan	Linda Hetzler	Marina Ratliff
Tracy Butler	Karen Johnson	Cindy Saiyadinejad
Marci Didlack	Julie Mastain	Barbara Sprague
Shelly Dugan	Kathy McQuillan	Brenda Struvan
Patti Gambetta	Lori Morse	Susan Watje

Practice for the Chico State women's cross country season began on the first day of school. Coach Cherrie Sherrard had thirteen runners signed up, but several others had expressed interest in joining the team. Of the initial cadre, only Barbara Sprague had run for Chico the previous cross country season. Sprague had attended Arcadia High School, and went to the State Track Championships her senior year as a member of her school's mile relay team. The team was also expected to be helped by five or six Lady 'Cats from the 1977 track team, and to be strengthened by Marina Lynn Ratliff, who had competed that summer in cross country meets in Europe.[11]

There was no conference for the 1977 season—because many schools did not have women's teams—and the Lady 'Cats would only compete in four invitational meets:
- Oct 1st: Cal-Berkeley Invitational
- Oct 8th: UC Davis Invitational
- Oct 15th: Stanford University Invitational
- Oct 22nd: University of Oregon Invitational, Redding[12]

Coach Sherrard was assisted by Mike Porter, who is mentioned earlier in *Stride Out*. Porter was Chico State's premier quarter-miler in the early 1970s, and remains so today. His school record for the 440-yard run, set in 1971, still stands over fifty years later. His 440-time converted to an equivalent 400 meters time (the distance run since the late 1970s) is 47.44—which proudly remains atop the Chico State Track and Field Top-Ten list for this event.

WORKOUT REGIME

> *A runner should not run from the toes but more off the heel as this allows more relaxation. In workouts we run 220s for pacing and then time the girls and let them know if they're going too fast or too slow. The goal is to average at least a 6:30 mile [over a standard 5,000-meter cross country course; different courses provide different challenges, which result in varied times].*
>
> —Coach Cherrie Sherrard.[13]

Regarding team training, Coach Sherrard noted, "There's no substitute for running," but the former Olympic competitor's team workouts were both vigorous, and incorporated a number of components to achieve a desired balance of speed, strength, and endurance. The team members often ran at Bidwell Municipal Golf Course (back then it was closed on Mondays for maintenance), and also did strength training focused on body weight exercises such as pull-ups and push-ups. Workout sessions for a typical week consisted of the following:

- Monday: Hill work
- Tuesday: Five to six mile run and weight training
- Wednesday: Three-mile warmup run, followed by intervals (3 x 220s and 3 x 330s) for pace work
- Thursday: 45-55 minutes of *fartlek* (Swedish word meaning "speed play"); a combination of different distances at different speeds to stress continuous movement, plus weight training
- Friday: Two miles of easy running and some stretching[14]

For women's cross country meets, teams could enter anywhere from eight to twelve competitors, depending on the race. Sherrard and Porter believed in ensuring that everyone had opportunity to compete.[15]

BERKELEY INVITATIONAL

The Lady 'Cats did well in their season opener, the Berkeley Invitational on October 1st, finishing second to UC Davis and ahead of Cal in the team competition. Chico State's top three finishers—Mastain, Aubuchan, and Sprague—all placed in the top five in the race. Chico's other finishers, which are not included in the summary table, were Brenda Struvan (11th, 22:40), Patti Gambetta (14th, 23:03), Tracy Butler (20th) and Kathy McQuillan, who was twenty-fourth.

UC Davis (35)	Chico State (37)	Cal-Berkeley (48)
1 – Tina Anex 19:38		
		2 – Sally Matteer 20:04
	3 – Julie Mastain 20:21	
	4 – Michele Aubuchan 20:45	
	5 – Barbara Sprague 21:17	
6 – Joan Gregg 21:21		
7 – Eileen Burger 21:27		
		8 – Carey 21:35
9 – Marilyn Brandt 21:47		
		10 – Campbell 22:15[16]

Coach Sherrard took her more experienced runners to Berkeley and, ascribing to the philosophy that "everyone participates," she sent a 'B' team to the Chico Invitational. In the women's 5,000-meter race, Marina Ratliff finished in seventh place (18:35), followed by teammates Cindy Saiyadinejad (12th, 19:50), Lori Morse (14th, 21:08), Marci Didlack (22nd), and Susan Watje in twenty-third place.[17]

FORMER "CHARLIE'S ANGEL"

Photo 19-3

"Charlie's Angels" from left to right: Luanne Park, Jill Symons, Joan Gregg, Darcy Burleson, Julie Selchau, Stacey Shols, and Suzanne Richter.
Chico Enterprise-Record

UC Davis freshman Joan Gregg (the Aggies' second runner that day) was a 1977 Chico High School graduate. During her senior year-cross country season there, she had been a member of the best group of Chico runners ever. These were the "Charlie's Angels" (a nickname derived from a popular television series at the time, and their coach, Chuck Sheley's first name, Charles).

Photo 19-4

Coach Chuck Sheley observing a track meet.
Courtesy of Dale Edson

This collection of extraordinarily talented, dedicated, and disciplined young ladies included:
- Suzanne (Richter) Reade: finished 5th in the mile at the State Meet in Bakersfield in 1978 with a time of 4:52.42; future standout UC Cal-Berkeley runner and All-American
- Jill (Symons) Hernandez: holder of swimming age-group world records and Olympic Trials competitor in 1976, and later Chico State All American in Cross Country
- Luanne Park: competitor in the 1984 U.S. Olympic T&F Trials marathon and later a triathlete and legendary ultrarunner

- Darcy Burleson: daughter of Chico State Track & Field Head Coach Larry Burleson, and niece of Dyrol Burleson, a several-time Olympian and former U.S mile record holder; ran Cross Country at Chico State
- Joan Gregg: Swam for UC Davis and also ran Cross Country
- Julie Selchau: No collegiate competitive running
- Stacey Shols: No collegiate competitive running

In autumn 1977, the "Charlie's Angels" were ranked second in the nation by *Harrier* magazine. As indicated in the above summary, two of their members—Jill Symons and Darcy Burleson, then still high school students—would subsequently run for the Lady 'Cats. More about them later in the book.

AGGIE INVITATIONAL AT DAVIS

Stanford won the UC Davis Invitational on October 8th with 48 points. Davis narrowly edged Chico 78-79 by one point to garner second place, and push the Lady 'Cats down into third. UC Berkeley was fourth (82), and Fresno State trailed with 149 points.[18]

Judy Graham, an unattached runner from San Jose (individual competitor without a team) won the race with a time of 17:49; she had also won the women's race at the Chico Invitational the previous weekend. Chico was led by Julie Mastain, who clocked a 19:06 over the 5,000-meter course to finish third. The finishing order of her teammates was Barbara Sprague 11th (19:47), Michele Aubuchan 13th (19:49), Brenda Struvan 22nd (20:50), Patti Gambetta 34th (22:12), and Cindy Saiyadinejad, thirty-fifth in 22:15.[19]

Kathy McQuillan, Lori Morse, Linda Hetzler, and Karen Johnson also ran in the 52-competitor field, but their finishes did not count toward Chico's point total.[20]

STANFORD INVITATIONAL

The meet was bigger [higher level] than we thought it would be.

If just two of those three [top team members, names not available] had run we would have beaten Cal.

—Coach Cherrie Sherrard, *Orion*, October 19, 1997.

On Saturday, October 15th, the Lady 'Cats found the slogging hard at Stanford, with three of their top runners unable to compete, and finished fifth of the five teams participating. The West Valley Track Club took top honors with 33 points—ahead of Cal-Poly San Luis Obispo in second with 48, Stanford (68), UC Berkeley (109), and Chico State with 126 points.[21]

Debbie Tearson of the University of Texas, El Paso, won the race with a time of 17:40. Julie Mastain clocked 19:38, good for 19th place. Behind her came Barbara Sprague (26th, 20:35), Marina Ratliff (39th, 21:54), Tracy Butler (48th, 23:22), and Cindy Saiyadinejad (49th, 23:32). Chico's sixth and seventh runners Lori Morse and Kathy McQuillan finished 51st and 53rd. (Cal termed its team's sixth and seventh finishers, "pushers." Although they were not scoring members in a race, if one or both came in ahead of the fifth-place runner on another team, they added one or two points to their opponent's score and, by doing so, ideally, "pushed" them down in the team standings.)[22]

OREGON INVITATIONAL AT REDDING

On Saturday, October 22nd, powerful University of Oregon hosted an invitational at Redding, a then-small city in northern California, located seventy-three miles north-northwest of Chico.[23]

The U of O's first five harriers all finished in the top 10 spots, easily winning the meet with 23 points. The San Jose Cindergals (an AAU team) were second with 77; Stanford third with 82; Oregon State fourth with 123; UC Berkeley fifth with 151; Humboldt State sixth with 158; UC Davis seventh with 162; and Chico State eighth with 179.[24]

Running unattached, Judy Graham (26:54) from San Jose State raced to victory over the three-mile course. Julie Mastain, 15th with a time of 18:22, led the Lady 'Cats. Chico's other runners were Michele Aubuchan (27th, 19:10); Shelly Dugan (58th, 21:37) competing in her first meet; Cindy Saiyadinejad (60th, 22:07); Lori Morse (63rd, 22:56); and Kathy McQuillan sixty-fifth (24:49).[25]

Although Mastain was still fighting off the effects of a cold, Sherrard believed that she might have a good chance of qualifying for the Nationals at the forthcoming regional meet.[26]

1977 AIAW REGION 8 COLLEGE CHAMPIONSHIPS

The 1977 Region 8 AIAW (Association for Intercollegiate Athletics for Women) Cross Country Championships were held on November 5th, at Tilden Regional Park in the San Francisco East Bay Area. Cal State North Ridge's Julie Brown finished first in the 5,000-meter race with a time of 17:38.4. Chico's Julie Mastain's 19:47 was good for 22nd place.

20

1978 Track and Field Season – Toni Ruggle's Finale

Photo 20-1

I feel running carries you over in life. It has given me more confidence in myself. I know because of my success in track I can do the same in the classroom and on the job.

There are more guys on the streets who have more talent than me but they don't put in the time I do.

—Toni Ruggle in a *Chico Enterprise-Record* article by Barry Punzal, titled "CSU's Ruggle Battles to Be Best."

Toni Ruggle competing as a Wildcat on the track. *Chico Enterprise-Record* photograph

Much of this chapter pays tribute to Toni Ruggle, a stalwart member of Wildcat track and field, and cross country programs over a bulk of the period covered in this book. Arriving on campus in autumn 1973, by season's end the quiet, eager, and wholly committed freshman was at the Cross Country National Championships helping his team to a sixth-place team finish. In spring 1978, he embarked on his final track and season. His four years of eligibility had been stretched out by missing one track and field season owing to an injury, and one cross country season because Chico State didn't have a cross country team that year.

Toni's tenure at Chico State was not without setbacks in athletics, as elucidated in the next few pages, of some material extracted from my book *Toe the Mark*, a companion to this one. While I was doing research for *Stride Out*, Kent Pease paid a nice tribute to his former teammate, simply stating to the author, "The teams were held together by Toni Ruggle; like an unofficial captain, he encouraged everyone and smoothed out rough patches when necessary."

INTERVIEW ABOUT RUGGLE'S STRUGGLES

In 1978, Toni Ruggle and high school classmate Scott Fairley, a pole vaulter, were co-captains of the Wildcat Track Team. Midway through the season, while relaxing in a home he shared with Scott and three other friends, Toni Ruggle described to a *Chico Enterprise-Record* reporter his remaining goals as a Wildcat. Arriving at Chico State in autumn 1973 (from Las Plumas High School in nearby Oroville), Ruggle was used to winning. As a prep athlete, he had twice represented the North Section in the California State Track & Field Championships and had a best of 4:18.8 in the mile.

EARLIER WILDCAT COMPETITIVE SEASONS

In the fall of his freshman year at Chico State, Toni was a member of the Wildcat team that finished sixth at the 1973 NCAA Division II Cross Country Championships at Wheaton, Illinois. Continuing to train hard and race well, at the conclusion of both the 1974 and 1975 track seasons, he qualified for, and competed in, the 1,500 meters at the Nationals. Toni wanted to earn All-American honors in these races, as presumably did the other competitors, and he considered that he had not performed well either year.

Then came a very discouraging junior year. Ruggle did not speak at length about it in the interview, only that 1977 had played a role in his current success, both in track and his life, commenting, "I've changed my attitude and reevaluated my training habits." He attributed his lack of success to inadequate training between the cross country and track seasons. As a result, distance runs during the track season were challenging. Moreover, the lack of sufficient base-conditioning hurt him physically and mentally. Toni summed up the preceding season (when interviewed in 1978) thus, "I didn't run under 4:10 for the 1,500 meters all season and didn't qualify for the Nationals." (He finished fifth in the Far Western Conference Championship race.)

FINAL OUTDOOR TRACK SEASON

The 1978 Season brought a resurgent Toni Ruggle as a result of increased work. He noted, "I have more confidence this season because I know I've done the training. The hard runs and the early morning training have paid off." By mid-point in the current season, Toni had won more races than in all the previous ones combined. His best seasonal marks were a 3:56 in the 1,500 and 4:13 in the mile (which is equivalent to a 3:54 1,500).

1978 INDOOR TRACK COMPETITION

On February 18th, at the *San Francisco Examiner* Games in Daly City, California, Toni had run a very impressive 4:18 to finish second in the mile, an event he characterized as "the biggest meet of my life." Although the time may not seem particularly impressive, one has to understand the conditions under which the race took place to appreciate it. The *Examiner* Games are held at the Cow Palace, an indoor arena in Daly City, situated on the city's northern border with neighboring San Francisco, and athletes must compete on a small track with tight turns.

Photo 20-2

Although of poor quality, this photograph of the "Devil Mile," which Toni Ruggle was then leading, evidences the excitement the event generates for fans, and for the runners competing in front of a loud and boisterous crowd.
Courtesy of Toni Ruggle

In the "Devil Mile" (Devil Take the Hindmost), competitors must negotiate tight turns while circling the track eleven times. Moreover, at the conclusion of the third lap and thereafter, the person in last place must step off the track. Because of this rule, running an even pace necessary to achieve best times is impossible, and spectators witness the excitement of a survival of the fittest contest, instead of a typical "tactical kickers race." Stanford's Tom Lobsinger won in 4:13.8, and Toni Ruggle was second (4:18.9), nipping Eric Hurst (4:19.0) of the Pacific Track Club in third.

1978 CHICO MEN'S OUTDOOR TRACK AND FIELD

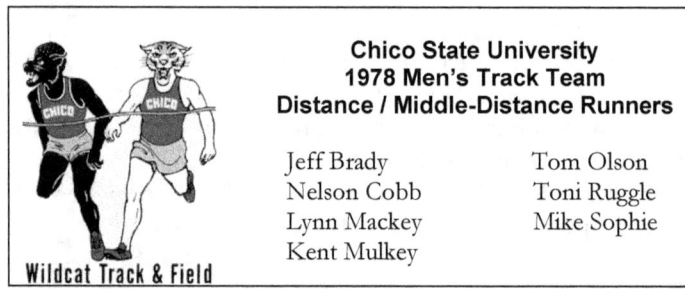

**Chico State University
1978 Men's Track Team
Distance / Middle-Distance Runners**

Jeff Brady
Nelson Cobb
Lynn Mackey
Kent Mulkey

Tom Olson
Toni Ruggle
Mike Sophie

The 1978 Chico State Men's Track Team opened their competitive season on Saturday, February 25, against San Francisco. The day started out cloudy and progressed to rain, but the Wildcats defied the weather, beginning with Mike Sophie's 34:19 victory in the 10,000-meter run. Toni Ruggle won the 1,500 meters in 4:03.1, and teammate Kent Mulkey was third at 4:35.8.[1]

Doubling back, Ruggle also won the 5,000 meters with a time of 15:59.83, and Chico's Lynn Mackey came in third in 16:25.31. Wildcats Nelson Cobb and Jeff Brady were second and third in the 800 meters, respectively, with times of 2:01 and 2:02.9. Continuing to pick up points in the distance events, Tom Olson (9:51.04) and Lynn Mackey (10:55.0) splashed to second and third places finishes in the steeplechase.[2]

STANFORD RELAYS

On March 18, 1978, against national-caliber competition in the Stanford Relays, Ruggle just missed qualifying for the Nationals in the 5,000 meters. In a field of twenty-five, he finished eighth in 14:40. The winner, Tom Wysocki of the University of Nevada crossed the finish line in 14:07.

HUMBOLDT STATE DISTANCE RUNNERS STRONG
Well into the season, Chico State defeated Humboldt State 87-76 in a Saturday dual-meet competition on April 29th. Most of Chico's points were gathered in the field events, whereas the 'Jacks ruled the track—winning seven races to the Wildcat's three. The majority of Humboldt's wins came in the distance events, including a particularly exciting 1,500-meter race. In it, Toni Ruggle put up a good fight against top-rated Ken Hammer, but the Lumberjack's ace was the victor in 3:52.71.[3]

WEST COAST RELAYS
After years of times of 4:11 to 4:14 for the mile, Toni finally went under the 4:10 barrier with a lifetime best of 4:08.1 at the West Coast Relays, May 5th-6th, in Fresno. It was an invitational mile with a loaded field on a dirt track won by Andy Clifford from Cal Berkeley in 4:03.3. Ruggle's time qualified him for the National Championships in Macomb, Illinois.

FAR WESTERN CONFERENCE MEET
The Far Western Conference Championships, hosted by the UC Davis Aggies, were held on May 11th-13th in Davis, California. Paul Heide of Humboldt won the 3,000-meter steeplechase in 9:05.1, followed by Wildcat Tom Olson (9:19.5) in second place. Ken Hammer from Humboldt, and Davis' Mike Pratt finished 1-2 in the 1,500-meter race with times of 3:53.8 and 3:55.1, respectively.

NCAA DIVISION II NATIONAL CHAMPIONSHIPS
The National Championships were held May 25th-27th at Macomb, Illinois. The participants included three Wildcats: Toni Ruggle and two "weightmen" (competitors in the shot put and/or discus throw). Interestingly, the distance events were dominated by athletes from Cal-Poly San Luis Obispo. Jim Schankel won both the 5,000- and 10,000-meter races with times of 14:12.6 and 30:01.5; and teammate Mitch Kingery (30:45.9) was third in the 10,000 meters.

In the 1,500-meter run, Cal-Poly's Dan Aldridge raced to victory with a time of 3:45.4. Toni narrowly missed making the Final, his 3:51 in his heat falling one place short. He had done his best in his final season as a Wildcat, and was nominated for Chico State Track & Field Outstanding Male Athlete.

> **1978 Chico State Women's Track and Field**
>
> **Distance / Middle-Distance Runners**
>
> Michele Aubuchan   Barbara Davis   Lori Morse
> Janet Bath   Shelly Dugan   Barbara Sprague
>
> **National Championships: May 25-27, Knoxville, Tennessee**

On Saturday, April 22, Chico State lost a dual meet 90-83 to the Sacramento State Hornets, despite strong performances by the Lady 'Cats distance squad which included school records being set. The first of these records came in a 1-2-3 sweep of the 800-meter run. Barbara Davis set a record with her win in 2:21.5, and taking second and third, teammates Lori Morse and Janet Bath also set personal records. Michele Aubuchan also set a school record in the 3,000 meters while placing second with a time of 10:48.4. Collecting still more points, Barbara Sprague won the 1,500 meters in 4:58.1; and she, Morse, Bath, and Shelly Dugan combined to win the two-mile relay—finishing one minute and 49 seconds ahead of the Sacramento team.[4]

The Chico State Lady 'Cats hosted the Golden State Conference Championships on Saturday, May 13th.

21

Jill Symons Arrives on Campus

Now that that has been resolved, runners won't shy away from Chico State's program.

—Coach Larry Burleson discussing the previous questionable future of the Wildcat cross country program, which Chico State had considered dropping from intercollegiate competition.[1]

Chico State University 1978 Men's Cross Country Team
Coach Larry Burleson, Assistant Coach Gene Meyers

Greg Durbin	Dave Luchenbill	Tom Olson
Dan Lemaroux	Kent Mulkey	Greg Schultz

As the dawn of the 1979 cross country season broke, there were questions about the viability of this fall sport on some campuses. A meet beween Chico State and conference champion Humboldt State, scheduled for September 16th, had been cancelled because Humboldt, a quarter-system school, had not begun its academic year.[2]

Regarding Wildcat prospects, Coach Burleson had high expectations of his top runner, Kent Mulkey, who had been plagued by illness and injury his entire college career, including the previous season when he underwent surgery to repair an Achilles tendon.[3]

On Saturday, September 23rd, Chico State's harriers placed second in a three-way meet hosted by San Francisco State. Two miles into the grueling 10,000-meter course at Crystal Springs, Mulkey had to drop out because of an asthma attack. Senior Tom Olson clocked 35:11 in finishing second behind the winner, and teammate Dan Lemaroux was fifth with a 37:55 time. Following on each other's heels came Greg Durbin (7th), Dave Luchenbill (8th) and Greg Schultz (9th), the Wildcat's third, fourth, and fifth runners.[4]

San Francisco State won the meet with 25 points, followed by Chico State (31), and Stanislaus State which had no score because none of its runners completed the course.[5]

HOME MEET ON COHASSET COURSE

On Saturday, October 14th, in Chico's only home meet, Kent Mulkey finished the race in sixth place with a time of 39:07. Sacramento State's 'B' team easily beat Chico State and UC Davis on the uphill Cohasset course. Non-conference member University of Southern Oregon collected 38 points for second place in the team competition. Tom Olson, Greg Shultz, Dave Luckenbill, and Dan Lemaroux were the other Chico runners.[6]

Photo 21-1

Kent Mulkey crosses the finish line.
Orion, October 18, 1978

Stanislaus State was host to the Far Western Conference Cross Country Championships on October 21st at Turlock. Sacramento State nipped Humboldt State 25-31 for the team championship, with both teams far ahead of the field. UC Davis was third with 103 points, followed by San Francisco State (117), Hayward State (128), and Chico State with 144 points.[7]

Sac State's Jim White won the individual title for the second straight year with a time of 31:21.8 over the 10,000-meter course. Everyone was expecting fast times, because the course was flat, but it was laid out through thick grass around the Stanislaus campus. Chico's Tom Olson was the first finisher for the Wildcats in tenth place.[8]

1978 LADY 'CATS CROSS COUNTRY SEASON

Over half of the team members are freshmen. One freshman, Jill Symons, did well at Chico High last year and is expected to turn out good times for Chico State this year.

Sherrard does have one returning runner, Julie Mastain. Mastain qualified for nationals held in Austin, Texas, last year.

—*Orion*, September 6, 1978. The author of this article in the student newspaper was likely unaware that Jill Symons had been named to the All-Northern California Second Team her previous cross country season while a high school senior, or that earlier, she had competed in the 1976 U.S. Olympic Swim Trials as a 16-year old.

Chico State University 1978 Women's Cross Country Team
Coach Cherrie Sherrard, Assistant Coach Mike Porter

Colleen Conners	Julie Mastain	Jill Symons
Cathie Fries	Alicia Munoz	Linda Wieking
Carrie Herd	Cathy Oddone	Janet Wilson
Ann King		Kim Woodland

As the women's cross country season opened, Coach Cherrie Sherrard believed that team members would need to achieve a 19-minute time in the three-mile race to qualify for the National Championships. In discussing what it took for someone to engage in and excel as a harrier, she remarked, "Cross country running is a totally self-motivating sport. "You have to really want to run and should be willing to push yourself beyond all known limits."9

To prepare her team for a successful season, she had the runners on a six-day-a-week workout program. Three of these days were devoted to distance running, while the remaining ones were used to condition with hill sprints and pace work.10

COMPETITION AGAINST FORMER TEAMMATE

Two former Chico High School "Charlie's Angels"—Suzanne Richter and Jill Symons—were running cross country that autumn. Richter was at Cal Berkeley leading a powerhouse team, and Symons at Chico State leading a relatively inexperienced one. The "Charlie's Angels" (moniker for the 1977 Chico High School girls cross country team ranked second in the nation by *Harrier* magazine) were introduced in Chapter 19. A summary of Suzanne Richter's accolades while in high school, follow:

- 1977 *Northern California Running Review* ranking as number 3 high school girl cross country runner in northern California
- 1978 California State Track and Field Championships 5th place finish in the mile; her time of 4:52.42 still stands as a school record
- First female Mid-Valley high school athlete to earn a full athletic scholarship to an NCAA Division I school

Photo 21-2

Suzanne Richter finishing a race.
Courtesy of Suzanne Richter

Often competing in the same meets, the former Panthers had occasion to see one another during warmups before races and would visit afterward. Three of these meets were the UC Berkeley, Fresno State, and Stanford University invitationals. A summary of their individual results in these races follows:

Berkeley Invitational	Fresno State Invitational	Stanford Invitational

September 23rd	September 30th	October 14th
Cal 1st (19)	Cal 1st (23)	Cal 1st (28)
Chico 4th (123)		Chico 4th (131)

Name	Time	Name	Time	Name	Time
Richter (2nd)	18:00	Richter (2nd)	17:15	Richter (2nd)	17:37
Symons (6th)	19:10	Symons (12th)	17:57	Symons (10th)	18:36

Cal "Golden Bear" Jan Oehm raced to a win in the UC Berkeley Invitational with a time of 17:54.9; teammate Suzanne Richer was second in 18:00. Jill Symons finished in sixth place (19:10). UC Berkeley (Cal) won its own meet with a low score of 19 points. Long Beach State (74) was second, followed by San Diego State (105), and Chico State (123).[11]

Oehm won again a week later at the Fresno State Invitational, with a time of 17:04 over the three-mile course. On her teammate's heels, Richter finished second in 17:15. Symons coming in twelfth (17:57), led the Lady 'Cats to the highest placing among Golden State Conference teams. Chico finished just one point behind Stanford, and one point ahead of Cal Lutheran, and ahead of rivals Davis and Hayward State.[12]

Powerful UC Berkeley won the invitational meet with 23 points, followed by Cal-Poly San Luis Obispo (52) and San Jose State (63).[13]

SYMONS WINS AGGIE INVITATIONAL AT DAVIS

On October 7th, the Chico State lady harriers travelled to Davis, 100 miles south of Chico, to compete in the Aggie Invitational hosted by UC Davis. Symons won her first major meet with a time of 17:47.4 over the course. Cathy Oddone was sixth in 18:30, helping Chico to a second place finish—albeit a distant 41 points behind first-place Sacramento State. Humboldt State was third.[14]

LADY 'CATS FOURTH AT STANFORD INVITATIONAL

On Saturday, October 14th at Stanford, the Cal Bears edged out Cal-Poly San Luis Obispo 28-37—led by 2-3-4-5-14 finishes by Suzanne Richter (17:37), Jan Oehm (17:50), Suzie Meek (17:50), Alice Trumbly (17:50), and Lynne Hjelte (18:44). Jill Symons (18:36) took tenth place, leading the Chico State women's team to a fourth-place finish in the 16-team meet, behind Cal, Cal-Poly, and a West Valley Track Club team.[15]

Maggie Keyes from Cal-Poly set a new course record with her time of 17:34 for first place. Other Chico finishers were Cathy Oddone (18th), Julie Mastain (20th), Colleen Conners (34th), and a fifth scoring runner, unidentified in results.[16]

GOLDEN STATE CONFERENCE CHAMPIONSHIPS

On Saturday, October 28th, Jill Symons captured first place at the Golden State Conference (GSC) Cross Country Championships, clocking 18:04 over the 5,000-meter course. She had been unbeaten against GSC competitors throughout the season. Among the eight teams competing, Chico State finished third with 65 points behind Sacramento State (41) and Cal State Hayward (56).

In addition to Symons, the Lady Wildcats had three other finishers in the top fifteen. Julie Mastain was fifth, Cathy Oddone tenth, and Colleen Conners fifteenth. Other Wildcat finishers were Janet Wilson (34th), Alicia Munoz (36th), Kim Woodland (39th), Linda Wieking (40th), Cathie Fries (48th), Ann King (50th), and Carrie Herd (52nd).

Symons, Oddone, and Conners qualified for the Region Eight Finals in Long Beach the following weekend. From that meet, the top three teams plus the top ten individuals would qualify for the National Championships in Boulder, Colorado.

Disappointment awaited in Long Beach after Symons, Oddone, Conners, and their coach arrived at the cross country course only five minutes before the gun—leaving no time to warmup either physically or mentally. The coach, who believed the race was at 11 A.M. instead of 10 A.M., later said about the incident, "I messed up, I really messed up." Symons failed to qualify for the Nationals, but would bounce back the following XC season, when she had the highest-ever finish to date of any Lady Wildcat in a National Cross Country Championship.

22

Final '70s Track Season

Coach Larry Burleson
Assistant Coaches Gene Meyers and Toni Ruggle

Chico State University
1979 Men's Track Team
Distance / Middle-Distance Runners

Nelson Cobb   Tom Olson
Danny Lemaroux   Greg Schultz

On Saturday, March 3th, the 1979 Chico Men's Track and Field Team opened their season with a win against Humboldt State at Arcata. The Wildcats gained the victory with strength in the sprints and field events; Humboldt swept every running event from the 800 meters up. Although Chico won this initial FWC meet, the rest of the season was expected to be more difficult. Hayward State had captured the conference title four consecutive years, with Davis second the past three years in a row.[1]

STANFORD RELAYS

This was the finest meet we've been to, very well run. We had hard competition, which we needed, and they treated us with respect. You don't always find that at the smaller college meets.

—Chico State Assistant Track Coach Gene Meyers.[2]

On Saturday, March 24th, Wildcat athletes competed in the Stanford Relays. At this meet, Chico's 800m relay team took second with a time of 1:27.5. Assistant Coach Gene Meyers was as pleased with this performance, as he was with other relay team and individual efforts. The 400m relay team ran 41.7, their best performance of the year; hammer thrower Dave Kennan achieved a mark of 168 feet, five inches; and steeplechaser Danny Lemaroux ran 9:45.[3]

COMBINED MEN'S AND WOMEN'S HOME MEET

> *It was one of those gorgeous Chico spring days with a little wind on the side, and the track was a bobbing sea of red warmups and sleek, black and white muscle. Clustered around the long jump pit were several athletic dandies wearing an assortment of black and red warmups and flowered shorts. One even sported a t-shirt that said "Dr. T. Jump," stood watching and followed each attempt with ardent expletives like "Alright!," Yeah!," and "Unhuh!" Big, Bad Hayward was here.*
>
> —Orion, 4 April 1979.

On Saturday, March 31st, the Chico State Men's and Women's Track and Field teams—which trained apart from one another, and normally competed in separate meets—hosted a joint home meet. In this competition, the Wildcat women's team easily beat Southern Oregon State 83-39 (their highlights are in a separate section), while the men faced Far Western Conference title holder, Hayward State. The men's team final score was Hayward 105, Chico 83.[4]

Chico just about swept the field events in both the men's and women's competition, but the men's thin distance squad eked out only a few points. Hayward's John Embody and Mike Plummer crossed the finish line together in the 10,000 meters, trailed closely for almost all of the 6.2-mile race by Greg Schultz, Chico's lone entry. Nelson Cobb was another Wildcat lone wolf; in a strong field of seasoned Hayward veterans in the 800 meters, he placed fourth.[5]

WOODY WILSON RELAYS AT DAVIS

Both Chico Men's and Women's Track teams competed in the Woody Wilson Relays at Davis on Saturday, April 21st.[6]

Coach Larry Burleson only travelled with about a third of his team. In the men's division, all seven Far Western Conference schools were entered, along with Sonoma State and Division I Fresno State. Wildcat Dave Kennan took second place in the hammer throw with a 52.03 meter effort, and Doug Silcox also claimed second place in the discus with a throw of 48.83 meters.[7]

Fresno State took the Woody Wilson title from two-time defending champion Hayward State 157-138½. Chico State and Humboldt State tied for sixth place with 40 points, behind Stanislaus State (57), Davis (54), and Sacramento State with 50½ points.[8]

The Wildcats' next competition would be on Saturday, April 28th, when the men's team hosted the Sacramento State Hornets at home, while the Lady 'Cats travelled to Sacramento State for their meet.[9]

HOME MEET AGAINST THE HORNETS

Warm weather and Pioneer Week (annual Chico State festivities and events) brought a fair turnout to University Stadium on Saturday night when the Wildcats tangled with the Sac State Hornets. One spectator commented "the meet was a cooker," regarding the competition in which Chico outscored Sacramento 96-68. Also taking part were some Humboldt runners trying to obtain qualifying times for the Nationals.[10]

As was common recently, Chico did well in the sprint, relay, and field events with little strength in middle-distance and distance events. The exception was lone Wildcat entrant in the steeplechase, Tom Olson, who won the race while running 9:14—his fastest time. Following the race, Olson observed, "This puts me six-tenths of a second away from the best guy in the conference. His time is 9:13.6 and he's never been beaten." Olson needed to cut his time another four-tenths of a second to achieve the qualifying mark for the National Championships.[11]

ALUMNI ATHLETES BACK ON THE TRACK

> *My biggest problem is in contacting the athletes. This year I tried to do it by mailing letters through school alumni departments, and it seems pretty hit or miss, mainly miss. Telephone calls would be expensive, but maybe I can find a way to do it next year.*
>
> —Mark Shuman explaining the difficulties in trying to contact former Wildcat athletes, and recruit them for competition against current Chico State Track and Field Team members in an annual meet.[12]

There was a friendly, informal air to proceedings at University Field on May 4th, when Chico State alumni athletes returned to compete against the Chico State men's team and a few competitors from Southern Oregon Tech, Humboldt State, and Sacramento State. Despite a freezing wind, the second annual IMAA (Inter-Mountain Athletes

Association) meet was held as past track and field greats were reunited with each other and old rivalries were renewed.[13]

All-American and former Wildcat Mark Shuman—affectionately referred to as "Shoe"—had organized the meet a year earlier to involve athletes who no longer held eligibility standing, in an annual meet against the regulars. He admitted that for some it was a bit painful to come back and confront the decline of athletic performance in relation to their past glory, but that the purpose of the IMAA was to compete for "fun, and the spirit of the thing, while reuniting old friends and encouraging friendly rivalry."[14]

A highlight of this meet was Sac State alumnus Lee Ferrero winning the 3,000-meter race in 8:41.8, against top-ranked Chico alumni Jack West and Toni Ruggle. West took second place with a time of 8:48.8, while Ruggle finished third in 8:56.3.[15]

FAR WESTERN CONFERENCE CHAMPIONSHIPS
On the weekend of May 12th and 13th, the Conference Championships held in Hayward boasted extreme summer heat and tough competition. Following the final tally of points at meet's completion, Chico had tied with UC Davis for fourth place with 73 points—behind Hayward State (204), Stanislaus State (105), and Sacramento State (102). Humboldt State scored 62 points and San Francisco State 31.[16]

The real heartbreaker of the meet was Tom Olson's steeplechase race. Olson entered the competition with a personal best of 9:14, was ranked second in the conference, and really wanted to win. This zeal caused him to go out too fast. He led the race until the last 600 yards, faded in the heat, and finished in fifth place. Sacramento State's Tim Farrell won with a time of 9:15.2; followed by Rob Anex (Davis, 9:23.4), Frank Dauncey (Humboldt, 9:24.3), Dan Martinelli (San Francisco, 9:25.0), Olson (9:25.6), and Ed Nicholson (Sacramento, 9:26.3).[17]

Final '70s Track Season   161

Coach Cherrie Sherrard, Assistant Coach Mike Porter

1979 Chico State Women's Track and Field

Distance / Middle-Distance Runners
Barbara Davis   Kathy Horn   Cathy Oddone   Jill Symons

National Championships: May 24-26, Cheney, Washington

SYMONS SETS CONFERENCE / SCHOOL RECORD

Photo 22-1

Jill Symons on her way to a new conference and school record for the 5,000-meter run on March 10, 1979. *Orion*, March 14, 1979

On Saturday, March 10, Chico State Women's Track and Field Team was defeated at home by visiting UC Davis, 102-74. One of the Lady

'Cats' meet highlights was Jill Symons winning the 5,000 meters in a time of 17:57.5, which was both a new conference and school record.[18]

A week later on March 17th, Chico State Women's Track Team easily beat Humboldt State 107-39 in a dual meet. The only event in which the Lady 'Cats did not place first was the 400-meter run. Jill Symons won the 5,000 meters in a time of 18:14.5, and the 800 meters with a 2:24.5. Teammate Barbara Davis took second in the two-lap race with a 2:27.2. Cathy Oddone won the 3,000-meter race with an 11:04.7, and a quartet of Chico middle-distance runners combined to capture first in the two-mile relay in 12:39.8.[19]

ALL-CAL WOMEN'S MEET

One week earlier on March 10th, Cal Women's Track Team members had competed against themselves in a meet at Berkeley. The below photos of four star distance runners puts faces to names listed in meet results in the previous chapter. At this inter-squad competition, Trumbly, Richter, and Metteer set school records.[20]

Photo 22-2

Left: Alice Trumbly (1,500 meters, 4:26.7); center: Suzanne Richter leading Jan Oehm (5,000 meters, 16:24.10); and right: Sally Metteer (10,000 meters, 35:46.0).
Nor-Cal Running Review, Spring 1979

FOUR-WAY WOMEN'S MEET

On March 24th (the same day as the Stanford Relays), the Chico State Women's Track Team was also in the San Francisco Bay Area—at Hayward competing in a four-way meet. In this competition, Jill Symons won both the 3,000 meters (10:43.0) and 1,500 meters (4:51.2), with Cathy Oddone (4:51.4) on her heels in the latter race. Oddone also placed fifth in the 800-meter run. Hayward State's Mary Rieboldt and Michele Aubuchon won the 800 meters (2:24.8) and 5,000 meters (17:57.7), respectively—demonstrating the strength of Lady Pioneers in the middle-distance and distance events. Hayward State (75) took team honors, followed by University of Nevada, Reno (50), Chico State (46), and Stanislaus State with thirteen points.[21]

COMBINED WOMEN'S AND MEN'S HOME MEET

> *It's becoming usual now for Becky Blankenship, Cathy Oddone, Barbara Davis, Golden Sizemore, and Jill Symons to win or take second in their events.*
>
> —Assistant Coach Mike Porter.[22]

In the quoted material, the Lady 'Cats' Assistant Coach, Mike Porter, implied that the individuals cited made it look easy, but it wasn't easy for some this Saturday. They had to fight, like Barbara Davis did when she struggled to take second in the 800 meters against a surprisingly strong Kathy Allen from Southern Oregon. But, at meet's end, as previously noted, the Chico Women's Track and Field Team prevailed over Southern Oregon State, 83-39.[23]

WOODY WILSON RELAYS

Among Chico's men and women athletes competing in the Woody Wilson Relays, only Kathy Kuchta came home a winner. She captured first place in both the shot put and discus throws, while setting a new meet record in the latter event. In the team competition, the Lady 'Cats finished fifth with 32 points behind winner Hayward State (60), Hawaii (56), Sacramento State (55), and host UC Davis with thirty-four points.[24]

GOLDEN STATE CONFERENCE CHAMPIONSHIPS

The Golden State Conference Track and Field Championships, held in Sacramento on Saturday, May 12, yielded some excellent individual performances, although Chico State only placed fifth overall in the meet. Assistant Coach Mike Porter was extremely pleased with some of his less-experienced runners who, "came on during the conference meet to run their personal fastest for the season." Kathy Horn ran a 2:30 leg of Chico's two-mile relay (which finished fifth with a time of 10:07.6) and "cooked" along with Cathy Oddone, who ran her leg in 2:25.[25]

23

End of a Decade – the 1979 Cross Country Season

Chico State University 1979 Men's Cross Country Team
Coach Larry Burleson

Al Masterson	Marcos Silva	Rich Watson
Steve Nygaard		Mike Wright

On Saturday, October 13th, the Chico State Men's Cross Country Team won its second consecutive home meet by defeating Stanislaus State and Humboldt State over the 10,000-meter course in Bidwell Park. The Wildcat's score of 38 points topped Humboldt's 41 points and the 45 accumulated by Stanislaus.[1]

Chico's top finisher for the third week in a row was Mike Wright, who placed second with a time of 30:47. Al Masterson was fifth (31:23), Rich Watson seventh (31:39), Steve Nygaard tenth (32:02), and Marcos Silva was the 'Cats' fifth scoring runner, clocking 33:41 for 14th place.[2]

Photo 23-1

Mike Wright competing in the steeplechase race during the following 1980 track and field season.
The Record 1980, CSU Chico Digital Collections

Photo 23-2

R-L: Marcos Silva leading teammates Kurt Vineyard and Eddie Teague while competing on the track.
The Record 1981, CSU Chico Digital Collections

The following Saturday, October 20th, the Wildcat harriers competed in the FWC Championships in Sacramento. Humboldt State's Dan Grimes was the individual winner with a time of 30:20.0 over the 10,000-meter course. A strong kick pushed him across the finish line one second ahead of Sacramento's Angel Coriallo, and gave the Lumberjacks the Far Western Conference Cross Country Championship title.[3]

The team scores were: Humboldt State (27), Sacramento State (28), Hayward State (111), UC Davis (121), San Francisco State (145), Stanislaus State (147), and Chico State (174).[4]

1979 LADY 'CATS CROSS COUNTRY SEASON

We've done very well. Jill Symons has won two meets in a row, and as a team we're right where I had hoped to be with two straight first places.

—Coach Cherrie Sherrard assessing prior to the third meet of the 1979 cross country season, how her team was doing thus far.[5]

Chico State University 1979 Women's Cross Country Team
Coach Cherrie Sherrard, Assistant Coach Mike Porter

Darcy Burleson	Annette Nielsen	Linda Ovegaard
Merrily Landers	Karen Noland	Joyce Scott
Katherine Langan	Cathy Oddone	Leann Secor
Brita Lindstrom	Julia Orri	Jill Symons
Alicia Munoz		Linda Wieking

On September 15th, Jill Symons and Cathy Oddone took first and third in a meet against the Sac State Hornets in Sacramento. The Wildcats captured the meet.[6]

A week later on the 22nd, Symons led a 1-2-3 sweep of Humboldt and Sonoma, as she covered the 5,000-meter Arcata course in 17:58.8; followed closely by teammates Cathy Oddone and Darcy Burleson in 18:20.9 and 18:50.7, respectively. Other Chico finishers were Julia Orri (8th), Linda Wieking (12th), Merrily Landers (20th), and Linda Ovegaard in twenty-second place.[7]

Photo 23-3

Lady Wildcats competing in a cross country race in 1980.
Sophomore Darcy Burleson is the second runner from the left in the photograph.
The Record 1980, CSU Chico Digital Collections

Darcy Burleson, daugher of Coach Larry Burleson, was another former member of the Chico High "Charlie's Angels" 1976 and 1977 cross country teams. As a sophmore in 1976, the year before the Angels' second in the nation ranking, she had led the team. In fact, she went unbeaten in cross country and, following completion of the 1976 Season, was named the All-Northern California Girl Runner of the Year, and to the All-Girls First Team. Joan Gregg and Luanne Park received Honorable Mention.

REMAINING THREE FORMER CHARLIE'S ANGELS

After delving into the subject of the Charlie's Angels, and previously introducing readers to Joan Gregg, Suzanne Richer, Jill Symons, and Darcy Burleson, it's appropriate to provide a thumbsketch of the other three of the seven former Charlie's Angels.

Luanne Park ran for Butte College, before accepting an athletic scholarship to Oregon State University for which she ran and played soccer. In 1984, she qualified for and ran in the inaugural U.S. Olympic Trials Marathon in Olympia, Washington. She qualified for, but did not participate in, the 1988 trials in Pittsburgh, Pennsylvania. By then, she had acquired a new passion—albeit one which included running 26.2 miles following a swim and bike ride.

In both 1987 and 1988, Luanne finished eighth among women at the Ironman World Championship in Hawaii. Apparently, the Iron Man was not challenging enough. In the late 1990s, Luanne began running, annually, the Western States 100-miler with other ultra-distance races sprinkled throughout the year.

Julie Selchau was named along with Jill Symons to the All-Northern Section Second Team in 1978. Suzanne Richter, on the First Team, was the third girl in all of northern California. Selchau had the talent, grit, determination, and other attributes necessary to be a top collegiate runner, and likely an All-American. Alas, she injured her Achilles tendon her senior year in high school, dashing any such hopes. Her competitive running over, she studied nursing in college and embarked on that noble, and caring profession.

Stacey Shols, principally a sprinter, but sufficiently accomplished at the longer distances to be the Angels' seventh runner, did not compete in track or cross country while attending college.

THREE-WAY MEET AT HOME

Photo 23-4

Julia Orri during a race against Humboldt State
and UC Davis on Chico's course in Bidwell Park.
Orion, October 3, 1979

Jill Symons led Chico State's Women's Cross Country Team to their third victory on September 29th, with a time of 18:58 on the Lady 'Cats' 5,000-meter home course in Bidwell Park. Chico scored 31 points in the three-way meet against Humboldt State (37), and UC Davis (63). Following closely behind Symons was Cathy Oddone in second (19:12). Darcy Burleson was fourth in 19:40, and Karen Noland, tenth (20:57).[8]

Julia Orri, Chico fifth scoring runner (16th, 21:17), led a large pack of teammates across the finish line. These were Annette Nielsen, 17th, Linda Wieking, 18th, and Leann Secor, 19th, all at 21:30; Katte Langon (22nd, 22:31); Brita Lindstrom (23rd, 22:36); Merrily Landers (27th, 23:34); and Joyce Scott with a time of 26:08 in twenty-ninth place.[9]

Among the large numbers of Lady 'Cats running cross country for Coach Sherrard were some sprinters—engaged in conditioning and strength building for the ensuing track season.[10]

Chico's next competition was to be the Cal-Aggie Invitational on October 6th. Sherrard remarked about her team's prospects at this meet: "This will be the first chance to know how well we'll do against other teams as a whole."[11]

CAL-AGGIE INVITATIONAL AT DAVIS

Jill Symons knows no place other than first place—and why not"

—*Orion*, October 10, 1979.

They all keep getting better and improving their times. They're running well and healthy. There have been no injuries...what else could you ask for?

—Coach Sherrard commenting on her team in the same article that paid tribute to Symons' great success.[12]

At the tenth annual Cal-Aggie Invitational Cross Country meet at UC Davis, Jill Symons set a new course record of 17:41 in finishing first in the 5,000-meter race. She bettered her previous year's winning time by six seconds and came in 31 seconds ahead of her closest rival. Chico placed second with 77 points among the nine schools competing. The meet was won by a team of women who had run in college—but now belonged to the Aggie Birds Running Club—with a score of 24 points.[13]

Chico's second and third team finishers, Cathy Oddone and Darcy Burleson placed sixth and seventh, respectively, with only five seconds between them, 18:23 and 18:28. Karen Noland (20:07), Annette Nielsen (20:18), and Julie Orri (20:24) came in 31st, 34th, and 35th. Other Lady 'Cat runners were Leann Secor, Katherine Langan, Linda Wieking, Brita Lindsrom, Merrily Landers, Joyce Scott, and Alicia Munoz.[14]

The following Saturday, October 13th, the Chico women's team was to take part in its biggest meet yet, the sixth annual Stanford Invitational. Up to this point, the Lady 'Cats had mainly been competing against schools in their own conference.[15]

STANFORD INVITATIONAL

That was the biggest and fastest meet we've had.... We finished in the top half.

—Coach Sherrard remarking on the results of the Stanford Invitational in which the Chico State Women's Cross Country Team placed a respectable 8th in the 18 team meet. Considering that they were running against many "scholarship schools," she thought her team did well.[16]

Of the 170 runners in the women's race at Stanford, Jill Symons placed 15th with a time of 18:07.6, thirty seconds faster than a year before. She needed to run particularly fast to do well, because the top five finishers ahead of her broke the previous year's course record. Cathy Oddone clocked 19:12.8 for 28th place, followed by Chico team members Darcy Burleson (19:59.1), Karen Noland (20:59), Julie Orri (21:07), Leann Secor (21:19) and Annette Nielsen with a time of 22:00.[17]

HAYWARD STATE INVITATIONAL

On October 20th, the host Hayward State team won the second annual Hayward State Women's Three-Mile Invitational with 23 points. The UC Berkeley 'B' team (57) was second, followed by the Woodside Track Club (57). Chico State (112) finished fourth among the fifteen teams.[18]

In winning the race—and leading her team to third in the college division and fourth overall—Jill Symons broke the course record by 28 seconds. Cathy Oddone finished in 8th place, Karen Noland in 30th, and Linda Wieking in 38th place. Also competing for Chico State were Julia Orri, Katherine Langan, and Merrily Landers.[19]

EVE OF THE REGIONAL CHAMPIONSHIPS

Thirty non-scholarship schools from California, Nevada, and Hawaii made up Divison Three, and they would all be competing on November 3rd at the Regional Championships for the top three team spots to qualify for the Nationals, to be held in Florida. The top fifteen individual runners would also qualify.[20]

A week earlier, the Chico State Women's Cross Country Team had won the Golden State Conference Cross Country Championships held on Saturday, October 27th, in Sacramento. Symons raced to victory in a close finish; her time of 17:43 was just two seconds ahead of Hayward's Michele Aubuchon.[21]

Coach Sherrard, when asked how she thought the team would do at Regionals, indicated that it was hard to say if Chico would qualify as a team. But, she was fairly certain that Jill Symons and possibly Cathy Oddone would qualify as individuals.[22]

REGION 8 AIAW CHAMPIONSHIPS DIVISION III – SYMONS AND ODDONE QUALIFY FOR NATIONALS

At the Regional Championships, Chico almost qualified to make the trip to Tallahassee, Florida, for the National Championships on November 17th. When points were tallied at race completion, the winning and second place teams—Hayward State and Sacramento State—were in. Chico State tied for third place with Cal Lutheran. In situations such as this, the finishing places of each team's fifth runner were compared, and whoever had placed higher decided the issue. Chico's Linda Wieking came in 54th in 21:04, while Cal Lutheran's fifth runner was nine spots ahead in 45th. Thus, Cal Lutheran got the nod as the qualifying team.[23]

Of great excitement to the Lady 'Cats and to fans of Chico State women's cross country, both Jill Symons and Cathy Oddone qualified for the Nationals, through the top 15 individuals.[24]

> **Division III:**
> 1. Jill Symons (Chico) 17:43; 2. Michelle Aubuchon (Hay) 17:50; 3. Connie Hester (Hay) 18:03; 4. Lisa Foy (Sac) 18:16; 5. Mary Scannell (Sac) 18:17; 6. Mary Tracy (Clare) 18:19; 7. Stephanie Strout (Hay) 18:28; 8. Marilyn Brandt (UCD) 18:40; 9. Diana Pappas (Sac) 18:45; 10. Cathy Fulderson (CLC) 18:45; 11. Fran Castro (Hay) 18:47; 12. Karey Robinson (Hay) 18:55; 13. Denise Bigelow (Hay) 18:59; 14. Shane Felix (Hay) 19:00; 15.0 Cathy Onone (Chico) 19:01.
>
> Team Scores: 1. Cal State Hayward 32; 2. Cal State Sacramento 54; 3. Cal Lutheran 99; 3. Cal State Chico 99; 5. UC Davis 120; 6. Humboldt State 121; 7. Pomona Pitzer 188; 8. Sonoma State 222.

JILL SYMONS MAKES ALL-AMERICAN

> *I've been written up so much that I think people must be tired of reading about me.*
>
> —*Orion*, December 12, 1979 article, noting about Jill Symons before the quoted sentence, "With such an impressive record, one is struck by her sincere modesty. She would rather talk of the team's success and of her teammates than herself."

Photo 23-5

Jill Symons, a 1979 Cross Country All-American.
California Track News, November 1979

Jill Symons—termed "Leader of the Pack," an appropriate moniker for someone who had won seven out of nine races in the past two months—finished 14th at the AIAW National Cross Country Championships in Tallahassee on November 17, 1979, earning All-American honors. Fellow sophmore and teammate Cathy Oddone placed a respectable 58th out of a field of 143 runners.[25]

Of Oddone, Coach Sherrard noted, "She ran well and placed in the top third. Cathy beat people she's never beaten before." The Lady 'Cats had truly a successful year, winning three out of eight meets. Sherrard summarized the season thus:

> I thought the team did quite well, placing third out of seven teams in their league. In our league, we competed against CSU Hayward, which won the division Three (nonscholarship schools) National Championship title this year. Sacramento State was the other [league competitor] team to go the the Nationals in division three. They came in sixth place.[26]

Jill Symons was the final and only woman Wildcat distance runner to earn All-American honors in the 1969-1979 period covered in *Stride*

Out. These ten individuals, beginning with Duwayne Ray and Gene Meyers, and ending with Symons, are honored in the book's postscript, which simply pictures them in successive pages.

Before leaving the text, a final visual reminder of a vibrant period, 1969-1979, when VW vans abounded.

Photo 23-6

Jack Leydig's 1968 VW Van, the only vehicle he's ever owned, bought after he earned a Master's degree at Southern Illinois University, and the first one without the "split" windshield. He did a lot of remodeling, including slide side windows, in 2009-2010, and the "Vdub" now has nearly 600,000 miles on it. Jack sold Nike shoes out of it in the early 70s prior to the establishment of Jack's Athletic Supply.
Courtesy of Jack Leydig

Postscript – Wildcat All-Americans, 1969-1979

Photo Postscript-1

Chico State's Duwayne Ray and Rob Laxson finishing first and second in the mile race at the 1969 Far Western Championship Meet. Ray won the mile at the 1969 NCAA College Division Track and Field Championships in Ashland, Ohio. (All-American and National Champion in the mile, 1969).
Wildcat, May 19, 1969

Photo Postscript-2

Wildcat Gene Meyers winning a race on the track for Chico State.
(All-American in the 880 in 1969, and mile in 1971)
Courtesy of Cathy Anderson-Meyers

Photo Postscript-3

Mike Dailey competing in a steeplechase race in 1970.
(All-American in Cross Country, 1969)
Courtesy of Bob Darling

Photo Postscript-4

Bob Darling racing to a 4th place finish in the 1969 Chico State Cross Country Invitational Meet in Bidwell Park.
(All-American in Cross Country, 1969)
Courtesy of Bob Darling

Photo Postscript-5

Jim Estes racing on the track in 1970.
(All-American in Cross Country, 1969. Estes finished 21st at the 1969 National Championships. At that time, only the top fifteen competitors made All-American. Subsequently that number was changed to twenty-five, and the U.S. Track & Field and Cross Country Coaches Association retroactively designated him an All-American to reflect the expanded allowances for achievement of this honor.)
Courtesy of Jim Estes

Photo Postscript-6

Wildcat Kim Ellison winning the mile race during a home meet on April 29, 1972. (All-American in the mile, 1971)
Chico Enterprise-Record photograph

Photo Postscript-7

Wildcat Mark Shuman finished in 23rd place finish at the 1973 NCAA Division II Cross Country Championships. He led the Chico State harriers to a sixth-place team finish and individually earned All-American honors.
(All-American in Cross Country, 1973)
Courtesy of Toni Ruggle

Photo Postscript-8

Tom Brown clearing a steeplechase barrier.
(All-American in the steeplechase, 1973 and 1974)
Chico Enterprise-Record photograph

Photo Postscript-9

Karl Schaechterle, location and date unknown.
(All-American in the steeplechase, 1976)
Courtesy of Bob Darling

Photo Postscript-10

Lady Wildcat Cross Country Team member Jill Symons in 1980.
(All-American in Cross Country, 1979)
The Record, 1980, CSU Chico Digital Collections

Appendix A: Wildcat Athletes' Track Times, 1969-1979

880-Yard Run

Name	Year		Time
Gene Meyers	1969		1:50.1
Jim Estes	1971		1:51.8
Rob Laxson	1969		1:51.9
Kim Ellison	1972		1:53
Dave Wood	1973		1:54.0
Duwayne Ray	1969		1:54.1
Scott McVey	1973		1:54.2
Mike Porter	1970		1:55.0
Juan Dura	1971		1:56.0
Dennis Butler	1975		1:55.2
Corbin Scott	1974		1:56.3
Tom Brown	1974		1:57.4
Karl Springer	1970		1:59.0
Manny Mahon	1971		1:59.0
Ralph Patten	1970	relay split	1:59.1
Darryl Brock	1970		1:59.4
Bob Darling	1971		2:02
Jack West	1973		2:05.5

800-Meter Run

Name	Year		Time
Kent Mulkey	1976		1:53.7
Dave Mills	1977		1:55.0
Lynn Ryan	1977		1:55.0
Nelson Cobb	1978		2:01
Toni Ruggle	1977		2:01.3
Jeff Brady	1978		2:02.9

Mile Run

Name	Year		Time
Kim Ellison	1972		4:01.4
Duwayne Ray	1969	anchor leg	4:02.9
Duwayne Ray	1969		4:05.5
Gene Meyers	1971		4:06.2
Rob Laxson	1969		4:06.7
Bob King	1973		4:08.1
Toni Ruggle	1978		4:08.1
Jack West	1973		4:12.1
Tim Stone	1976		4:12.9
Eddie Silva	1973		4:13.4
Jim Estes	1971		4:13.8
Mike Dailey	1971	anchor leg	4:14.7

Name	Year	Time
Scott McVey	1972	4:15.1
Bob Wear	1970	4:18.4
Jim Price	1974	4:19
Bob Darling	1971	4:24
Joe McNally	1969	4:26.2
Karl Springer	1969	4:27.4
Burt Hume	1974	4:30
Nick Vogt	1972	4:30.3

1,500-Meter Run

Name	Year	Time
Toni Ruggle	1978	3:51
Tom Keller	1977	3:52.5
Tim Stone	1976	3:53.6
Lynn Ryan	1977	3:54.0
Kent Pease	1977	3:56.2
Kent Mulkey	1978	4:35.8

2-Mile Run

Name	Year	Time
Kim Ellison	1972	8:57
Eddie Silva	1973	9:00.7
Pat Stordahl	1972	9:09.2
Gene Meyers	1970	9:24.5
Mike Dailey	1971	9:25.6
Ralph Patten	1971	9:25.6
Bob Darling	1970	9:39.5
Mark Shuman	1973	9:39.8
Nick Vogt	1971	9:45.1

3,000-Meter Steeplechase Run

Name	Year	Time
Tom Brown	1974	8:55.7
Karl Schaechterle	1976	8:57
Mike Dailey	1971	9:02.8
Tom Olson	1979	9:14
Joe McNally	1969	9:36
Danny Lemaroux	1979	9:45
Scott McVey	1972	9:46.8
Mike Fornaciari	1973	9:47.2
Tom O'Connor	1970	9:53.3
Charlie Griffin	1977	10:00.0
Jim Moyle	1970	10:08.0
Bob Darling	1971	10:10
Gene Gilligan	1969	10:21.3
Lynn Mulkey	1978	10:55.0

3-Mile Run

Name	Year		Time
Pat Stordahl	1972		14:06.4
Gene Meyers	1971		14:07.2
Eddie Silva	1973		14:12.0
Greg Griffin	1975		14:19.0
Mike Dailey	1971		14:23.7
Duwayne Ray	1969		14:26.2
Bob Darling	1971	race split on way to 6-mile time	14:33
Mark Shuman	1973		14:35.6
Kim Ellison	1972		14:46.0
Howard Miller	1970		14:55.4
Nick Vogt	1972		15:05.4
Bob Wear	1970		15:06.2
Karl Springer	1969		15:34.1
Jim Moyle	1969		15:56.8

5,000-Meter Run

Name	Year	Time
Toni Ruggle	1978	14:40
Greg Griffin	1976	14:46.8
Tom Keller	1977	15:24.8
Tony Webb	1977	15:31.7
Dave Mills	1977	16:38.8
Lynn Mackey	1978	16:25.31

6-Mile Run

Name	Year	Time
Bob Darling	1971	29:22.8
Pat Stordahl	1973	30.35.0
Nick Vogt	1972	30:34.4
Mark Shuman	1973	30:36.0
Howard Miller	1971	30:37.6
Dan Chapman	1972	31:08.5
Junior Torres	1972	31:08.5
Calvin Lantrip	1974	33:44.2

10,000-Meter Run

Name	Year	Time
Greg Griffin	1976	31:04.2
Mike Sophie	1978	34:19

Appendix B: Lady 'Cat Athletes' Track Times, 1969-1979

800-Meter Run

Name	Year	Time
Barbara Davis	1978	2:21.5
Jill Symons	1979	2:24.5
Barbara Sprague	1977	2:25.6
Berni Phillips	1977	2:44.4

880-Yard Run

Name	Year		Time
Sandy Wiseman	1973		2:19
Barbara Sprague	1977		2:21
Lisa Foy	1976		2:23
Cathy Oddone	1979	relay leg	2:25
Kathy Horn	1979	relay leg	2:30
Kathy Spence	1976		2:35
Toni Crumbo	1976		2:36.4
Regina Robinson	1972		2:40.9
Nancy Wedel	1969		2:41.2
Vicki Hobbs	1976		2:45.5
Nancy Hartwig	1969		2:49.6

1,500-Meter Run

Name	Year	Time
Jill Symons	1979	4:51.2
Cathy Oddone	1979	4:51.4
Barbara Sprague	1977	4:56.8
Pat Donald	1977	5:52.0

Mile Run

Name	Year	Time
Sandy Wiseman	1974	5:22.8
Barbara Sprague	1977	5:29.7
Laurie de Ghetaldi	1975	5:38
Stacy Sudduth	1974	5:41
Lisa Foy	1976	5:50.2
Stacy Fitzgerald	1975	5:50.3
Kathy Sullivan	1976	5:53
Nancy Wedel	1969	6:18.9
Kathy Spence	1976	6:21.3
Darlene Wallach	1972	6:21.9
Shirley Miller	1972	6:45.9

3,000-Meter Run

Name	Year	Time
Michele Aubuchan	1978	10:48.4
Cathy Oddone	1979	11:04.7
Kelly Butler	1977	12:48.2
Dolores Diaz	1977	13:16.6

2-Mile Run

Name	Year	Time
Merill Cray	1974	11:36.0
Kathy Sullivan	1977	12:05.5
Darlene Wallach	1973	12:47
Liz Belyea	1976	14:12.7

3-Mile Run

Name	Year	Time
Kathy Sullivan	1977	18:32.2

5,000-Meter Run

Name	Year	Time
Jill Symons	1979	17:57.5
Kathy Sullivan	1977	19:27.6

Chapter Notes

PREFACE NOTES:
[1] Northeastern California Historical Photograph Collection
California State University, Chico
https://calisphere.org/item/d5a93c1e49faccb724cee5afeed81bba/
[2] "Long-time ARC coach helped bring Olympic Trials to town" (https://runsra.org/2014/01/09/baeta-joins-sra-hall-of-fame-2/: accessed 5 February 2023).
[3] "Gary Towne Head Cross Country Coach" (https://chicowildcats.com/sports/2008/9/11/MXC_0911084903.aspx?path=mcross: accessed 5 February 2023).
[4] Ibid.

CHAPTER 1 NOTES:
[1] *The Record 1969*, CSU Chico Digital Collections.
[2] *Wildcat*, 27 February 1969.
[3] *The Record 1968*, CSU Chico Digital Collections.
[4] *Wildcat*, 13 March 1969.
[5] Ibid.
[6] Ibid.
[7] *Wildcat*, 24 April 1969.
[8] *Wildcat*, 16 April 1969.
[9] Ibid.
[10] Ibid.
[11] *Wildcat*, 21 April 1969.
[12] Ibid.
[13] Results provided by Hank Lawson (http://lynbrooksports.prepcaltrack.com/ATHLETICS/CTRN/ctrn.htm: accessed 15 February 2023).
[14] *Wildcat*, 2 May 1969.
[15] *Wildcat*, 7 May 1969.
[16] Ibid.
[17] *Wildcat*, 7 May 1969; *Wildcat*, 8 May 1969.
[18] Ut supra.
[19] *The Record 1969*, CSU Chico Digital Collections.
[20] *Wildcat*, 8 May 1969.
[21] Ibid.
[22] *The Record 1969*, CSU Chico Digital Collections.
[23] *Wildcat*, 15 May 1969.
[24] *Wildcat*, 19 May 1969.
[25] Ibid.
[26] Ibid.

[27] "U.S. Track & Field and Cross Country Coaches Association 1969 All-Americans College Outdoor Track & Field" (http://www.ustfccca.org/assets/awards/div2/allamericans/cd_allamOT_1969.pdf: accessed 8 February 2023.
[28] *Wildcat*, 25 April 1969.
[29] *Wildcat*, 7 May 1969.
[30] Ibid.
[31] *Wildcat*, 12 May 1969.
[32] *Wildcat*, 19 May 1969.
[33] Mike Hubbard and Jack Pfeifer, *Statistical Review of the Early Years of Women's Collegiate Track & Field in the U.S.* (Baltimore, MD, Federation of American Statistics of Track, 1984). https://trackandfieldnews.com/wp-content/uploads/2018/11/WCollegiateTrack.pdf: accessed 16 February 2023.
[34] Ibid.

CHAPTER 2 NOTES:
[1] *Wildcat*, 6 November 1969.
[2] Ibid.
[3] Ibid.
[4] Ibid.
[5] *Wildcat*, 8 October 1969.
[6] Ibid.
[7] Ibid.
[8] *Wildcat*, 20 October 1969.
[9] Ibid.
[10] Ibid.
[11] *Wildcat*, 27 October 1969.
[12] *Wildcat*, 7 November 1969.
[13] *Wildcat*, 7 November 1969; *Wildcat*, 27 October 1969.
[14] *Wildcat*, 7 November 1969.
[15] *Wildcat*, 5 November 1969.
[16] Ibid.
[17] *Wildcat*, 14 November 1969.
[18] Ibid.
[19] *Wildcat*, 17 November 1969.
[20] Ibid.
[21] *Wildcat*, 24 November 1969.
[22] Ibid.
[23] Ibid.

CHAPTER 3 NOTES:
[1] *Wildcat*, 26 February 1970.
[2] Ibid.
[3] Ibid.
[4] *Wildcat*, 6 March 1970.

[5] Ibid.
[6] *Wildcat*, 11 March 1970.
[7] *Wildcat*, 18 March 1970.
[8] *Wildcat*, 3 April 1970; Meet results provided by Jim Estes.
[9] *Wildcat*, 6 April 1970.
[10] *Wildcat*, 10 April 1970.
[11] *Wildcat*, 6 April 1970.
[12] *Wildcat*, 10 April 1970.
[13] Ibid.
[14] *Wildcat*, 13 April 1970.
[15] Ibid.
[16] *Wildcat*, 24 April 1970.
[17] Ibid.
[18] *Wildcat*, 4 May 1970.
[19] *Wildcat*, 6 May 1970.
[20] Ibid.
[21] "Track leads the season; takes third in FWC" in *The Record 1970*.
[22] *Wildcat*, 13 May 1970.
[23] Ibid.
[24] Ibid.
[25] *Wildcat*, 20 May 1970.
[26] *Wildcat*, 18 May 1970.
[27] "Track leads the season; takes third in FWC" in *The Record 1970*.
[28] Undated clipped *Chico Enterprise-Record* article.

CHAPTER 4 NOTES:
[1] *Wildcat*, 21 September 1970.
[2] *Wildcat*, 18 September 1970; *Wildcat*, 21 September 1970.
[3] *Wildcat*, 18 September 1970.
[4] *Wildcat*, 21 September 1970.
[5] *Wildcat*, 28 September 1970.
[6] "Larry Burleson 1938-2022" (https://www.legacy.com/us/obituaries/chicoer/name/larry-burelson-obituary?id=35829808: accessed 7 February 2023).
[7] *Wildcat*, 28 September 1970.
[8] Ibid.
[9] *Wildcat*, 5 October 1970.
[10] *Wildcat*, 5 October 1970; Wildcat, 9 October 1970.
[11] *Wildcat*, 9 October 1970.
[12] *Wildcat*, 12 October 1970.
[13] *Wildcat*, 9 October 1970.
[14] *Wildcat*, 12 October 1970.
[15] Ibid.
[16] *Wildcat*, 16 October 1970; *Wildcat*, 19 October 1970.
[17] *Wildcat*, 19 October 1970.
[18] *Wildcat*, 5 October 1970.

[19] *Wildcat*, 23 October 1970.
[20] *Wildcat*, 26 October 1970.
[21] Ibid.
[22] *Wildcat*, 2 November 1970.
[23] Ibid.
[24] *Wildcat*, 13 November 1970.
[25] *Wildcat*, 20 November 1970.

CHAPTER 5 NOTES:
[1] *Wildcat*, 22 February 1971; *Wildcat*, 26 February 1971.
[2] *Wildcat*, 26 February 1971.
[3] Ibid.
[4] Copy of meet results provided by Mike Dailey.
[5] Ibid.
[6] Copy of meet results provided by Jim Estes.
[7] Ibid.
[8] *Wildcat*, 8 March 1971.
[9] *Wildcat*, 19 March 1971.
[10] *Wildcat*, 24 March 1971.
[11] *Wildcat*, 14 April 1971; meet results provided by Mike Dailey.
[12] Meet results provided by Mike Dailey.
[13] *Wildcat*, 20 April 1971.
[14] *Wildcat*, 20 April 1971; *Wildcat*, 27 April 1971.
[15] *Wildcat*, 4 May 1971.
[16] *Wildcat*, 11 May 1971.
[17] Ibid.
[18] Ibid.
[19] *Wildcat*, 11 May 1971; Kim Ellison correspondence of 16 February 2023.
[20] *Wildcat*, 21 May 1971.
[21] *Wildcat*, 25 May 1971.
[22] Ibid.
[23] *Chico Enterprise-Record*, May 4, 1971.
[24] Laura de Ghetaldi correspondence, March 5, 2023.
[25] Ibid.
[26] Ibid.

CHAPTER 6 NOTES:
[1] *Wildcat*, 29 September 1971.
[2] Ibid.
[3] Ibid.
[4] *Wildcat*, 5 October 1971.
[5] *Wildcat*, 5 October 1971; *Wildcat*, 15 October 1971.
[6] *Wildcat*, 22 October 1971.
[7] *Wildcat*, 27 October 1971.
[8] *Wildcat*, 22 October 1971.

[9] *Wildcat*, 27 October 1971.
[10] Ibid.
[11] *Wildcat*, 2 November 1971.
[12] *Wildcat*, 5 November 1971.
[13] *Wildcat*, 9 November 1971.
[14] Ibid.

CHAPTER 7 NOTES:
[1] *Wildcat*, 1 March 1972.
[2] *Wildcat*, 15 March 1972.
[3] *Wildcat*, 21a March 1972.
[4] Ibid.
[5] Ibid.
[6] *Wildcat*, 6 April 1972.
[7] *Wildcat*, 14 April 1972.
[8] *Wildcat*, 19 April 1972.
[9] *Wildcat*, 26 April 1972.
[10] *Wildcat*, 28 April 1972.
[11] Ibid.
[12] *Wildcat*, 10 May 1972.
[13] *Wildcat*, 25 May 1972.
[14] *Wildcat*, 12 April 1972.
[15] Ibid.
[16] Ibid.
[17] Ibid

CHAPTER 9 NOTES:
[1] *Wildcat*, 28 September 1972.
[2] *Wildcat*, 3 October 1972.
[3] *West Valley Newsletter*, December 1969.
[4] *Wildcat*, 10 October 1972; *Wildcat*, 12 October 1972.
[5] *Wildcat*, 10 October 1972.
[6] Ibid.
[7] *Wildcat*, 26 October 1972.
[8] *Wildcat*, 2 November 1972.
[9] Ibid.
[10] *Wildcat*, 9 November 1972.
[11] Ibid.
[12] "The Doobie Brothers" (https://thedoobiebrothers.com/news/273303#:~:text=The%20set%20includes%20more%20than,Closer%20(1980)%2C%20and%20Farewell: accessed 3 March 2023).
[13] Laura de Ghetaldi correspondence, March 6, 2023.
[14] Ibid.

CHAPTER 10 NOTES:
[1] *Wildcat*, 13 March 1973.
[2] *Wildcat*, 22 March 1973.
[3] *Wildcat*, 20 March 1973.
[4] *Wildcat*, 5 April 1973.
[5] Ibid.
[6] *Wildcat*, 5 April 1973; *Wildcat*, 10 April 1973.
[7] *Nor-Cal Running Review* May-June 1973.
[8] *Nor-Cal Running Review* February 1973, May-June 1973.
[9] *Nor-Cal Running Review* May-June 1973.
[10] *Wildcat*, 8 May 1973.
[11] *Wildcat*, 15 May 1973.
[12] *Wildcat*, 22 May 1973.
[13] Ibid.
[14] Ibid.
[15] Ibid.
[16] Ibid.
[17] *Wildcat*, 1 June 1973.
[18] *Nor-Cal Running Review* July 1973; "TrackNewsletter and TrackStats," June 7, 1973.
[19] Correspondence from Laurie de Ghetaldi, March 2, 2023.
[20] *Wildcat*, 10 April 1973.
[21] Clipped, undated article from the *Chico Enterprise-Record*.
[22] Clipped, undated article from the *Chico Enterprise-Record*; Correspondence from Laura de Ghetaldi.
[23] *Wildcat*, 15 May 1973.

CHAPTER 11 NOTES:
[1] *Wildcat*, 13 September 1973.
[2] *Nor-Cal Running Review*, October-November 1973.
[3] *Wildcat*, 2 October 1973.
[4] *Wildcat*, 4 October 1973; *Nor-Cal Running Review*, October-November 1973.
[5] *Nor-Cal Running Review*, October-November 1973.

CHAPTER 12 NOTES:
[1] *Wildcat*, 19 March 1974.
[2] *Wildcat*, 18 April 1974.
[3] *Wildcat*, 2 May 1974.
[4] *Wildcat*, 7 May 1974.
[5] *Wildcat*, 9 May 1974.
[6] *Wildcat*, 21 May 1974.
[7] *Wildcat*, 18 April 1974.
[8] *Wildcat*, 25 April 1974.
[9] *Wildcat*, 2 May 1974.
[10] Ibid.
[11] Ibid.

[12] *Wildcat*, 7 May 1974; undated, clipped newspaper article.

CHAPTER 13 NOTES:
[1] *Wildcat*, 15 October 1974.
[2] Cross Country team meet schedule and roster proved by Hank Lawson.
[3] *Wildcat*, 3 October 1974.
[4] *Wildcat*, 8 October 1974.
[5] *Wildcat*, October 15, 1974; results provided by Hank Lawson.
[6] *Wildcat*, 29 October 1974.
[7] Ibid.
[8] Ibid.
[9] *Wildcat*, 7 November 1974.
[10] *Wildcat*, 12 November 1974.
[11] *Nor-Cal Running Review*, November-December 1974.
[12] "Division II Men's Cross Country Championships Records Book (http://fs.ncaa.org/Docs/stats/m_cross_country_champs_records/2018-19/D2.pdf: accessed 18 February 2023).
[13] Ibid.

CHAPTER 14 NOTES:
[1] *Orion*, 13 March 1975; *Orion*, 20 March 1975; "NCAA Division 1 Track and Field Championships 1974 Jun 4, 1974 - Jun 8, 1974" (https://tx.milesplit.com/meets/191275-ncaa-division-1-track-and-field-championships-1974/results/344593/raw#.Y_EzfmTMKM9): accessed 18 February 2023.
[2] *Orion*, 3 April 1975.
[3] *Orion*, 8 April 1975.
[4] *Orion*, 15 April 1975.
[5] *Nor-Cal Running Review*, March-April 1975.
[6] *Orion*, 29 April 1975.
[7] *Nor-Cal Running Review*, March-April 1975.
[8] Ibid.
[9] Ibid.
[10] *Wildcat*, 7 November 1974.
[11] *Wildcat*, 7 November 1974; "History of US National Results: 100 Hurdles – Women" (https://trackandfieldnews.com/history-of-us-nationals-results-100-hurdles-women/: accessed 19 February 2023).
[12] *Wildcat*, 15 April 1975.
[13] *Wildcat*, 22 April 1975.
[14] *Wildcat*, 29 April 1975.
[15] Ibid.

CHAPTER 15 NOTES:
[1] *Wildcat*, 9 September 1975.
[2] Ibid.
[3] Ibid.
[4] *Wildcat*, 14 October 1975.
[5] Ibid.
[6] *Wildcat*, 18 November 1975.
[7] Ibid.
[8] "Randy Watt" (https://chicowildcats.com/sports/2008/10/16/GEN_1016080254.aspx?id=95: accessed 21 February 2023).

CHAPTER 16 NOTES:
[1] *Nor-Cal Running Review*, March-April 1976.
[2] Ibid.
[3] *Nor-Cal Running Review*, May-June 1976.
[4] *Orion*, 5 May 1976.
[5] *Orion*, 29 April 1976.
[6] Ibid.
[7] *Orion*, 11 May 1976.
[8] *Nor-Cal Running Review*, May-June 1976.
[9] Ibid.
[10] *Orion*, 7 April 1976.
[11] Ibid.
[12] *Orion*, 16 March 1976.
[13] *Orion*, 7 April 1976; *Orion*, 30 March 1976.
[14] Ut supra.
[15] *Orion*, 7 April 1976.
[16] *Orion*, 5 May 1976.
[17] *Orion*, 4 May 1976.
[18] Ibid.

CHAPTER 17 NOTES:
[1] *Orion*, 11 October 1976; Orion, 5 October 1976.
[2] Ut supra.
[3] *Orion*, 11 October 1976.
[4] Kent Pease correspondence, February 21, 2023.
[5] Ibid.
[6] *Nor-Cal Running Review*, September-October 1976.
[7] Ibid.
[8] *Orion*, 10 November 1976.
[9] *Wildcat*, 4 November 1976.
[10] *Nor-Cal Running Review*, November-December 1976.
[11] *Orion*, 10 November 1976.
[12] *Nor-Cal Running Review*, November-December 1976.

CHAPTER 18 NOTES:
[1] Results provided by Hank Lawson (http://lynbrooksports.prepcaltrack.com/ATHLETICS/TRACK/1977/RESULTS/Chico_vs_UNReno.pdf: accessed 16 February 2023).
[2] *Orion*, 30 March 1977.
[3] Results provided by Hank Lawson.
[4] Ibid.
[5] *Orion*, 20 April 1977.
[6] *Nor-Cal Running Review*, March-April 1977; *Orion*, 4 May 1977.
[7] Ut supra.
[8] *Orion*, 18 May 1977; Results provided by Hank Lawson; *Nor-Cal Running Review*, May-June 1977.
[9] Ut supra.
[10] Kent Pease correspondence, February 21, 2023.
[11] *Orion*, 16 March 1977.
[12] Ibid.
[13] Ibid.
[14] *Orion*, 23 March 1977.
[15] *Orion*, 22 March 1977; *Nor-Cal Running Review*, March-April 1977.
[16] *Orion*, 22 March 1977.
[17] *Orion*, 23 March 1977.
[18] *Orion*, 31 March 1977.
[19] Results provided by Hank Lawson (http://lynbrooksports.prepcaltrack.com/ATHLETICS/TRACK/1977/RESULTS/Cal_vs_Chico_women.pdf: accessed 16 February 2023).
[20] *Orion*, 20 April 1977; *Nor-Cal Running Review*, March-April 1977.
[21] Ibid.
[22] *Orion*, 27 April 1977.
[23] Ibid.
[24] *Orion*, 4 May 1977.
[25] Ibid.
[26] *Nor-Cal Running Review*, May-June 1977; *Orion*, 10 May 1977.
[27] Ut supra.

CHAPTER 19 NOTES:
[1] *Orion*, 14 September 1977.
[2] *Orion*, 5 October 1977.
[3] Ibid.
[4] Ibid.
[5] *Nor-Cal Running Review*, September-October 1977.
[6] *Orion*, 19 October 1977.
[7] *Orion*, 26 October 1977.
[8] *Orion*, November 2, 1977.
[9] Mike Darling correspondence, February 24, 2023.
[10] Results provided by Toni Ruggle.
[11] *Orion*, 7 September 1977.

[12] *Orion*, 7 September 1977; *Orion*, 12 October 1977.
[13] *Orion*, 12 October 1977.
[14] Ibid.
[15] Ibid.
[16] *Nor-Cal Running Review*, September-October 1977; *Orion*, 5 October 1977.
[17] *Orion*, 5 October 1977.
[18] *Orion*, 12 October 1977.
[19] Ibid.
[20] Ibid.
[21] *Orion*, 19 October 1977.
[22] Ibid.
[23] *Orion*, 26 October 1977.
[24] Ibid.
[25] Ibid.
[26] Ibid.

CHAPTER 20 NOTES:
[1] *Orion*, 1 March 1978.
[2] Ibid.
[3] *Orion*, 3 May 1978.
[4] *Orion*, 26 April 1978.

CHAPTER 21 NOTES:
[1] *Orion*, 13 September 1978.
[2] Ibid.
[3] Ibid.
[4] *Orion*, 27 September 1978.
[5] Ibid.
[6] *Orion*, 18 October 1978.
[7] *Orion*, 18 October 1978; undated clipped articles from the *Modesto Bee*, and *Special to the Bee*.
[8] Ut supra.
[9] *Orion*, 6 September 1978.
[10] Ibid.
[11] *Nor-Cal Running Review*, November-December 1978.
[12] *Orion*, 4 October 1978.
[13] Ibid.
[14] *Orion*, 11 October 1978.
[15] *Nor-Cal Running Review*, November-December 1978.
[16] *Orion*, 18 October 1978.

CHAPTER 22 NOTES:
[1] *Orion*, 7 March 1979.
[2] *Orion*, 28 March 1979.
[3] Ibid.
[4] *Orion*, 4 April 1979.

[5] Ibid.
[6] *Orion*, 25 April 1979.
[7] Ibid.
[8] Ibid.
[9] Ibid.
[10] *Orion*, 2 May 1979.
[11] Ibid.
[12] *Orion*, 9 May 1979.
[13] Ibid.
[14] Ibid.
[15] Ibid.
[16] *Orion*, 16 May 1979.
[17] Ibid.
[18] *Orion*, 14 March 1979.
[19] *Orion*, 21 March 1979.
[20] *Nor-Cal Running Review*, Spring 1979.
[21] *Nor-Cal Running Review*, Spring 1979; *Orion*, 28 March 1979.
[22] *Orion*, 4 April 1979.
[23] Ibid.
[24] *Orion*, 25 April 1979.
[25] *Orion*, 16 May 1979.

CHAPTER 23 NOTES:
[1] *Orion*, 17 October 1979.
[2] Ibid.
[3] *Orion*, 17 October 1979; *The Modesto Bee*, October 21, 1979.
[4] *The Modesto Bee*, October 21, 1979.
[5] *Orion*, 26 September 1979.
[6] *Orion*, 19 September 1979.
[7] *Orion*, 26 September 1979.
[8] *Orion*, 3 October 1979.
[9] Ibid.
[10] Ibid.
[11] Ibid.
[12] *Orion*, 10 October 1979.
[13] Ibid.
[14] Ibid.
[15] Ibid.
[16] *Orion*, 17 October 1979.
[17] Ibid.
[18] *Orion*, 24 October 1979.
[19] Ibid.
[20] *Orion*, 31 October 1969.
[21] Ibid.
[22] Ibid.
[23] *Orion*, 7 November 1979.

[24] Ibid.
[25] *Orion*, 12 December 1979.
[26] Ibid.

Index

Adams, Bill, 14
Adams, Steve, 11, 13
Albrecht, Bonnie, 96-97
Aldridge, Dan, 149
Aldridge, John, 65
Alexander, Suzie, 115
Anderson, Barry, 104
Andrews, Mike, 115
Anex, Rob, 160
Anex, Tina, 124, 133-134, 140
Aubuchan, Michele, 138, 140, 142-143, 150, 190
Aubuchon, Michele, 162, 171
Avrit, Doug, 123
Barth, Wayne, 111-112
Banister, Roger, 54
Barham, Brett, 29-34, 47-48
Batie, Don, 19
Bath, Janet, 150
Bauhs, Scotty, 56
Belyea, Liz, 117, 119, 190
Berta, Agnes, 121-122
Best, Dan, 62
Birnbaum, Jim, 124
Blake, Herman, 105
Bobick, Duane, 129-130
Brady, Jeff, 148, 185
Brandt, Lorna, 119-120
Brandt, Marilyn, 140
Brignolo, Dick, 22, 25-26
Britten, Bill, 124, 130
Brock, Darryl, 23, 185
Brown, Julie, 143
Brown, Tom, 47-48, 51-57, 65-68, 73-79, 83-94, 100-105, 143, 182-186
Bulbeck, Karen, 58
Burk, Frank, 115
Burleson, Darcy, 140, 142, 167-171
Burleson, Dyrol, 31, 99, 142
Burleson, Larry, 1-3, 6, 11-15, 19-21, 26, 29-35, 38, 40, 47-48, 53, 64, 66 68, 83-88, 92-93, 99-101, 111, 115, 121-124, 135, 142, 151, 157-158, 165, 168
Butler, Dennis, 91, 103-104, 185
Butler, Kelly, 131, 133, 190

Butler, Tracy, 138, 140, 143
Calandi, Kevin, 63
Caldwell, John, 52, 77
Call, Rick, 22, 40
Carlos, John, 25
Carlsen, Deanne, 27-28, 44-46, 58, 80, 106, 118
Carter, Rich, 6
Cary, Renda, 96-97, 108, 117, 120
Castro, Tom, 5, 21
Chapman, Dan, 51-52, 65, 67, 187
Clark, Bill, 64
Clifford, Andy, 149
Cobb, Nelson, 127, 135-137, 148, 157-158, 185
Cola, Sandy, 58
Colborn, Tony, 92
Conners, Colleen, 153, 156
Covert, Mark, 63-64
Crawford, Don, 38, 52, 79, 94
Cray, Merill, 70, 95-96, 98, 106-108, 190
Crumbo, Toni, 117, 119, 189
Dailey, Mike, 11-42, 177, 185-187
Darling, Bob, 11-42, 61-64, 77, 112, 177-178, 183-187
Dauncey, Frank, 160
Davis, Barbara, 150, 161-163, 189
Davis, Glenn, 118
Davis, Otis, 118
de Ghetaldi, Laurie, 28, 59, 70, 80, 82, 95, 97-98, 106-108, 127, 189
Devol, Michelle, 82, 96-97, 117, 120
Diaz, Dolores, 131, 133, 190
Didlack, Marci, 138, 140
Dion, Larry, 115
Donald, Pat, 131, 133, 189
Duffy, Peter, 38, 75-76
Dugan, Shelly, 138, 143, 150
Dura, Juan, 37-42, 51-52, 139, 185
Durbin, Greg, 151
Elijah, Ron, 34, 68, 77, 114
Ellison, Kerry, 54
Ellison, Kim, 37-43, 47-57, 64, 73-77, 85-86, 114, 180, 185-187
Eashman, Willie, 41, 43, 52-53, 57, 78
Embody, John, 158
Engel, Vince, 20-21, 26
Escoto, Gil, 51-52
Estes, Jim, 13-25, 29-30, 37-43, 47, 179, 185
Faeth, Dave, 93
Fairley, Scott, 146

Farrell, Tim, 160
Felson, Deamon, 75
Ferrero, Lee, 160
Finn, Pat, 65-66, 83, 87-89, 100-102
Fitzgerald, Stacy, 106-107, 189
Fornaciari, Mike, 47-48, 65-66, 76, 83, 86, 186
Foy, Lisa, 114, 117, 119, 121, 132, 189
Frankienich, Steve, 105, 113
Franson, Terry, 79
Frazier, Joe, 130
Freitas, Kirk, 5, 22, 25, 40
Fries, Cathie, 153, 156
Furey, Kevin, 35, 43, 87
Gambetta, Patti, 138, 140, 142
Genet, Mark, 100
Giannini, Mario, 123
Gilbert, George, 135-136
Gilligan, Gene, 1, 4, 11-12, 186
Gillingham, Bill, 7
Glenesk, Neil, 65-68, 111-112
Graham, Judy, 125, 142-143
Gregg, Joan, 140-142, 168
Griffin, Charlie, 111-113, 117, 121, 125, 127, 186
Griffin, Greg, 83, 86-89, 100-104, 111-113, 187
Hagenbuch, Dan, 19
Hammer, Ken, 149
Hamilton, Sheila, 120
Hammond, Kathy, 58
Hansen, Bill, 68
Harms, Dwayne, 56, 68, 86-87
Hartman, John, 68
Hartwig, Nancy, 9, 189
Haver, Ed, 22, 26, 33, 43
Heide, Paul, 149
Herd, Carrie, 153, 156
Hetzler, Linda, 138, 142
Hitchcock, Noel, 35, 52
Hjelte, Lynne, 156
Hobbs, Vicki, 117, 119, 189
Horn, Kathy, 161, 163, 189
Hossack, Michael, 68
Hulbert, Mark, 121, 125, 127, 128
Hulsey, Mike, 4-6
Hume, Burt, 9, 186
Hunter, Dick, 14
Hurst, Eric, 148

Innes, Gordon, 114, 130
Ipsen, Mike, 62
Jenkins, Hersh, 52, 87
Jhanson, Lloyd, 40
Johnson, Flynn, 6-8, 26
Johnson, Karen, 138, 142
Johnston, Tom, 68-71
Jones, Mark, 79, 93
Jones, Mel, 44-45
Keller, Tom, 127-130, 135-137, 186-187
Kennan, Dave, 158
Keyes, Maggie, 156
King, Ann, 153, 156
King, Bob, 29-37, 40, 47, 51, 56, 65-68, 76-77, 185
Kingery, Mitch, 62, 149
Knox, Carl, 105
Koch, Djorn, 75
Kohl, Gary, 111-112
Labrie, Howard, 34
Ladd, Doug, 105
Landers, Merrily, 167-171
Langan, Katherine, 167, 170-171
Lantrip, Calvin, 57, 83-94, 187
Lathrop, Greg, 135-136
Laxson, Rob, 1-25, 175, 185
Lemaroux, Danny, 157-158, 186
Lindstrom, Brita, 167-170
Leonard, Mike, 32, 47-48, 65-66, 73-74, 151-152
Lepp, Tara, 118
Lindgren, Gerry, 63
Liquori, Marty, 42
Lobsinger, Tom, 148
Loene, Ken, 100
Lowry, Conrad, 78, 87
Luchenbill, Dave, 151
Lydiard, Arthur, 116
MacKenzie, Norm, 85
Mackey, Lynn, 148, 187
Mahon, Manny, 29-40, 185
Malain, Keith, 135-136
Marshall, Dick, 111
Martinelli, Dan, 160
Martinez, Angelo, 87, 124-125
Mastain, Julie, 138, 140-143, 153, 156
Masterson, Al, 165
Mathews, Will, 26

Farrell, Tim, 160
Felson, Deamon, 75
Ferrero, Lee, 160
Finn, Pat, 65-66, 83, 87-89, 100-102
Fitzgerald, Stacy, 106-107, 189
Fornaciari, Mike, 47-48, 65-66, 76, 83, 86, 186
Foy, Lisa, 114, 117, 119, 121, 132, 189
Frankienich, Steve, 105, 113
Franson, Terry, 79
Frazier, Joe, 130
Freitas, Kirk, 5, 22, 25, 40
Fries, Cathie, 153, 156
Furey, Kevin, 35, 43, 87
Gambetta, Patti, 138, 140, 142
Genet, Mark, 100
Giannini, Mario, 123
Gilbert, George, 135-136
Gilligan, Gene, 1, 4, 11-12, 186
Gillingham, Bill, 7
Glenesk, Neil, 65-68, 111-112
Graham, Judy, 125, 142-143
Gregg, Joan, 140-142, 168
Griffin, Charlie, 111-113, 117, 121, 125, 127, 186
Griffin, Greg, 83, 86-89, 100-104, 111-113, 187
Hagenbuch, Dan, 19
Hammer, Ken, 149
Hamilton, Sheila, 120
Hammond, Kathy, 58
Hansen, Bill, 68
Harms, Dwayne, 56, 68, 86-87
Hartman, John, 68
Hartwig, Nancy, 9, 189
Haver, Ed, 22, 26, 33, 43
Heide, Paul, 149
Herd, Carrie, 153, 156
Hetzler, Linda, 138, 142
Hitchcock, Noel, 35, 52
Hjelte, Lynne, 156
Hobbs, Vicki, 117, 119, 189
Horn, Kathy, 161, 163, 189
Hossack, Michael, 68
Hulbert, Mark, 121, 125, 127, 128
Hulsey, Mike, 4-6
Hume, Burt, 9, 186
Hunter, Dick, 14
Hurst, Eric, 148

Innes, Gordon, 114, 130
Ipsen, Mike, 62
Jenkins, Hersh, 52, 87
Jhanson, Lloyd, 40
Johnson, Flynn, 6-8, 26
Johnson, Karen, 138, 142
Johnston, Tom, 68-71
Jones, Mark, 79, 93
Jones, Mel, 44-45
Keller, Tom, 127-130, 135-137, 186-187
Kennan, Dave, 158
Keyes, Maggie, 156
King, Ann, 153, 156
King, Bob, 29-37, 40, 47, 51, 56, 65-68, 76-77, 185
Kingery, Mitch, 62, 149
Knox, Carl, 105
Koch, Djorn, 75
Kohl, Gary, 111-112
Labrie, Howard, 34
Ladd, Doug, 105
Landers, Merrily, 167-171
Langan, Katherine, 167, 170-171
Lantrip, Calvin, 57, 83-94, 187
Lathrop, Greg, 135-136
Laxson, Rob, 1-25, 175, 185
Lemaroux, Danny, 157-158, 186
Lindstrom, Brita, 167-170
Leonard, Mike, 32, 47-48, 65-66, 73-74, 151-152
Lepp, Tara, 118
Lindgren, Gerry, 63
Liquori, Marty, 42
Lobsinger, Tom, 148
Loene, Ken, 100
Lowry, Conrad, 78, 87
Luchenbill, Dave, 151
Lydiard, Arthur, 116
MacKenzie, Norm, 85
Mackey, Lynn, 148, 187
Mahon, Manny, 29-40, 185
Malain, Keith, 135-136
Marshall, Dick, 111
Martinelli, Dan, 160
Martinez, Angelo, 87, 124-125
Mastain, Julie, 138, 140-143, 153, 156
Masterson, Al, 165
Mathews, Will, 26

McAlister, Don, 6
McClintock, Lynn, 96-97
McCollum, Art, 52
McGrath, Michael, 87, 104
McGuire, Bob, 78
McLain, Bruce, 26
McNally, Joe, 1, 3-4, 20, 186
McQuillan, Kathy, 120, 138, 140-143
McVey, Scott, 48-57, 65-66, 73-78, 83, 86, 185-186
Mead, Steve, 67
Metcalf, Jerry, 68
Medlin, Kathy, 58
Meek, Suzie, 156
Metteer, Sally, 124, 162
Meyers, Gene, 1-8, 11, 13-14, 18-26, 29-31, 33-38, 40-43, 48, 56, 73, 83, 93, 95, 135-136, 151, 157, 174, 176, 185-187
Mezzapelle, Tony, 128
Michael, Mathyas, 37-38
Mik, Cynthia, 120
Miller, Gary, 34
Miller, Howard, 11-22, 29-39, 187
Miller, Shirley, 57-58, 189
Mills, Dave, 113, 121-122, 127, 129, 185, 187
Morse, Lori, 138, 140, 142-143, 150
Mossbacker, Ken, 92
Moyle, Jim, 4, 11, 13-15, 19, 23, 186-187
Mulkey, Kent, 111-113, 117, 121-129, 148, 151-152, 185-186
Mullen, Nancy, 58
Mullens, Daniel, 43, 51, 78
Mulloy, Dan, 11-12
Munoz, Alicia, 153, 156, 167, 170
Myers, Bob, 105, 117, 131
Nicholson, Ed, 160
Nielsen, Annette, 167, 169-171
Noland, Steve, 23
Noland, Karen, 167, 169-171
Norton, Ken, 130
Nuccio, Jim, 86
Nygaard, Steve, 165
O'Connor, Tom, 1, 4, 11, 14, 19, 23, 29, 32, 186
O'Halloran, Toni, 121-122
Oddone, Cathy, 153, 156, 161-163, 167-173, 189-190
Oehm, Jan, 155-156, 162
Olson, Tom, 135-137, 148-153, 157-160, 186
Orri, Julia, 167-171
Ovegaard, Linda, 167

Index

Park, Luanne, 140-141, 168
Patten, Ralph, 11-25, 29-40, 185-186
Pease, Kent, 122-131, 146, 186
Peters, Ron, 90
Peters, Scott, 136
Phillips, Berni, 131, 133, 189
Pick, Mike, 103
Plummer, Mike, 158
Porter, Mike, 19-25, 38-40, 138-139, 153, 161, 163, 167, 185
Porter, Steve, 105, 130
Porter, Tirian, 68
Pratt, Mike, 149
Prefontaine, Steve, 63
Price, Jim, 32, 47-48, 65, 73-77, 83, 86-92, 186
Purcell, Dick, 37
Ratliff, Marina, 138, 140, 143
Ray, Duwayne, 1-8, 11-13, 42, 56, 174, 175, 185, 187
Rieboldt, Mary, 162
Remillard, Jim, 115
Richardson, Peter (E.P.), 130
Richey, Don, 115
Richey, Val, 119
Richter, Suzanne, 140-141, 154-156, 162, 168
Ricketts, Eric, 90
Robertson, Robert, 135-136
Robinson, Regina, 57-58, 82, 189
Rogers, George, 100, 112
Roulsten, Jim, 54
Rowland, Flip, 4-6, 19-25, 38, 40, 42
Ruby, Mary, 9-10
Ryan, Lynn, 127-130, 185-186
Ryun, Jim, 54
Saiyadinejad, Cindy, 138-143
Sanchez, Silas, 6
Schaechterle, Karl, 113-117, 183, 187
Schafer, Walt, 114-115
Schankel, Jim, 149
Schipper, Bill, 3
Schultz, Greg, 135-137, 151, 157-158
Scobey, Bill, 7, 13, 16, 20-21, 26, 32-35, 62, 64
Scott, Corbin, 91, 100, 185
Scott, Joyce, 167, 169-170
Secor, Leann, 167-171
Selchau, Julie, 140, 142, 168
Sheehan, John, 49, 68, 77, 87
Sheley, Chuck, 115, 123, 141

Sherrard, Cherric, 118, 120-121, 132, 134, 138-143, 153, 161, 167, 169-173
Sherrard, Mike, 118
Shols, Stacey, 140, 142, 168
Shorter, Frank, 63
Shuman, Mark, 65-68, 73-78, 83-90, 11-114, 121-125, 159-160, 181, 186-187
Silcox, Doug, 158
Silva, Eddie, 65-68, 73-78, 86, 185-187
Silva, Marcos, 165-166
Simmons, Pat, 68
Smead, Chuck, 68, 77-78, 87, 93
Smith, Brian, 131
Smith, Mike, 135-137
Smith, Rich, 83
Snell, Peter, 114-116
Sophie, Mike, 135-137, 148, 187
Spradlin, Byron, 26, 33, 42-43
Spence, Kathy, 117, 119, 121, 125, 189
Sprague, Barbara, 131-143, 150, 189
Springer, Karl, 1-6, 19-23, 36, 74, 185-187
Stanley, Carol, 58
Staples, John, 45-46
Stevens, Dan, 5-6, 22, 25
Stohr, Diana, 134
Stokes, Mike, 105
Stone, Tim, 100-104, 111-117, 185-186
Stordahl, Pat, 51-57, 65-68, 73-78, 83, 186-187
Stordahl, Roger, 111-112
Streichman, Craig, 34
Struvan, Brenda, 138, 140, 142
Sudduth, Stacy, 96, 189
Sullivan, Kathy, 114-119, 121, 131-134
Sullivan, Paul, 79, 105
Symons, Jill, 90, 140-142, 151-156, 161-174, 184, 189-190
Taxiera, Jox, 101
Teague, Eddie, 166
Teague, Ron, 113
Tearson, Debbie, 143
Thrupp, Ann, 124
Tibaduiza, Domingo, 75-76
Torres, Junior, 47-48, 51-52, 65, 187
Trachok, Rich, 75
Tremaine, Tom, 73, 75
Trumbly, Alice, 156, 162
Tuttle, Gary, 64
Urmann, Stan, 91-93, 105
Vagmonde, Linda, 58

Vanderford, Mike, 29, 32
Vogt, Nick, 29, 32, 37, 47-48, 51, 57, 186-187
Waldon, Bob, 13
Wallach, Darlene, 57-58, 79-80, 95, 189-190
Walters, Vanita, 96-97, 108
Washington, Randy, 25
Watje, Susan, 138, 140
Watson, Rich, 165
Watt, Randy, 79, 111-112
Wear, Bob, 11-14, 18, 23, 29-35, 186-186
Webb, Tony, 100, 111-112, 121-129, 187
Wedel, Nancy, 9-10, 58, 189
West, Jack, 73-78, 83-86, 91-92, 160, 185
Wieking, Linda, 153, 156, 167, 169-172
Wilson, Clay, 24
Wilson, Janet, 153, 156
Wilson, Tom, 6
Wiseman, Sandy, 70, 79-82, 95-98, 189
Wood, Dave, 47-53, 56, 65, 73, 76, 78, 83, 86, 185
Woodland, Kim, 153, 156
Woods, Larry, 5, 26
Wright, Mike, 165
Wysocki, Tom, 148
Vineyard, Kurt, 166
Yeo, Matt, 101
Yerman, Jack, 118
Young, Charlie, 24
Young, Earl, 118
Young, George, 63
Yourek, Bob, 79, 92

About the Author

Commander David D. Bruhn, U.S. Navy (Retired) served twenty-two years on active duty and two in the Naval Reserve, as both an enlisted man and as an officer, between 1977 and 2001.

He is a graduate of California State University, Chico, and has Masters degrees from the U.S. Naval Postgraduate School and U.S. Naval War College.

During his career, Bruhn served aboard six ships including command of the mine countermeasures ships USS *Gladiator* (MCM-11) and USS *Dextrous* (MCM-13) in the Persian Gulf. Ashore, he did two three-year tours in the Pentagon. During the first one, he was assigned to Secretary of the Navy and Chief of Naval Operation staffs as a budget analyst and resources planner. His final assignment was to the Secretary of Defense staff as executive assistant to a senior (SES 4) executive at the Ballistic Missile Defense Organization in Washington, D.C.

Following military service, he was a high school teacher and track coach for ten years, and remains an avid Track & Field fan. He lives in northern California with his wife Nancy and has two grown sons, David and Michael.

A prolific writer, Bruhn has authored twenty-five books on naval history; one on shipboard engineering; and two related to sports, *Toe the Mark* and *Stride Out* about competitive running in the 1970s.

www.ingramcontent.com/pod-product-compliance
Lightning Source LLC
Chambersburg PA
CBHW060601230426
43670CB00011B/1914